· Discovering ·
Classic
fantasy
fiction

*Essays on the Antecedents
of Fantastic Literature*

Edited by

Darrell Schweitzer

WILDSIDE PRESS
P.O. Box 45
Gillette, NJ 07933-0045

WILDSIDE PRESS
P.O. Box 45
Gillette, NJ 07933-0045

*　*　*　*　*　*　*　*

CONTENTS

DEDICATION

For Jason Van Hollander,
A True Original (Not a Print)

INTRODUCTION

Discovering Classic Fantasy Fiction is intended to be, of course, entertaining, and also, quite frankly, propagandistic. Its very existence is a kind of polemic in a time when the enormous boom in commercial fantasy publishing has proven a very mixed blessing.

It used to be that fantasy books or stories were rare treasures, often difficult to find, and that the few fantasies which successfully fought their way into print were exotic creatures indeed, anything but routine commercial fiction bashed out for a buck.

Nowadays, most fantasy seems to be bashed out for a buck. We are buried in look-alike trilogies tailored to meet very specific generic expectations. This is harmful in several ways: first, it degrades the audience's taste, building up an expectation for just such bland pablum. Second, it causes publishers to expect and even demand bland pablum, thus hampering the development of any really original writers. There is no doubt much good fantasy buried among the avalanche. The problem is finding it. Many readers now sneer at the whole mass, and don't even try. Many *writers*, one suspects, could do a lot better if either they, their editors, or their audience had higher expectations.

Many years ago the late Lin Carter, otherwise a commercial pablum-writer of the worst sort, redeemed himself by editing the Ballantine Adult Fantasy Series which played a major role in *creating* the commercial genre of fantasy. It was a wonderful series, which educated a generation of fantasy readers and writers, introducing them to such giants as James Branch Cabell, Lord Dunsany, William Hope Hodgson, Evangeline Walton, Arthur Machen, Ernest Bramah, and many others. Which is where the present volume comes in. *Educated* is the key word.

Carter's successors at Ballantine had nowhere near the taste he did, and have spent much of the intervening years educating the audience to the glories of Terry Brooks. Most of the classics are again out of print and nearly as difficult to find as they ever were. The devotee has to go digging.

Discovering Classic Fantasy Fiction is intended as a guide to help you in your explorations. Read these essays, then hunt down the books. There is a lot more to the fantasy field than a trip to your local chain bookstore might suggest.

—Darrell Schweitzer

ACKNOWLEDGMENTS

"Lord Dunsany: The Career of a Fantaisiste" originally appeared in somewhat different form in *The Weird Tale*. This version is Copyright © 1996 by S. T. Joshi.

"James Branch Cabell: No Fit Employment for a Grown Man," "Villains of Necessity: The Works of E. R. Eddison," and "Henry Kuttner: Man of Many Voices" are Copyright © 1996 by Don D'Ammassa.

"Mervyn Wall and the Comedy of Despair" first appeared in somewhat different form in *Fantasy Review* no. 93 (July/August, 1986), and is Copyright © 1986 by Florida Atlanta University. This version is Copyright © 1996 by Darrell Schweitzer.

"John Collier, Fantastic Miniaturist" is Copyright © 1996 by Alan Warren.

"A. Merritt: A Reappraisal" originally appeared in *Ibid* no. 23 (July, 1978). This version is Copyright © 1996 by Ben P. Indick.

"Subtle Perceptions: The Fantasy Novels of Algernon Blackwood" is Copyright © 1996 by Jeffrey Goddin.

"David Lindsay and the Quest for Muspel-Fire" originally appeared in *Nightshade* no. 5, and is Copyright © 1979 by Galad Elflandsson.

"Classic American Fairy Tales: The Fantasies of L. Frank Baum" is Copyright © 1996 by Neal Wilgus.

"Of the Master, Merlin, and H. Warner Munn" is Copyright © 1996 by Don Herron.

I.

LORD DUNSANY

THE CAREER OF A FANTAISISTE

by S. T. Joshi

1. The Career of a Fantaisiste

The career of Lord Dunsany (1878-1957) is a peculiar one. After achieving spectacular fame with early short stories and plays about "the edge of the world," he continued to write for several decades—novels, tales, plays, articles, reviews—with considerable success but without the sort of thundering recognition that had greeted his early work. In the 1930s and 1940s Dunsany was certainly a respected enough writer—his work appeared in *The Spectator*, *Life and Letters*, *Time and Tide*, and other distinguished journals, and his books were reviewed by Evelyn Waugh, Elizabeth Bowen, and Sean O'Faolain— but even his admirers seemed to wish that he had continued to write more *Gods of Pegana* and *Dreamer's Tales*. H. P. Lovecraft, his most ardent supporter, labelled Dunsany's Jorkens tales "tripe,"[1] and never stopped expressing wistful regret at what he felt was Dunsany's waning power. Lovecraft seems to have continued to read Dunsany dutifully into at least the early thirties, but without much enthusiasm; and other critics responded with a similarly stony silence. The articles of the teens that had marvelled at the phenomenon of Dunsany ceased abruptly when Dunsany began his novel writing in the 1920s; Broadway, which had once staged five of his early plays simultaneously, took no interest in his dramas after *If* (1921). I know of no significant article on Dunsany from the mid-1920s until well after his death.

Now all this is both unfortunate and unfair. It is unfortunate because some of Dunsany's later work—*The Blessing of Pan*, *The Curse of the Wise Woman*, *The Story of Mona Sheehy*—is very brilliant, and in fact there are few works of Dunsany's that do not offer some interest to the critic and the enthusiast; and unfair because it is foolish and unjust to expect an author to adhere to a single style and manner over a career of fifty years. In the fantasy field, the course of Dunsany's writing is in its way even more remarkable than that of Lovecraft: whereas we can see that Lovecraft's later novelettes and novels, although light-years ahead of his early tales, nevertheless are clearly similar to them in theme and substance, the work of Dunsany is constantly expanding—in style, execution, and even philosophical orientation. Whether or not Dunsany felt oppressed by the success of his early work—and I have received no impression that he did—he was constantly experimenting with new modes of narration, new tones and manners, new ways of saying the many things he had to say. In fact, from a critical perspective it is very hard to say anything about the early work: one can simply rhapsodize over it as an unrivalled and unique body of fantasy literature. The later work is considerably more amenable to analysis, and I hope to be excused if I spend much of my time on the later novels, plays, and stories.

What we need initially, however, is a brief critical survey of Dunsany's entire career, so that the whole of his work can be put in perspective. We need only mention the early volumes of tales—*The Gods of Pegana* (1905), *Time and the Gods* (1906), *The Sword of Welleran* (1908), *A Dreamer's Tales* (1910), *The Book of Wonder* (1912), *Fifty-One Tales* (1915), *The Last Book of Wonder* (1916), and *Tales of Three Hemispheres* (1919)—plus the two drama collections, *Five Plays* (1914) and *Plays of Gods and Men* (1917), to be aware of the awesome achievement of Dunsany's first decade or so of work. Although *Tales of Three Hemispheres* postdates World War I, the tales in it seem to have been written before or during the war; whether that conflict, in which Dunsany served, had anything to do with his abandonment of this vein of writing is hard to tell, for Dunsany is one of the most reticent of all fantaisistes. Whatever the cause, after *Tales of War* (1918) and *Unhappy Far-Off Things* (1919), his first purely non-fantastic writings, Dunsany abandoned the short story for the novel. "Abandon" is perhaps too strong a word, for Dunsany was stupefyingly prolific and continued to write many short tales, some collected much later and many not collected; but, to be sure, he abandoned *The Gods of Pegana* style of tale. Its swan song may be *The King of Elfland's Daughter* (1924), criticized by some contemporary reviewers precisely for its attempted maintenance of the jewelled, quasi-biblical prose of his early tales over the course of an entire novel; but on the whole, the work is as successful a recapturing of that gorgeous early style as can be imagined.

Don Rodriguez (1922) and *The Charwoman's Shadow* (1926), both pseudo-historical novels set in the Spain of the "Golden Age," represent a transition from the never-never land of Pegana to the realities of the modern world. In fact, it is remarkable that it took Dunsany so long to discover that fantasy can also be achieved by juxtaposing the real and the dream worlds—a juxtaposition tentatively achieved in the play *If* and in *The King of Elfland's Daughter*, but first exploited to the full in *The Blessing of Pan* (1927). In a sense the rest of Dunsany's career can be seen as the gradual banishing of fantasy in the ordinary sense of the term: in style Dunsany has entirely given up any attempts at pseudo-archaism, while in substance there is a greater and greater tendency to use the supernatural less for its own sake than to underscore a philosophical point. In *The Curse of the Wise Woman* (1933), there is no strict need to explain events supernaturally; the curious novel *Up in the Hills* (1935) is purely non-fantastic in its tale of a mock-war amongst boys in the hills of Ireland; while, as Darrell Schweitzer has pointed out, *The Story of Mona Sheehy* (1939) is a watershed in overtly denying anything fantastic in the incidents it tells. A similar thing occurs in many of the tales in *The Man Who Ate the Phoenix* (1949); all but one of the tales in *The Little Tales of Smethers and Other Stories* (1952) are non-supernatural. Of the very late novels, *The Strange Journeys of Colonel Polders* (1950) is supernatural, *His Fellow Men* (1951) is non-fantastic, and *The Last Revolution* (1952) is quasi-science fiction. The later plays correspond to this trend: while *The Old Folk of the Centuries* (1930) is definitely supernatural, *Mr. Faithful* (1935; written in 1922) is definitely not; *Lord Adrian* (1933; written in 1922-23) is somewhere in between. All the *Seven Modern Comedies* (1928) and the *Plays for Earth and Air* (1937), when they use the supernatural at all, use it as a vehicle for conveying a particular point.[2]

In a sense, though, the distinction between what is supernatural and non-supernatural in Dunsany is an artificial one: the transition from the one to the other is not systematic, and Dunsany used either whenever he felt it would best get his point across. What we can note in Dunsany is a constant sensitivity to *style*, and in particular to the question of how a style that has abandoned the "crystalline singing prose" (Lovecraft's memorable phrase) of the early tales can nevertheless create that atmosphere of shimmering fantasy that we find in the whole of Dunsany. The later work also reveals a quite pervasive interest in the question of the "suspension of disbelief": how is a tale, set in the prosy world of London or the less prosy but still obtrusively real world of Ireland or (as in the Jorkens tales) Africa or the Near East, and without the benefit of the quasi-biblical rhythm and imagery that so effortlessly transports us to Bethmoora or Pegana, to convince us of the bizarre events it is relating? If the magic of the early Dunsany makes us look for feeble parallels in the fairy tales of Oscar Wilde or, later, the convoluted prose of E. R. Eddison, the later Dunsany tempts us to look for comparisons in the starkness of Hemingway or Sherwood Anderson. This problem of *belief* is a very real one that Dunsany quite knowingly posed for himself, and he solved it in ways that, I think, will make us marvel the more at his ingenuity and versatility.

2. Nietzsche in a Fairy Tale

One of the difficulties in studying Dunsany at all is that he has left behind remarkably few sustained statements of his motives and purposes in writing fantasy. His three autobiographies—*Patches of Sunlight* (1938), *While the Sirens Slept* (1944), and *The Sirens Wake* (1945)—tell much less about his work than about his wide-ranging travels and hunting expeditions;[3] the *Donnellan Lectures* (1945) on poetry, fiction, and drama are very general; and of his relatively few (few, that is, in comparison to the voluminous Lovecraft and Machen) essays and reviews, we can learn only very indirectly of his theory of literature. Such an essay as "Nowadays" (1912) is very pretty, even poignant, in its condemnation of industrialism, and a paean to the expressive powers of poetry; but it is hard to apply these *dicta* in any precise way to the interpretation of Dunsany's own work. Lovecraft, at the opposite extreme, has left such an ocean of philosophical and literary comment in his letters and essays that critics seem to have had a difficult time getting beyond his own views on his work; it does not help that Lovecraft is almost invariably his own best commentator. The extremes to which Dunsany went in avoiding interpretation of his own work—aside from some routine disavowals of allegory in his early fantasies—may actually be of significance from a critical standpoint; for I see it as part of a rather thoroughgoing tendency on Dunsany's part to portray himself as an *ingénu*, a child of Nature who wrote whatever came to mind without any thought of pointing a moral. Lovecraft, at the height of his "art for art's sake" phase, sensed this, remarking that Dunsany's tales "are fashioned in that purely decorative spirit which means the highest art"; adding, significantly, "About his work Dunsany spreads a quaint atmosphere of cultivated naiveté and child-like ignorance."[4] "Cultivated naiveté" is exactly right; for the dominant note in Dunsany's early work is the tension between his apparently artless manner of expression and the worldly, cynical, even nihilistic message underlying it.

The Gods of Pegana is a perfect example. This book, Dunsany's first, is a fascinating farrago of biblical sonority and very advanced philosophical views—Nietzsche in a fairy tale. In what purports to be the Bible of an imaginary race dwelling on the "islands in the Central Sea" we do not expect to find such conceptions—derived from nineteenth-century science—as the infinity of time (the gods "sat in the middle of Time, for there was as much Time before them as behind them") and space ("Pegana was The Middle of All, for there was below Pegana what there was above it, and there lay before it that which lay beyond"[5]), determinism[6] (a Greek idea, to be sure, but emphasized in the teachings of the Social Darwinists), and this very strange conception, which a god utters to a mortal:

> "There is an Eternity behind thee as well as one
> before. Hast thou bewailed the aeons that passed
> without thee, who are so much afraid of the aeons that
> shall pass?"[7]

This exact notion is attributed to Hume, that most sceptical and "modern" of eighteenth-century philosophers, in Boswell's *Life of Johnson*: "David Hume said to me, he was no more uneasy to think he should *not be* after this life, than that he *had not been* before he began to exist."[8] It is a notion that the atheist Lovecraft is endlessly fond of citing in his polemics against the idea of life after death.

But, of course, the profoundest cynicism comes in the very hierarchy of the gods and its attendant cosmology. As the preface to *The Gods of Pegana* states, life is only a "Game" to Mana-Yood-Sushai, the Jupiter of the gods; the other gods confess themselves to be merely the "little games"[9] of Mana-Yood-Sushai, but they decide to "make worlds to amuse Ourselves while Mana rests."[10] The gods and all they create are nothing but the dreams of Mana-Yood-Sushai. Nor are we comforted by the fact that the god Hoodrazai knows "the wherefore of the making of the gods" and becomes "mirthless"[11] as a result. The gods are cruel gods:

> Thousands of years ago They were in mirthful
> mood. They said: "Let Us call up a man before Us
> that We may laugh in Pegana."[12]

The god Slid sends death as a reward, for he "will not forget to send thee Death when most thou needest it."[13]

Later collections only hammer home this bleak message—but always in that exquisitely lyrical prose that is like a smiling goddess handing us a daisy while summoning lightning to blast us. "The Dreams of a Prophet" (*Time and the Gods*) effectively conveys the precise idea of Nietzsche's eternal recurrence. After "Fate and Chance had played their game and ended, and all was over," they decide to play it all over again:

> So that those things which have been shall all be
> again, and under the same bank in the same land a
> sudden glare of sunlight on the same spring day shall
> bring the same daffodil to bloom once more and the
> same child shall pick it, and not regretted shall be the
> billion years that fell between. .

In "The Journey of the King," a lengthy tale that concludes *Time and the Gods*, a king asks various prophets to tell him what comes after death; again, every prophet speaks in the sweetest possible prose, but the core of every prophet's message is the extinction and nothingness that follow death.

Much of Dunsany's early work suggests his dim—or perhaps intentionally skewed—recollections of his classical learning. Dunsany, in one of his few candid moments, seems to suggest that his failure to master the Greek language as a boy was ultimately a source for the creation of his imaginary pantheon:

> It may have been the retirement of the Greek gods
> from my vision after I left Eton that eventually drove
> me to satisfy some such longing by making gods unto
> myself.[14]

To be sure, his early collections, for all their biblical prose, bring the Graeco-Roman pantheon more to mind than Jesus and the Apostles. Several early tales—"The Revolt of the Home Gods" in *The Gods of Pegana*; "The King That Was Not" in *Time and the Gods*—are textbook cases of hubris. The gods in Dunsany also seem to have a certain Epicurean air to them: Mana-Yood-Sushai "is the god of Having Done—the god of Having Done and of the Resting,"[15] reminding one of Epicurus's ethereal gods who do nothing but seek repose in the spaces between the stars. And note this passage In "The Vengeance of Han" (*Time and the Gods*):

> All feared the Pestilence, and those that he smote
> beheld him; but none saw the great shapes of the gods
> by starlight as They urged Their Pestilence on.

This is, I think, an echo of the celebrated passage in Book 11 of the *Aeneid* where Venus tells Aeneas that the destruction of Troy is being caused not only by the Greeks but by the gods:

> "Look—for the cloud which, o'er thy vision drawn,
> Dulls mortal sight, and spreads a misty murk,
> I will snatch from thee utterly...
> > here where thou but seest
> Huge shattered fragments and stone rent from stone,
> And dust and smoke blent in one surging sea,
> Neptune with his vast trident shakes the walls,
> And heaves the deep foundations, from her bed
> O'ertopping all the city. Juno here
> Storms at the entrance of the Scaean gate,
> Implacable, and raging, sword on thigh,
> Summons her armed confederates from the ships.
> Now backward glance, and on the embattled height
> Already see Tritonian Pallas throned.

Flashing with storm-cloud and with Gorgon fell...."[16]

But there is more to these early tales than echoes of half-remembered classics. In fact, I think we have to ask ourselves why Dunsany chose to invent this decadent cosmology to begin with. I am not at the moment concerned with any possible literary influences: I frankly know of nothing in earlier literature that is even remotely like *The Gods of Pegana* or *Time and the Gods*; and even if viable antecedents could be found, that would not answer the question of why Dunsany was led to create his own pantheon and give it the traits he did. The early essay "Romance and the Modern Stage" (1911) may suggest an answer, and we see Dunsany arguing for the "romantic drama" as an antidote to the modern age:

> ...all we need, to obtain romantic drama, is for the dramatist to find any age or any country where life is not too thickly veiled and cloaked with puzzles and conventions, in fact to find a people that is not in the agonies of self-consciousness. For myself, I think it simpler to imagine such a people, as it saves the trouble of reading to find a romantic age, or the trouble of making a journey to lands where there is no press.[17]

What else is Pegana and its gods but a repudiation of modernism? The archaism of style immediately banishes us from the present, and engulfs us in a world where we are, to be sure, the playthings of the gods, but where things are cleaner, purer, simpler, and more august than the world of workaday London. Later stories of Dunsany's early phase begin to suggest this social satire more explicitly: in "The City on Mallington Moor"

> there was none of that hurry of which foolish cities boast, nothing ugly or sordid so far as I could see. I saw that it was a city of beauty and song (*The Last Book of Wonder*).

But the city on Mallington Moor does not exist.

Another uncollected story or prose poem, "Jetsam" (1910), encapsulates another possible motive for Dunsany's early work:

> ...the cliffs of destiny wholly hem us in, they are beautiful in the morning lit by the rising sun, but they grow darker and darker as evening falls behind them. And therefore let us run swiftly along the shore and gather pretty things or build sand castles and defy the sea, for those mutable waves are coming up the beach

and sweeping away the children's paper ships and sweeping away the navies of the nations and curving their beautiful crests and calling for us.[18]

We seem to have heard this all before—"*Après nous le deluge*"; "Let us eat and drink, for tomorrow we die." But this is Dunsany at his most nihilistic, and I do not think we are to take him quite at his word here. The view that Dunsany is—exaggeratedly—expressing might be adequately summed up as the *aesthetic interpretation of life*. The aesthete lives for beauty; beauty and ugliness, not good and evil, are his moral opposites. We all know that Dunsany the aesthete does not believe, and does not expect us to believe, in the literal reality of the Pegana pantheon (in this sense his repudiation of allegory becomes somewhat disingenuous, for it is either as allegory or symbolism or parable that we must interpret his work); but we believe *aesthetically* because Dunsany, while capturing perfectly the tone of naive earnestness that characterizes all primitive religious writing, is hammering home a profoundly "modern" message.

It is, I think, the aesthetic interpretation of life that is at the bottom of what turns out to be a systematic criticism or mockery of conventional religion. This is a tendency that can be traced through the whole of Dunsany's career, and it may be well to pursue this entire thread here. What Dunsany's actual religious beliefs were, I have no idea: I suspect he was an atheist, but he never says so. Perhaps he need not have bothered, for his anti-religious (or, at the very least, anti-clerical) polemic lies very close to the surface of much of his work. We have already seen the cruel and capricious nature of the gods of Pegana; in *Time and the Gods* they continue to play out "the game of the gods, the game of life and death" ("When the Gods Slept"). "The Sorrow of Search" is a transparent allegory about the quest for truth and the inability of religion to satisfy it. King Khanazar "would know somewhat concerning the gods," and a prophet tells him a parable: there is a long road with temples all along its course, and the keeper of each temple believes that the road ends there; but one traveller walks past them all:

> It is told that the traveller came at last to the utter
> End and there was a mighty gulf, and in the darkness
> at the bottom of the gulf one small god crept, no bigger than a hare, whose voice came out in the cold:
> "I know not."
> And beyond the gulf was nought, only the small
> god crying.

In "For the Honour of the Gods" we find that the only happy people are those with no gods; all the other folk are ruled by capricious gods who compel them to fight and kill in their name. In "The Relenting of Sardinac" a lame dwarf comes to be hailed as a god: this is no retelling of the Greek story of lame Hephaestus (he was not a dwarf), but a vicious jab at (morally) deformed gods.

Some of the plays enforce the anti-religious diatribe in a different way. King Argimenes, now a slave of King Darniak, remarks mournfully: "I have no...hope, for my god was cast down in the temple and broken into three pieces on the day they surprised us and took me sleeping." How fragile are the gods! But Argimenes's fellow slave speaks of Darniak's god:

> "Yet is Illuriel a very potent god....Once an enemy cast Illuriel into the river and overthrew the dynasty, but a fisherman found him again and set him up, and the enemy was driven out and the dynasty returned." (Act I)

The Glittering Gate, Dunsany's first play, makes the point even more bluntly. Jim and Bill, both criminals who have died, are at the Gate of Heaven; Bill, who has just arrived, thinks there may be a way to break in (he is master lock-picker), but Jim, who has been there a long time, has no hope. Bill manages to pick the lock, and finds nothing but an abyss: "Stars. Blooming great stars." Bill concludes: "There *ain't* no Heaven, Jim." At this, the "faint and unpleasant laughter" that has been heard constantly in the background bursts forth into a "cruel and violent laugh" which "increases in volume and grows louder and louder." Actually, Dunsany leaves open the question of whether we are really to imagine this as the gate of a non-existent Heaven or the gate of a very real Hell.

Dunsany's novels, both early and late, continue the anti-religious polemic. *The Blessing of Pan* presents a clear-cut confrontation of conventional religion and paganism. Tommy Duffin's Pan pipes ultimately lure the inhabitants of an entire village to revive ancient pagan rituals, until finally even the vicar, Elderick Anwrel, submits. But Anwrel is not the butt of the attack, and at one point Dunsany even extends sympathy toward his quest to preserve his religion:

> The old ways were in danger; something strange had come and was threatening the old ways, and they were gathered there to defend the things they knew, the old familiar ways that were threatened now by this tune that troubled the evenings. (Chapter 14)

The real satire is directed at the bishop and his underlings who refuse to believe what is going on and rest comfortably in their pious conventions. The rector Hetley, sent to replace Anwrel when he is forced by the bishop to take a vacation, never hears the pipes at all: he is deaf to the spiritual plight of the community. After even his wife deserts him to join the others in the hills, Anwrel's resistance is undermined and he comes to lead the ceremony.

The non-fantasy novel *His Fellow Men* (1952) is Dunsany's last exhaustive statement on religion. Here we are presented with a hopelessly naive and idealistic young man, Mathew Perry, who roams the world searching for a religion that practises "tolerance"; of course, he finds it nowhere—certainly not in the Ireland he is compelled to flee because he cannot accept the conventional enmity of Catholic and Protestant, and not in Africa, Arabia, India, or England. Although Dunsany commits the aesthetic mistake of supplying a contrived happy ending, we are left with the impression that Perry's quest was doomed to failure.

We have reached the end of Dunsany's career, but we have by no means finished discussing his early work. In particular we must demolish the notion that all his early collections, from *The Gods of Pegana* to *Tales of Three Hemispheres*, represent a uniform body of work. It is not merely that the Pegana mythos is not sustained after *Time and the Gods*; it is that Dunsany's attitude toward his work changes, and does so rather early on. I think it would have been impossible for Dunsany to have maintained his biblical prose or his otherworldly subject matter for very long, and sure enough we find exceptions so early as the third collection, *The Sword of Welleran* (1908). "The Kith of the Elf-Folk" is the first tale that actually acknowledges the existence of the "real" world, and presents the conflict between the "Wild Thing" of the title and the conventional human beings who do not understand what she is. "The Highwayman," later in the collection, is Dunsany's first tale set entirely in the "real" world.

Further curious things happen in *A Dreamer's Tales* (1910). By now much of the biblical archaism of style has slipped away, and the sense of fantasy is created almost wholly by exoticism of setting ("Idle Days on the Yann," "Bethmoora"). "The Hashish Man" is a somewhat disturbing tale, and not entirely for the reasons Dunsany intended: it is a conscious sequel to "Bethmoora," and signals the beginning of a strain of self-cannibalization that would reach a height in *Tales of Three Hemispheres*.

With *The Book of Wonder* and *The Last Book of Wonder* something disastrous has occurred. Dunsany can no longer summon the perfect naiveté that made us marvel at *The Gods of Pegana*, and his growing sophistication (or, more likely, his increasing disinclination to suppress his sophistication) leads him to mar his creations with ever-increasing doses of whimsy, irony, and deflation. The first two paragraphs of "The Quest of the Queen's Tears" (*The Book of Wonder*) tell it all:

Sylvia, Queen of the Woods, in her woodland palace, held court, and made a mockery of her suitors. She would sing to them, she said, she would give them banquets, she would tell them tales of legendary days, her jugglers should caper before them, her armies salute them, her fools crack jests with them and make whimsical quips, only she could not love them.

This was not the way, they said, to treat princes in their splendour and mysterious troubadours concealing kingly names; it was not in accordance with fable; myth had no precedent for it. She should have thrown her glove, they said, into some lion's den, she should have asked for a score of venomous heads of the serpents of Licantara, or demanded the death of any notable dragon, or sent them all upon some deadly quest, but that she could not love them—! It was unheard of—it had no parallel in the annals of romance.

I think it is passages like this that led Lovecraft to rue the passing of Dunsany's early manner:

As he gained in age and sophistication, he lost in freshness and simplicity. He was ashamed to be uncritically naive, and began to step aside from his tales and visibly smile at them even as they unfolded. Instead of remaining what the true fantaisiste must be— a child in a child's world of dream—he became anxious to shew that he was really an adult good-naturedly pretending to be a child in a child's world.[19]

Lovecraft is, I suspect, right as to the result but wrong as to the motive: I believe Dunsany simply found *The Gods of Pegana* vein running dry, so that the only thing to do was to poke fun at it. This comes out especially well in an exquisite self-parody, "Why the Milkman Shudders When He Perceives the Dawn" (*The Last Book of Wonder*), where we are never given the answer to the question implied in the title. In both "The City on Mallington Moor" and "The Long Porter's Tale" we find that it is possible to get to the Edge of the World with a ticket from Victoria Station—a ticket "that they only give if they know you." There is complete deflation at the end of "The Long Porter's Tale," where we are told flatly that the "grizzled man" who told it is "a liar"; while the interminable "A Story of Land and Sea" concludes with a pompous "Guarantee to the Reader" whose final paragraph reads:

> Meanwhile, O my reader, believe the story, rest-
> ing assured that if you are taken in the thing shall be a
> matter for the hangman.

Tales of Three Hemispheres continues the lamentable tendency, with abrupt shattering of the atmosphere by direct addresses to the reader, transparent social satire, and, on occasion, an intentionally flat and pedestrian style used for comic effect. Self-cannibalization continues with two moderately interesting but ultimately vacuous continuations of "Idle Days on the Yann."

Accompanying this shift of attitude is a shift in Dunsany's whole conception of fantasy. In *The Gods of Pegana*, aside from a curious mention of Olympus and Allah on the very first page, one would have no idea that the "real" world ever existed. Indeed, this mention—"*Before* there stood gods upon Olympus, or ever Allah was Allah, had wrought and rested Mana-Yood-Sushai" (my italics)—obviously states a chronological priority of Pegana to the world. Although this conception is maintained in a few other stories—note the reference to "the days of long ago" in "The Fortress Unvanquishable Save for Sacnoth" (*The Sword of Welleran*)—it is not consistent in Dunsany. Indeed, Dunsany has singularly little concern with the relation of his invented realms to the "real" world. Babbulkund was known to Pharaoh and Araby, and received gifts from Ceylon and Ind. There were Europeans in Bethmoora before its desertion. The narrator of "Idle Days on the Yann" comes "from Ireland, which is of Europe, whereat the captain and all the sailors laughed, for they said, 'There are no such places in all the land of dreams.'" So at least Yann is in a dream-world. And we have seen how it is possible to get to the Edge of the World from Victoria Station. I wonder which way the route lies. North? Does Dunsany think, with Samuel Johnson, that the Hebrides are the Edge of the World? I don't know, and it hardly matters. There is, of course, no reason why Dunsany should be consistent in the establishment of his fantasy lands: he is not writing a connected epic like Eddison or Tolkien, and he would be the first to scorn the notion that trains, maps, or any such appurtenances of the rational world have any application to his realms.

But what is more important than the precise location of Pegana is why it and similar imaginary realms gradually disappear from Dunsany's work. A glancing reference in *The Queen's Enemies* to "fairy Mitylenë," uttered by Queen Nitokris of Egypt, may be our starting-point: it does not take a classical scholar to know that Mitylene was a very real city in ancient Greece, and this is our first suggestion in Dunsany that the realm of fantasy is dependent upon perspective and imagination. *The Last Book of Wonder* brings this point home emphatically. In "A Tale of London" London is spoken of in the same exotic terms as any fabled Eastern city; in "A Tale of the Equator" a Sultan finds greater satisfaction in hearing his court poets describe a wondrous city than in actually building it. "The Last Dream of Bwona Khubla," in *Tales of Three Hemispheres*, completes the circle: here again a mirage of London seen in the depths of Africa inspires all the awe and wonder that Babbulkund or Sardathrion ever did.

Later works continue to develop and enrich the idea. *The King of Elfland's Daughter*, if stylistically a striking resumption of Dunsany's early biblical manner, is thematically quite different. One would think that this tale of a mortal man winning the hand of Lirazel, the daughter of the King of Elfland, would provide an opportunity for contrasting the prosiness of the "real" world with the wonder of an imaginary realm; but in large part the reverse is the case. To be sure, Elfland is a place of magic; but the very name of the "real" country involved—Erl, the German for "elf"—already signals a very tenuous distinction between our world and fairyland. Similarly, the names of characters in Erl—Narl the blacksmith, Guhic the farmer, Oth the hunter, Vlel the ploughman (Chapter 5)—remind us pointedly of certain inhabitants of Pegana and its congeners. And to Lirazel and the other denizens of Elfland, the real world is just as much a source of wonder as their realm is to us:

> He [a troll] told of cows and goats and the moon, three horned creatures that he found curious. He had found more wonder in Earth than we remember, though we also saw these things once for the first time; and out of the wonder he felt at the ways of the fields we know, he made many a tale that held the inquisitive trolls and gripped them silent upon the floor of the forest, as though they were indeed a fall of brown leaves in October that a frost had suddenly bound. They heard of chimneys and carts for the first time: with a thrill they heard of windmills. They listened spell-bound to the ways of men; and every now and then, as when he told of hats, there ran through the forest a wave of little yelps of laughter. (Chapter 24)

In *Don Rodriguez* and *The Charwoman's Shadow* Dunsany solves—or, rather, evades—the problem by setting the tale in a half-fantastic historical time—the "Golden Age past its wonderful zenith" (*The Charwoman's Shadow*, Chapter 1), whenever that is—but the matter is taken up again in *The Curse of the Wise Woman* and later novels. *Wise Woman* is, strangely, the first of Dunsany's novels to deal explicitly with Ireland; and with its two companions, *Rory and Bran* (1936) and *The Story of Mona Sheehy* (1939), we reach the culmination and resolution—a very curious one—of Dunsany's approach to fantasy.[20] Has Dunsany here merely replaced Pegana with Ireland? The answer is not quite as simple as that. Certainly Dunsany's lyric descriptions of Ireland in these novels creates a certain sense of shimmering fantasy, but his approach is really subtler than this. In all three novels we are quite clearly dealing with a real Ireland of farmers, tinkers, and estates. The contrast to this reality is provided, firstly, by the dialect speech put in the mouths of the Irish characters, and, secondly, by the allusions to names out of Irish folklore or topography—the half-imaginary realm of Tir-nan-og in *Wise Woman*, the mountain Slievenamona in *Rory and Bran* and *Mona Sheehy*. The first replaces Dunsany's archaistic prose, the second his resonant imaginary place-names. The Wise Woman's ponderous utterances now supply the only escapes into prose-poetry that Dunsany allows himself:

> "We walked down the river, Mother," said Marlin.
> "Aye, the river," said she, "and one of the great rivers of the world, though it's small here. For it widens out on its way, and there's cities on it, high and ancient and stately, with wide courts shining by the river's hanks, and steps of marble going down to the ships, and folk walking there by the thousand, all proud of their mighty river, but forgetting the wild bog-water." (Chapter 10)

The Story of Mona Sheehy seems to represent a dramatic shift in Dunsany's attitude to fantasy: here we are concerned with a young girl who believes herself to be a child of the fairies, when in fact Dunsany makes it abundantly—almost excessively—plain to us that she is merely the product of an illicit liaison between Lady Gurtrim and Dennis O'Flanagan. The opening and closing sentences are identical—"'I never saw a more mortal child'"—and Dunsany never tires of reminding us that Mona's belief in her magical birth is all a delusion.

It is not merely that fantasy has become relative, as in the "fairy Mitylenë" reference: fantasy here is explicitly denied. I am not sure that this novel is not the sole representative of an anomalous new genre, which might be called "psychological fantasy," on analogy with "psychological horror." Just as psychological horror is horrific but non-supernatural (Bloch's *Psycho*, Campbell's *The Face That Must Die*), so in psychological fantasy the fantasy does not exist except in the mind—here, in the mind of Mona Sheehy and the many townspeople who share her delusion. Dunsany even provides some simple-minded anthropology to account for the phenomenon:

> ...the story of many a fairy, many an elf, is probably but the history of the small things dwelling in woods,

altered a little by the eye of man, for he saw them in
dim light, altered again by his mind as he tried to explain them, and altered again by frailties of his memory, when he tried for his children's sake to remember
the stories that his grandmother told him. (Chapter
20)

I think, though, that this climax to Dunsany's fantasy work has
some possible antecedents. Thematically Mona Sheehy is very similar
to Lirazel in *The King of Elfland's Daughter*: both are outcasts from
conventional society, Lirazel supernaturally, Mona non-supernaturally.
In *The Curse of the Wise Woman* the role of the supernatural is highly
problematical: Dunsany leaves entirely open the question of whether
the titanic storm concluding the novel is a natural occurrence or the result of the Wise Woman's curses. Some highly significant passages in
Rory and Bran also anticipate the renunciation of fantasy in *Mona
Sheehy*: "The world is full of wonders, and all the wonders that our
imagination paints are but the mirages of them" (Chapter 2). And note
the constant use of similes when fairyland is invoked: "the notes of
thrushes [seemed] *like* notes from the horns of Elfland" (Chapter 20;
my italics). What in the early Dunsany would have been a bold
metaphor explicitly identifying the thrushes with Elfland has now become a mere simile which precisely negates such an identification.
Mona Sheehy, then, has its predecessors.

The shift, of course, is not irrevocable, and with many later
short stories and the novel *The Strange Journeys of Colonel Polders* we
are back amongst the supernatural; but the manner in which Dunsany
now approaches the supernatural is very different, and must be discussed when we study the notion of "belief" in Dunsany's later work.

3. Man vs. Nature

A curious coherence can be noticed in Dunsany's novels, stories, and plays of the late twenties and thirties, a coherence whose central theme is what might be called *the non-human perspective of life*.
The plays *The Old Folk of the Centuries* (1930), *Lord Adrian* (1933),
Mr. Faithful (1935), and *The Use of Man* (1937), and the novels *My
Talks with Dean Spanley* (1936), *Rory and Bran* (1936), and the very
late *The Strange Journeys of Colonel Polders* (1950) all focus around
the conflict of man with the animal world. But in truth the theme is
broader than this, and the use of a non-human perspective—seeing the
world as, say, a dog or a fox might see it—is merely a vehicle for Dunsany's wholesale criticism of modern man and the industrialized civilization he has erected; and the focal point for this criticism is nothing

less than the very brief play *The Evil Kettle* (in *Alexander and Three Small Plays*, 1925).

This powerful little play asks us to imagine the young James Watt as he notices his mother's tea kettle boiling and begins to realize the awesome potential of steam. Later the Devil comes to him and shows him apocalyptic visions of the future with the familiar "dark, Satanic mills" marring the natural environment. The symbolism of this play is very obvious (steam = factory smoke = the fires of Hell), but it nevertheless lays the groundwork for two fundamental and related principles in Dunsany's later work: one, the tragic and increasing separation of man from his natural environment; and two (evidently the cause of the first), the dominance of the machine in modern civilization. The first theme is developed in a much more interesting and dynamic way than the second, and it is worth studying in detail.

The Blessing of Pan and *The Curse of the Wise Woman*, two of Dunsany's strongest novels, portray the cleavage between man and Nature very poignantly. In *The Blessing of Pan* it is clear that the elfin tune played by Tommy Duffin, a tune that ultimately summons the inhabitants of an entire town to follow him up the hills and re-enact ancient rituals, is a means for reintegrating himself and his listeners with primal Nature. In an early scene Tommy finds it impossible to take a game of chess seriously: chess presents merely an *artificial* problem and solution; as Lovecraft once remarked in a letter, games are pointless because "after I solve the problem...I don't know a cursed thing more about Nature, history, and the universe than I did before."[21] In Dunsany the game is a symbol for the meaningless artificiality of modern civilized life: it is too far from Nature. Such a simple thing as taking off one's shoes holds great significance for Tommy: "Somehow in bare feet he felt a little closer to that mystery of which the pipes were the clue" (Chapter 6). And the ending leaves no doubt of Dunsany's message:

> Tommy Duffin's curious music...seems to have come at a time when something sleeping within us first guessed that the way by which we were then progressing t'wards the noise of machinery and the clamour of sellers, amidst which we live today, was a wearying way, and they turned from it. And turning from it they turned away from the folk that were beginning to live as we do. (Chapter 35)

Similarly, *The Curse of the Wise Woman* particularizes the conflict of man vs. Nature in the struggle of the Wise Woman to defeat a developing company which plans to drain an ancient bog—the precise theme, curiously enough, of Lovecraft's early story "The Moon-Bog" (1921). Here the Wise Woman herself is described as "something akin to those forces that ruled, or blew over, the bog, and that cared nothing for man" (Chapter 3); and the storm that in the end destroys both her and the development project points to the bitter and perhaps mutually destructive conflict in which man dares to take on Nature. And, however repulsive it may be to modern sensibilities, we must admit that the narrator's hunting expeditions across the face of Ireland—the bulk of the novel deals with them—reinforce the harmony that can be established between man and the natural world. Yes, the narrator—he is perhaps the only significantly autobiographical character in all Dunsany—kills, and kills frequently, but in some strange way he establishes a bond between himself and the world around him. Many of us perhaps find Dunsany's enthusiasm for hunting very repellent, but he never made apologies for it, and never regarded it as an aberration. It is true that the narrator of *The Curse of the Wise Woman* kills principally for food, not for sport (fox hunting is defended on the ground that the fox is a menace to sheep and poultry); but, more importantly, his hunting compels him to learn the ways of Nature, and in the end he is no more—or less—predatory than the animals he hunts and shoots.

From a slightly different perspective many of the plays in *Seven Modern Comedies* (1928) display "modern" attitudes only to condemn them. In *Atalanta in Wimbledon* a girl advertises in the paper challenging prospective husbands to a ping pong game: if he wins, he marries her; if he loses, he dies. The title becomes witheringly ironic, for not only do we have a jarring juxtaposition of ancient goddess and modern suburb, but this modern Atalanta sets up a contest for herself that obtrusively lacks the profound mythic dimensions of her predecessor. In *The Raffle* a man's soul is bartered about with unbelievable cynicism by the "business mentality" of the characters—even a bishop—as they debate how much money is worth spending to buy the soul back from the Devil. In *The Journey of the Soul*, a virtual metadrama, an acting company hopelessly misconstrues a play that does not provide the frivolous amusement and titillation expected by cast and audience alike from modern plays. In *His Sainted Grandmother* the ghost of a man's "sainted grandmother" tells the man's daughter that she was by no means as strait-laced and conventional as he has imagined: here the satire is double-edged, directed both at the old fogy's pious reverence for the "old ways" and at the callowness of the younger generation. But the unifying feature of these plays—emphasized by the almost grating modernity of diction employed in them—is the greed, shallowness, and hypocrisy of the modern world: as in many of Dunsany's later plays, there is not a single admirable character in them, not a single one who is not mercilessly caricatured.

Man's alienation from the world of Nature has entailed a concurrent polarization with the animal world: this is the theme of a whole series of works of the twenties, thirties, and later, and it is here that

Dunsany uses the non-human perspective, with varying degrees of effectiveness. Curiously, an uncollected early tale or prose poem, "From the Mouse's Point of View" (*The Open Window*, Sept.-Oct. 1911), anticipates the trend, picturing very prettily the towering vastness of a house and the shuddersome presence of the huge cat as seen from a mouse's perspective. The otherwise very slight play *The Old Folk of the Centuries*, where a boy has been turned into a butterfly, does little more than show sympathy with non-human life-forms: the boy, while being irked at his transformation, finds the situation itself comfortable and even enjoyable. It is in *Lord Adrian* (composed in 1922-1923)—where a man, injected with the gland of an ape to rejuvenate himself, begets a son (Lord Adrian) who, although perfectly normal-looking, shows disturbing affinities to animals—that the point is first made significantly; indeed, if anything, rather too obviously. Adrian makes such utterances as "I don't love men" (Act III, Scene 1) and "I regard the domination of all life by man as the greatest evil that ever befell the earth" (Act III, Scene 2), and finally concludes:

> Nature's scheme is clear enough. You see it in every bird and every flower. Every city you build, every noisy invention you make, is a step away from the woods, is a step away from Nature, is a step that is wrong. (Act III, Scene 2)

There is some vicious satire in this play—at one point Adrian is trying to explain to his sweetheart Nellie his deep sense of sympathy with the animal world, and she replies with the appallingly platitudinous "I'm awfully fond of animals too" (Act II, Scene 3)—but on the whole the play lacks subtlety and comes across as naively moralistic. Much better is the outrageously funny *Mr. Faithful* (composed in 1922), where a man desperate for work takes on the job of a watchdog, presenting the argument that, as an intelligent human being, he can do the job far better than a mere animal. The artificial and self-serving way in which man makes use of animals is, for all the rollicking hilarity of the play, brutally underscored here; and this play is far more effective in depicting the evils of man's domination of beast than is *Lord Adrian*. A final play, *The Use of Man* (in *Plays for Earth and Air*, 1937), is even more viciously satirical. Here a man is transported in dream to a meeting of the spirits of animals, who all demand what the "use" of man is, just as he and his friends could find no especial use—from the human perspective—of badgers. None of the animals, save the obsequious dog, speaks up for man: the bird hates his cages, the mouse his traps, the cat is too aloof and indifferent to man's fate. Finally the mosquito speaks for man—he is its food.

A trilogy of novels completes the man-beast dichotomy in Dunsany. *Rory and Bran* tells of a boy and a dog as they lead cattle to a fair and back; but we are never told that Bran is a dog, and through the course of the entire novel it is possible to interpret Bran as simply Rory's brother or (human) companion. But this novel is more than a vast *tour de force* or practical joke (although evidently some reviewers never saw through the ploy); the point Dunsany is making is the senseless artificiality of distinguishing the animal and the human. This is not a contradiction of such a work as *Mr. Faithful*, but a confirmation of it from a different perspective: the world of Nature makes no distinction between man and animal—and Rory, the farmer's son, is ultimately indistinguishable from Bran because both are part of the natural landscape; it is only when men become civilized that they lose the link with Nature. I am reminded of Dunsany's statement about the Irish poet Æ, a statement that could apply more precisely to Dunsany himself: "He had a prophetic feeling that cities were somehow wrong."[22]

My Talks with Dean Spanley (1936) is an entertaining but rather slight work where a man believes himself to have been a dog in a previous incarnation. Dunsany is certainly uncannily precise in "getting into" a dog's state of mind, but this novel ends up as simply a trial run for the more exhaustive *The Strange Journeys of Colonel Polders*. Here an Indian pundit causes Colonel Polders to experience dozens of incarnations into all manner of animals—dog, cat, eel, butterfly, stag, and on and on. Again, Dunsany is enormously clever at depicting the lives and putative thoughts of various animals; but, like *Rory and Bran*, all this is more than an exercise in ingenuity. The one message hammered home again and again in Polders's account of his various incarnations is the *natural comfort* of animal life. When he is made an eel he remarks:

> "To be frank, I was perfectly comfortable. I will say that for the fellow; he always made me comfortable. No credit to him of course. It's merely that animals lead comfortable lives. And, when he sent me there, I was naturally comfortable. Not that an eel is an animal. But you know what I mean. Why animals should be any more comfortable than us I don't know. With all our conveniences, it should be the other way about." (Chapter 14)

Earlier Polders notes that "it takes so much money and so many drinks and smokes and comforts, and machinery of different sorts, to get [the] comfort" (Chapter 8) of a fox in his den. Throughout the novel, too, infallible inhuman instinct—the instinct that allows geese to fly south, an eel to reach the open sea, a sparrow to return to his home—is compared invidiously to the slow-moving human reason; and the animal's immediacy of experience leads Polders to claim that the life of a dog is "a more ample life than any, I am sorry to say, that any of us can live.

More full, more ample, life with a grander scope" (Chapter 3). As a dog Polders finds absolute contentment chasing a ball; as a sparrow he finds flies "delicious" (Chapter 6) because they are a sparrow's natural food; and Polders's keenness of sight and smell as a butterfly prompts his exclamation, "How blunt our senses are!" (Chapter 17). *The Strange Journeys of Colonel Polders* may seem formless, but Polders's kaleidoscopic shifting from one incarnation to the next—with each incarnation designed for maximum contrast with its predecessor—is all the form a novel of this sort needs.

The other branch of Dunsany's criticism of modern man—the dominance of machines—is not handled with nearly the richness or subtlety as the theme of man's alienation from Nature. It is, of course, man's increasing mechanization that has initiated this alienation to begin with, and it is a notion that can be found as early as his essay "Romance and the Modern Stage" (1911). The evils of industrialism randomly and tangentially enter many of Dunsany's works, but one must wait until *The Last Revolution* (1951) before it is treated comprehensively. And yet, this novel of machines developing an intelligence of their own and challenging man's supremacy is not a success: the theme is handled too obviously, and Dunsany's ever-placid narrative tone never produces the requisite tension and sense of dramatic conflict, in spite of one exciting scene where the protagonists are besieged in a house by the machines. It is almost as if the theme was so close to Dunsany's heart that he could never treat it except in this blunt and obvious way. As it is, a much more successful handling of the idea occurs in a very late story, "The Ghost of the Valley" (1955), which ends poignantly:

> "Times are changing," it [the ghost] said. "The old firesides are altering, and they are poisoning the river, and the smoke of the cities is unwholesome, like your bread. I am going away among unicorns, griffons, and wyverns."
> "But are there such things?" I asked.
> "There used to be," it replied.
> But I was growing impatient at being lectured to by a ghost, and was a little chilled by the mist.
> "Are there such things as ghosts?" I asked then.
> And a wind blew then, and the ghost was suddenly gone.
> "We used to be," it sighed softly.[23]

This is a fine conceit: the disappearance of the creatures of the imagination is a powerful symbol for the disappearance of wonder and mystery in the industrial age, and brings full circle the pensive warning that Dunsany made at the beginning of his career: "I know of the boons that machinery has conferred on man, all tyrants have boons to confer, but service to the dynasty of steam and steel is a hard service and gives little leisure to fancy to flit from field to field."[24]

4. Jorkens

The five volumes of tales about the clubman Joseph Jorkens must be considered as a unit. Lovecraft may not be the only one to find it odd, even vaguely repellent, that Dunsany could have written these light-hearted *jeux d'esprit*; but again such a reaction is to deny the diversity of Dunsany's literary work. If many of the Jorkens tales are quite frivolous and "clever" in the pejorative sense of the term, many of them underscore in a lighter vein the central themes of Dunsany's work. In particular we note, in three tales in *The Travel Tales of Mr. Joseph Jorkens* (1931), the preoccupation with the man-beast dichotomy dominant in Dunsany's work of the 1930s. In "The Tale of the Abu Laheeb" Jorkens stumbles upon a species, unknown to science, that like man has learnt the control of fire. Jorkens refuses to shoot the beast precisely because of this unholy but inescapable relation to man. One is immediately reminded of *Lord Adrian*, where Adrian is at the end killed just as he is beginning to teach animals the use of fire: man's domain must not be usurped in this way.

In "Our Distant Cousins," a rather peculiar science fiction tale, a man discovers that the humanoid inhabitants of Mars are *not* the dominant species on the planet. In "The Showman" apes in Africa capture a circus showman and display him in a cage; the title becomes a pun, as it does in "Elephant Shooting" (*Jorkens Has a Large Whiskey*, 1940), where an ancient four-tusked elephant sees through a trap and shoots a hunter with his own rifle. Two other tales reveal the fragility of our supremacy over the natural world. In "The Walk to Lingham" (*Mr. Jorkens Remembers Africa*, 1934) Jorkens is unnerved as he senses a line of poplars following him menacingly along a deserted road: he feels that these trees do not grant "the respect that is due to man"; but the trees withdraw as Jorkens approaches a town, and he remarks with a significant political metaphor—"I knew at once that there had been no revolution"—that anticipates *The Last Revolution*. Finally, in "On Other Paths" (*Jorkens Borrows Another Whiskey*, 1954) Jorkens, having angered some African gods, is given a glimpse of the state of things if man had not secured domination over beasts; and he reflects:

It was very likely a nearer thing than we think, our getting the domination. We had to beat the mammoth and the tiger. It might easily have gone some other way.

There is less development, stylistically and thematically, in the Jorkens tales than in the rest of Dunsany's work; perhaps necessarily so, given the nature of the serial character. The trick that Dunsany has to accomplish in these tales is to amaze us with highly remarkable events and inventions and yet conclude the tale with Jorkens—and the world—not significantily different from how they were at the beginning of the story. As a result, Jorkens finds and loses many fortunes ("A Large Diamond," "The Pearly Beach," "A Nice Lot of Diamonds," and several others), he marries a mermaid but she swims away at the end ("Mrs. Jorkens"), and he is a witness to countless fantastic inventions which are either lost or destroyed. One story, "Making Fine Weather" (*The Fourth Book of Jorkens*, 1948), offers a variation on this theme. Here we are asked to believe in a man who has discovered the secret of controlling the weather, and who produces a torrential rainstorm on a clear day: "You may remember that year, when all the oats in England were laid flat." But whereas the occurrence might conceivably have been real (as the Vermont floods of 1927 in Lovecraft's "The Whisperer in Darkness" were real), only Jorkens knows the "real" cause of it. A man goes to Mars in "Our Distant Cousins," but of course no one believes him; in "The Slugly Beast" the man goes back to Mars, never to return.

It would be false to say that the Jorkens tales all deal frivolously with themes dealt with seriously elsewhere in Dunsany. True enough, the later Jorkens tales begin to become parodies of themselves, as in "The Sultan, the Monkey, and the Banana," where the strange story hinted in the title is never in fact told, or in "An Unrecorded Test Match" (*Jorkens Borrows Another Whiskey*), a shaggy dog story where a man claims that the Devil has given him great prowess in cricket in exchange for a single virtue—"That of always speaking the truth." This is a wry version of the "All Cretans are liars" paradox; unfortunately, Dunsany uses precisely the same punch line in another story.25 Similarly, "The Lost Romance" is a purely non-supernatural tale of Jorkens's being outwitted by a group of clever nuns. But in at least one story the lightness of tone actually enhances the power of the message. In "A Life's Work" we are told of a man who spends thirty years single-handedly shovelling away a hill, then deciding to spend thirty years shovelling it back. Behind the frivolity we get a glimpse of the monstrous futility of all human effort; and again the title becomes grotesquely ironic.

A final curious feature of the Jorkens tales is the possibility— and it is, I think, nothing more—that we are to read them sequentially. All the tales were of course written over many years, and they seem to be arranged in rough chronological order; but Dunsany is careful, in the first four of the Jorkens collections, to label each story a "chapter" and not a separate entity. I am not sure that much is really to be made of this: the first several tales in *The Travel Tales of Mr. Joseph Jorkens* are meant to be read in sequence; some stories are conscious sequels of others; but beyond this it may not be possible to go. As it is, *Jorkens Has a Large Whiskey* seems to exhibit the greatest unity of arrangement: "The Grecian Singer" is the tale of a modern Siren; "The Development of the Rillswood Estate" deals with a satyr in the suburbs; and in "A Doubtful Story" Pan talks to Jorkens in Homeric Greek and goes with him to London.

No one would want to read all five volumes of the Jorkens tales in succession; but it is remarkable how fresh and vigorous even the later tales remain. Some of these later stories are nothing but written-out jokes ("On the Other Side of the Sun," "Out West"), but Dunsany's imagination is as dynamic as ever. And it is worth serious thought whether the tone of bland casualness that, as we shall see, dominates Dunsany's later work is a result of the Jorkens tales, begun in 1925 and continued sporadically to the end of his career. The relation between the Jorkens tales and Dunsany's other work is perhaps too subtle for so simplistic an analysis, but these stories do have a place, and possibly a significant place, in Dunsany's literary output.

5. Style

Style in Dunsany is a massive issue, and we can only touch upon some central features. The magic of Dunsany's early style is close to unanalyzable, for to say that he uses the cadences of the King James Bible explains almost nothing. Certain features are very obvious—sonorous repetition, a staggeringly bold use of metaphor, just the right *soupçon* of archaism (much less, say, than in E. R. Eddison)—and can be illustrated by a single quotation from "A Legend of the Dawn" (*Time and the Gods*), that exquisite fable of the rising and setting of the sun:

> Again the Dawnchild tossed the golden ball far up into the blue across the sky, and the second morning shone upon the world, on lakes and oceans, and on drops of dew. But as the ball went bounding on its way, the prowling mists and the rain conspired together and took it and wrapped it in their tattered cloaks and carried it away. And through the rents in their garments gleamed the golden ball, but they held it fast and carried it right away and underneath the world. Then on an onyx step Inzana sat down and wept, who could no more be happy without her golden ball. And again the gods were sorry, and the South Wind came to tell her tales of most enchanted islands, to whom she listened not, nor yet to the tales

of temples in lone lands that the East Wind told her, who had stood beside her when she flung her golden ball. But from far away the West Wind came with news of three grey travellers wrapt round with battered cloaks that carried away between them a golden ball.

This passage illustrates two further aspects of Dunsany's early style: the relatively sparing use of adjectives and the exhaustive use of paratactic construction. The early Dunsany probably has significantly fewer adjectives per square inch than similar work of its kind—Wilde's fairy tales, Eddison, Lovecraft's "Dunsanian fantasies"—and Dunsany was always careful never to have mere catalogues of jewelled words and phrases. As for paratactic construction—the conscious avoidance of subordination of clauses, as contrasted with the syntactic construction of the periodic style derived from classical models—it was something Dunsany retained throughout his career, and is exemplified perfectly in a passage from *The King of Elfland's Daughter*:

> When Alveric understood that he had lost Elfland it was already evening and he had been gone two days and a night from Erl. For the second time he lay down for the night on that shingly plain whence Elfland had ebbed away: and at sunset the eastern horizon showed clear against turquoise sky, all black and jagged with rocks, without any sign of Elfland. And the twilight glimmered, but it was Earth's twilight, and not that dense barrier for which Alveric looked, which lies between Elfland and Earth. And the stars came out and were the stars we know, and Alveric slept below their familiar constellations. (Chapter 12)

There is more to this than merely the old joke of beginning every sentence with "and": there may actually be no less imagery in this passage than in one of similar size in the syntactic construction; but the effect is one of simplicity, because the failure to subordinate clauses creates the impression of linear sequentiality. This is, incidentally, the principal reason why Lovecraft's "Dunsanian fantasies," for all their close derivation from—and in some cases near plagiarism of—Dunsany's work, never ring true: Lovecraft, nurtured from infancy on the Graeco-Roman classics and their stylistic imitators of Augustan England, was too wedded to the syntactic construction to abandon it, even for the sake of imitation. Paratactic construction is really the fundamental element Dunsany himself derived from the King James Bible, and it is this element that gives to his work its distinctive air of child-like simplicity. Padraic Colum's antithesis—"We are all fictionists nowadays: Lord

Dunsany, however, is that rare creature in literature, the fabulist"[26]—is exactly right as far as this feature of style is concerned.

As Dunsany's style develops, the first thing to be sloughed off is the archaism. I do not mean to imply by this either that there is anything intrinsically wrong with archaism of diction (one only has to point to Lucretius and Spenser) or that Dunsany was at all clumsy in his early use of it: *The Gods of Pegana* could be a textbook for that sort of thing. But so early as *A Dreamer's Tales* almost all the thee's and thou's are gone. Surprisingly little is lost by this procedure, for to the end of his career Dunsany's style remained one of the most musical and subtly rhythmical in all English, and I think it can hardly be questioned that his is, quite simply, some of the greatest prose (*qua* prose) in world literature. But the loss of archaism is not immediately felt because the exoticism of setting continues to dazzle us; this carries us through Dunsany's work of the mid-1920s, at least through *The Charwoman's Shadow*.

In the plays, interestingly enough, the progression is quite otherwise. His first play, *The Glittering Gate* (1909), presents two Cockney plebeians in all their dialectic colloquialism, something one would never have expected from the author of "Poltarnees, Beholder of Ocean." But this aberration gives way to the richly melodious and atmospheric plays of Dunsany's early period—*Five Plays*, *Plays of Gods and Men*, and *Alexander* (written in 1912)—although even here *The Lost Silk Hat* (1913) seems an anticipation of his later work. But the real watershed seems to be *Plays of Near and Far*, whose plays were composed around 1919 and 1920. Here we have the archaistic plays—*The Compromise of the King of the Golden Isles*, *The Flight of the Queen*—juxtaposed with plays in modern idiom: *Cheezo*, *A Good Bargain*, *If Shakespeare Lived To-day*, *Fame and the Poet*. There is much reason for this, for all these plays quite obviously satirize various features of the modern world. In *If* Dunsany can have his cake and eat it, too, for the plot allows him to go from modern London to the Near East and back again. In fact, a large part of the success of this play is the startling contrast between modernism and archaism, as in the following bit of dialogue:

> JOHN: ...But who is your master?
> ALI: He is carved of one piece of jade, a god in the greenest mountains. The years are his dreams. This crystal is his treasure. Guard it safely, for his power is in this more than in all the peaks of his native hills. See what I give you, master.
> JOHN: Well, really, it's very good of you. (Act I, Scene 2)

31

This sort of device is found in diluted form in one late play—*Golden Dragon City*, in *Plays for Earth and Air*—but otherwise Dunsany abandons the prose-poetic style entirely in his remaining dramas: *Mr. Faithful, Lord Adrian, Seven Modern Comedies, The Old Folk of the Centuries*, and the remaining *Plays for Earth and Air*.

In the novels and later stories a similar tendency is at work, but the break is not quite so clear-cut. *The Blessing of Pan* is one of Dunsany's most carefully written works, and its subtly modulated and understated prose is as effective in creating an atmosphere of fantasy as the most involved archaism would have been. Here Dunsany's earlier bold metaphors have given way to an equally bold and precise symbolism:

> Very soon he [Anwrel] saw the trees rising over the hedges, both of which encircled the rectory and church of Rolton. Great fields lay around it, stretching far away, and the trees seemed guarding that part of the parish from the level waste of the eternal fields. A few farmhouses straggled away behind. (Chapter 20)

The hedges encircle the rectory and church because in the end the forces of Nature, symbolized by Tommy's tunes on the Pan pipes, will overwhelm Anwrel's conventional religion and lead him to partake of the ancient rituals; the few farmhouses suggest the tenuous hold of modern civilization over the "great fields" of Nature. A later reference to the music of the pipes as "that awful messenger" (Chapter 26) brilliantly suggests two things at once: the messenger "awful" in the modern sense to Anwrel, but "awful" in the archaic sense ("aweful") to the rest of the community; and this punning antithesis is all the more apt in that Anwrel represents the modern world and the other inhabitants the ancient world of primitive Nature-worship.

We have seen how, in *The Curse of the Wise Woman*, the utterances of the Wise Woman allow Dunsany a few moments of archaism and prose-poetry. The narrative itself occasionally bursts forth into restrained lyricism, and Dunsany can still coin breathtaking metaphors, as in the description of a sunset as "that unseen finger lifted to still the world" (Chapter 17), or, during the apocalyptic storm: "I seem to remember the sound of the crash of the strides of Time" (Chapter 32). Obvious as this sort of dactylic prose is, it is yet effective in context. And one earlier passage must be quoted at length:

> So we went further into the bog. And Marlin found a place for me, and there I waited, with no thought but for the coming of the geese, while Earth darkened and the sky became like a jewel of a magi-

cian in which some apprentice to magic gazes deeply, but comprehends nothing. And while I waited the hush of the evening seemed to deepen, until quite suddenly into that luminous stillness there stepped the rim of the moon, stepped flashing like the footsteps of a princess of faery coming into our world from her own, shod in glittering silver. And, as it rose, it slowly became golden, a vast orb holding me breathless, no pallid wanderer of the wide sky now, but huge on the edge of Earth like an idol of gold on its altar. I gazed at that magical radiance, forgetting the geese. And just as the lower edge of the great disc left the horizon I turned to Marlin to say something of what I felt, but said no more than: "It's a fine moonrise, Marlin." (Chapter 17)

All the features of Dunsany's earlier style—paratactic construction, boldness of metaphor and simile, utter simplicity of diction—are here, but modernized; more importantly, the lyricism is now brought to bear in describing a very real occurrence.

    Rory and Bran and *The Story of Mona Sheehy* seem more archaistic because of their greater use of Irish dialect, which—at least in Dunsany's rendition—seems, if not more archaic, at least more metaphorical than normal speech, as in Mona's memorable phrase defending her supposedly fantastic lineage: "Sure, we have nothing to do with Heaven" (Chapter 9). But in Dunsany's short stories and novels of the 1930s and 1940s the modernism of tone has yielded to a positively flat and almost pedestrian style. Again, even this style is still inherently musical, but if we did not know better we would think we were dealing with an English Hemingway. The Jorkens stories are the prime examples here, but other works confirm the tendency. Dunsany remarked that the humor of *My Talks with Dean Spanley* stems from the contrast between the dean's "rather polished language"[27] and the dog's thoughts he claims to utter. This statement is interesting because, firstly, it points to the fact that Dunsany chose his laconic, conversational style deliberately (note that two of his last three novels, *The Strange Journeys of Colonel Polders* and *The Last Revolution*, are very largely dialogue); and secondly, it indicates that humor has become a prime concern with Dunsany. The role of humor in the late works will be studied later, but we can note here that virtually all his fiction of the 1940s and 1950s—the Jorkens tales, the short stories in *The Man Who Ate the Phoenix* and *The Little Tales of Smethers* (although several were written in the 1920s and 1930s), the two novels mentioned above, and many uncollected stories, especially those contributed to *Punch*—are avowedly comic; only the anomalous *His Fellow Men* stands apart amongst his late works. And the means Dunsany chose to convey his dry humor was the deadpan tone exemplified in the following passage from *Colonel Polders*:

> We were again in the reading-room, where I had persuaded our little party to adjourn as soon as possible, because I had seen the colonel looking too often towards the pundit; and, when one reflected that Polders had been a tiger and was but just now remembering it, while Sinadryana had caused him more than one violent death, it was easy to realize how inharmonious, and detrimental to the best interests of the club, a meeting between them might be. There was of course no guarantee that the pundit would not enter the reading-room; indeed, there was a probability that he would; but trouble in the future somehow seemed better than immediate trouble now. I think all of the colonel's little audience saw my motive, and did what they could to further it. Over our coffee and some liqueurs we sat silent awhile. And then the colonel looked up from his coffee. "Yes, I was a tiger," he said. (Chapter 16)

How successful this is, I have no especial interest in deciding: for my part I think *Colonel Polders* a masterpiece of comic fantasy (or fantastic comedy), and many stories in *The Man Who Ate the Phoenix* are very amusing; but Dunsany was writing a great deal in this period, and some—perhaps much—necessarily falls flat. I do not think that many of the parodic detective stories in *The Little Tales of Smethers* are particularly successful; in any case, Dunsany's style in this last decade and a half of work becomes, for once, too uniform and monotonous to be consistently effective. It is foolish to criticize Dunsany for developing this vein of writing: it was in many senses a logical development of his stylistic and aesthetic conceptions of the 1920s and 1930s, with, firstly, the emergence of Jorkens and, secondly, the repudiation of fantasy in plays and novels alike. But I think Dunsany's writing becomes rather mechanical after a while, especially in his endless *Punch* sketches (many of them neither funny nor clever) and other uncollected tales. But works like *Colonel Polders* and the wickedly funny "The Two Bottles of Relish" (1932) redeem almost any amount of routine hackwork.

6. Dunsany the Dramatist

Something must be said of Dunsany the dramatist. It is by the drama that he initially achieved his tremendous popular acclaim of the teens and twenties, and throughout his career Dunsany provided eminently actable plays for "little theatres" both in America and England. And although his playwriting career began almost by accident—Yeats casually asked him to write a play for the Abbey Theatre—Dunsany seems to have known from the beginning that a novelist or short-story writer, however successful, is not necessarily a successful playwright; and it was Dunsany's ability to adapt his skills for the stage that makes him one of the most powerful dramatists of his period. Some of his dramatic touches are mind-numbingly simple: we have observed the "faint and unpleasant laughter" that is heard in the background throughout *The Glittering Gate*: the chilling hideousness of this effect has to be heard or imagined to be perceived. Then there is the simple device, early in *Alexander*, of Alexander the Great sitting casually upon "some fallen pillar or stone" (Act I)—what a powerful anticipation of his eventual doom!

Dunsany knew that even the finest prose in dialogue could never make a successful play; indeed, he advises strongly against making fine dialogue an end in itself:

> The essential thing is the drama...it is the sudden manifestation of one of Destiny's ways...Dialogue is the means whereby such things are shown on the stage, and is to dramatists what canvas is to the painter, or bricks to the architect. You seldom praise the canvas of a painter, indeed you do not see it, and one never says of a fine house that the bricks are very good, well baked and square at the ends, for a heap of bricks is not architecture. Let us be equally sure that brilliant dialogue is not drama.[28]

This is not to say that dialogue in Dunsany is not fine, but it is always subordinate to the dramatic point. The magnificently jarring opening of *King Argimenes and the Unknown Warrior*, where Argimenes, now enslaved, says with great satisfaction, "This is a good bone; there is juice in this bone," brings home the awfulness of his fate more powerfully than pages of high-flown lament could have done. A more elaborate example is *If*, a meditation on the nature of Time. John Beal, an ordinary London salesman, is offered the chance to change a single incident in his past, although this alteration will still allow him to return (in some fashion) to his present home and circumstances. Beal chooses to relive a moment ten years before when he was not permitted to board a train to work—a harmless enough incident, one supposes. The result, of course, changes his entire life and takes him to the East in company with a *femme fatale*, Miralda Clement. The shift in Beal's circumstances is conveyed almost entirely by language: as the play opens Beal is the typical suburban Englishman ("By jove!"; "Very good of you"; "Cater's rather an ass"); as the scene shifts to the east, so too does Beal:

> And I will exalt myself. I have been Shereef
> hitherto, but now I will be king. Al Shaldomir is less
> than I desire. I have ruled too long over a little coun-
> try. I will be the equal of Persia. I will be king; I
> proclaim it. The pass is mine; the mountains shall be
> mine also. And he that rules the mountains has mas-
> tery over all the plains beyond. If the men of the
> plains will not own it let them make ready; for my
> wrath will fall on them in the hour when they think
> me afar, on a night when they think I dream. (Act
> III, Scene 2)

But as Beal returns to London after the ten years of his altered life, so
too do his old habits of language return:

> I had been intended for work in the City. And
> then, then I travelled, and—and I got very much taken
> with foreign countries, and I thought—but it all went
> to pieces. I lost everything. Here I am, starving.
> (Act IV, Scene 2)

This is a brilliant example of how Dunsany can use dialogue
not only to enhance the drama but to draw character: the inherent
weakness of Beal's personality is signalled by these radical shifts in his
speech. I think it ought to be pointed out that Dunsany is in fact one of
the few fantaisistes who can draw character at all. Machen was never
successful at portraying any character that did not resemble himself;
Lovecraft sidestepped the whole issue by vaunting "phenomena" as the
real characters in his stories. But Dunsany, both in his fiction and his
dramas, could vivify just about any character he chose. I think one of
the most delicate examples is Queen Nitokris in *The Queen's Enemies*.
It seems that this sort of character—the woman who, under a guise of
helplessness, masks her vengeful and ruthless nature—held a fascination
for Dunsany, for we find it again in the Miralda of *If*. But the Queen is
even subtler than Miralda, and is one of Dunsany's masterful creations:
throughout the play she debases herself before her enemies as they dine
in her underground chamber; but even at the end, when she lets in the
Nile to carry them off, she does not relinquish her façade—after all, it
was simply her sensitive nature that could not bear to have enemies.
Dunsany was right to take pride in the conclusion:

> ACKAZARPSES: Illustrious Lady, the Nile has
> taken them all.
> QUEEN (with *intense* devotion): That holy river.
> ACKAZARPSES: Illustrious Lady, will you sleep to-
> night?

QUEEN: Yes. I shall sleep sweetly.

Dunsany was most proud, however, of *The Gods of the Mountain*: "Was this not something new to the English stage?"[29] The absolute flawlessness of this play beggars analysis, and I shall say nothing about it save to note that both Lovecraft and Dunsany himself seem to have been mesmerized by that portentous utterance "Rock should not walk in the evening" (Act III), as a character sees the real gods of the mountain come to take vengeance on the beggars who have set themselves up *as* the real gods. Dunsany quite elegantly justifies this utterance by remarking, "When people are terrified they are likely to say simple things"[30]—a secret to much of the effectiveness of Dunsany's entire work. *The Gods of the Mountain*, more than any of his other plays, is magnificent in its dramatic modulation, its sense that Destiny is commanding Dunsany's pen. It is as close to Greek tragedy as the twentieth century will ever get.

The Gods of the Mountain also uses what proves to be a favorite dramatic device of Dunsany's—the rapid multiple elimax. This effect is seen to good advantage in the otherwise peculiar play *Cheezo*. Here we have two threads of action: one, the quest of an unscrupulous businessman to invent a substitute for cheese; and two, an Anglican preacher's desire to win the hand of the businessman's daughter. Both threads are resolved brilliantly and simultaneously in the dynamic conclusion. The businessman opposes the marriage because the preacher cannot bring himself to accept the notion of eternal punishment, a stance that hinders his advancement; there seems no way round this impasse until the cleric sees that the cheese substitute, Cheezo, has indeed been eaten by some mice, but that it has killed them. (What Dunsany would have done with Cheeze Whiz, I have no idea.) This unfortunate result, far from deterring the businessman, only goads him the more defiantly to market his product. It is at this point that the preacher says, "suddenly with clear emphasis": "I THINK I DO BELIEVE IN ETERNAL PUNISHMENT."

Alexander concludes not with a multiple climax but a deliberate anticlimax. Throughout the play we witness Alexander's growing belief, fostered by his sycophantic supporters, in his own divinity; but the climax of the play is not his lingering death from fever, but the bourgeois reflections of his party after he has died. It is not merely that Alexander is mortal; it is that he must posthumously suffer the scorn and contempt that is the natural pendant to his former elevation:

1ST ARCHER: It is a hard thing, comrade, that none will bury Alexander.
2ND ARCHER: What matters it what becomes of Alexander now that we are governed by plain honest men.

1ST ARCHER: Indeed you are right, comrade. And
    yet he was worthy perhaps of burial. (Act IV,
    Scene 2)

But Alexander remains unburied, his body ignored by all save Rhododactilos, Queen of the Amazons.

The later plays tend to be less intense—inevitably so, what with their almost abrasively modern diction and their pervasive irony and deflation—but still dramatically effective. Some of the *Plays for Earth and Air* were adapted from earlier short stories, one not so successful (*Golden Dragon City*, adapted from "The Wonderful Window") and one very successful (*The Bureau de Change*, from "The Bureau d'Echange de Maux"). In this latter case the play is more effective than the story—as Dunsany recognized[31]—because the play creates an almost kaleidoscopic effect as various characters discuss the exchanging of their "evils," some trivial and some quite otherwise, with each other. The dialogue is the key to this play, and the narrative prose of the story cannot come close to duplicating the effect. Similarly, the insubstantial short story "The Use of Man"[32] was turned into a magnificent little play; again the secret is dialogue, especially the dialogue of the silly young fool upon whom has been thrust the unenviable task of defending the "use" of the human race.

7. Satire and Philosophy

Dunsany found it irksome when critics labelled his early work allegorical; he was, I suppose, right to do this, but some of his early work, if it is not allegory, must be termed parable, and there is certainly a preponderance of irony, satire, and scarcely veiled philosophy in the whole of Dunsany's work. It may seem a little late in the game to discuss Dunsany as philosopher; but the fact is that he never evolved—and never claimed to evolve—a coherent philosophy and made it the foundation of his whole work, as Machen and Lovecraft did. We have seen bits of philosophy come out in our previous discussions—Dunsany's aestheticism as the source for his easygoing atheism and his hatred of industrialism and advertising; his sense of man's alienation from the natural world—but some works are so consciously philosophical, so endowed with an obvious "message," that they deserve to be studied separately.

But before doing so we should address a related question. I can never escape the nagging sensation, especially in reading his early work, that much of Dunsany does not "mean" anything in particular. What I am trying to say is that some of his work is so exquisitely and transcendentally beautiful that it seems to serve as its own justification; if there is any "meaning" behind it, it may be only to exemplify Wilde's great dictum, "The artist is the creator of beautiful things." There is, in the end, nothing wrong with this, although some serious critics may find this thematic or philosophical vacuity (if it is that) annoying. Take a story like "A Legend of the Dawn" (*Time and the Gods*): its sole function is to present a heartrendingly beautiful account of the rising and setting of the sun as represented by the child Inzana as she plays with her golden ball. In this ease Dunsany is perfectly correct in stating that no allegorical interpretation can be made; or, rather, that the allegory is so obvious and explicit that it is useless in the interpretation of the story. All we can do here is simply stand back and enjoy the effect, as we would some flawlessly chiselled Greek statuary.

Even some of his novels seem to be impervious to analysis. *Don Rodriguez* and *The Charwoman's Shadow* are merely (merely!) entertaining stories. Yes, I suppose one can say that the charwoman who has lost her shadow can symbolize the social outcast who is not accepted by conventional society; some such interpretation is even hinted in one passage:

> All this ridiculous fuss about a trifle, and not a trifle that they even set any store by themselves; for who prizes his shadow, who compares it with that of others, who shows it, who boasts of it? A trifle that they knew to be a trifle, the least useful thing on earth; a thing that nobody sold in the meanest shop and that nobody would if they could, and that nobody would buy, a thing without even a sentimental value, soundless and weightless and useless. (Chapter 15)

The same might be said of Lirazel in *The King of Elfland's Daughter*; but does such an interpretation really get to the heart of these novels? I don't think so, and I think that we as critics shall have to rethink this whole issue of whether an explicit "message" must be tied to every work. There is something to be said for pure expression.

But there are other works where the philosophical message is dominant, and Dunsany can use various forms of irony and satire to convey the message. The most concentrated of such works is the collection of prose-poems, *Fifty-One Tales* (1915). I am not sure that this is not in the end Dunsany's finest collection, as every story is one flawless facet of Dunsany's whole approach to life and literature. In under 500 words each of these stories distills a certain essence of the Dunsanian world-view: really speaking, it is as close to philosophy as he ever came.

Dunsany brings all his known tools into play here—simplicity of utterance, boldness of metaphor, a sprinkling of archaism, and all the rest. Many tales deal with the concept of Time—Time as the foe to beauty but also as the cleanser of ugliness; Time in conflict with Art for supremacy and survival. In "The Raft-Builders" writing is likened to rafts, but "Oblivion's Sea" deals mercilessly with most of them; the conclusion can only be quoted:

> Our ships were all unseaworthy from the first.
> There goes the raft that Homer made for Helen.

What can one say when faced with prose like this? Or take "The Prayer of the Flowers," one of Lovecraft's favorites: the message is heart-stoppingly simple—the flowers see the rise of great cities with their smoke and noise, but Pan calms them by saying, "Be patient a little, these things are not for long." It is this offhand way that Dunsany can speak of the destruction of civilization that makes many of these tales so powerful; and he does not require even his understated prose to achieve the effect. In "The Workman" the ghost of a man who has fallen from a scaffolding comes to the narrator and says bluntly: "Why, yer bloomin' life 'ull go by like a wind, and yer 'ole silly civilisation 'ull be tidied up in a few centuries." The secret of this passage is "tidied up": not only is it shockingly colloquial, but it implies that civilization is some contemptible stain that must be cleaned up. One could write essays on every one of the *Fifty-One Tales*: they are all parables, devastating in their simplicity.

A somewhat anomalous use to which Dunsany puts philosophy is in a group of tales whose point is nothing less than literary criticism. Methodologically this is different from parody—Lovecraft's "Sweet Ermengarde," for example, a send-up of the Horatio Alger-type story—although the end result is the same, the emphatic underscoring of a particular critical stance. The first example seems to be the Jorkens tale "The Club Secretary" (*Mr. Jorkens Remembers Africa*), where Jorkens stumbles upon a very exclusive club—a club for famous poets, so rigid in its membership qualifications that Pope is only a hall porter. There is no need to cite passages from Dunsany's nonfiction to show his dislike of Pope and the "school of wit" he represented. Late in his career Dunsany produced many tales of this type, most rather crude and obvious, but some quite successful, or at least mildly amusing. "Darwin Superseded"[33] displays a man who has proved that modern poetry is a sure sign that man has begun to reverse the course of evolution and return to primitivism; he concludes: "In fact, if my theory is sound, as I feel sure it is, this should bring us back to the trees before the end of the century." This was a theme Dunsany never tired of uttering, not only in countless articles and diatribes against what he felt was the irrationality of modern poetry, but in stories like "A Fable for Moderns" (1951),[34] a scathing attack on T. S. Eliot (never named, of course), or "The Awakening," where a man, listening to a pianist, senses that he is finally beginning to understand modern music and spins a grandiose philosophical interpretation of the piece—but the "pianist" is only the piano-tuner. Obvious as this is, it is redeemed by its unrelenting ferocity.

The issue of irony and satire in Dunsany is a large one, and we have earlier pointed out certain examples. Again we must say that much of the effectiveness of Dunsany's satire comes from the unnerving contrast between the viciousness of the irony and the mild and gentle manner of its expression. Some of the later plays exhibit this tendency brilliantly. Throughout the *Seven Modern Comedies* and the *Plays for Earth and Air* we look in vain for an admirable character; the success of several of these plays lies in the fact that *everyone* is the target of satire. *Golden Dragon City*, in the latter collection, portrays each of its three characters as shallow and unimaginative fools. A man has bought a window from a strange Arab and sets it up in his flat; and the window magically reveals a fantastic city under siege from an invading army. But the miracle of this sight escapes everyone—Bill, his landlady, and his sweetheart Lily—and it becomes nothing but a carnival amusement. A single bit of dialogue will be enough:

> BILL: Won't you take another look at your city, Mrs. Lumley?
> MRS. LUMLEY: Not now, thank you, sir. I've a few things to do. I'll take a good look later. I'm glad we've got it down there. Come to think of it, I really am. I'll be going now, sir. (EXIT)
> BILL: Well, Lily, when you've finished your muffin we'll take another look at the city.
> LILY (mouth full): Yes.

A Matter of Honour is a vicious parody of a deathbed scene, as a dying man confesses, "as a matter of honour," that he once succeeded in seducing a bishop's wife, thereby winning an old bet from his two friends. And we have seen how, in *The Raffle*, all the characters are mercilessly flayed as they bandy about the monetary value of a man's soul.

When Dunsany shifted to a lighter and more overtly humorous style in the 1940s and 1950s, the ferocity of his satire tended to wane and yielded occasionally to a wistful pensiveness that is almost reminiscent of *Fifty-One Tales*. Three tales collected in *The Man Who Ate the Phoenix* are good examples. In "The Policeman's Prophecy" (first published 1930) Dunsany uses the casual remark of a policeman to a reckless driver, "You'll kill yourself and everybody else," as a springboard to imagine a world without human beings; concluding with the reflection, "What a noise we made! But it will all be forgotten." "Poseidon" (first published 1941) speaks of a man travelling in Greece who meets the ancient god of the title; but Poseidon is a weak and insubstantial god now, no longer having any worshippers, and at the end he quite literally fades away. In a more amusing vein is "The Honorary Member," where we find the god Atlas an honorary member of a London club. The message is the same as in "Poseidon"—Atlas has no place in the world because, as he remarks, "The world's got too scientific for all that"—but the effect is achieved by the brutal yet comic juxtaposition of the incongruous. I want to single out one further example where the lighter approach can nonetheless be devastating. I refer to the late work "The Speech" (*The Little Tales of Smethers and Other Stories*), one of the most remarkable stories in Dunsany's entire corpus. In pre-World War I days a firebrand member of the House of Commons plans a speech that will almost certainly bring war to Europe; the government is determined to let the man speak, but a shadowy group is equally determined to stop him in the interests of peace. This group resorts to nothing so crude as assassination—not, at any rate, of the M.P. Instead, they murder the man's father, Lord Inchingthwaite; the M.P. is suddenly a peer and cannot speak in the lower house. At this point the tale is merely amusingly clever; but we have not reached the end:

> "So war was averted," said one of us.
> "Well, yes," said old Gauscold.   "Not that it made any difference in the end."

The Great War came anyway.

8. Belief

The question of *belief* is an important and complex one in Dunsany. By this I mean the manner by which Dunsany convinces us of the reality—or at least the probability—of the supernatural or fantastic events he is describing. There seem, fundamentally, to be two ways in which this can be done in fantasy writing: one, the use of a lavish, richly textured prose style which acts almost as an incantation; and two, the minute accumulation of background details, whether accompanied by a dense prose style (Machen, Lovecraft) or by a colloquialism or flatness of diction so as to make the events more believable (M. R. James, Kipling). Dunsany, of course, makes extensive use of the first in his early work, but never fully utilizes the second once he abandons his quasi-biblical prose; in fact, what Dunsany does in his late work is to evade the question of belief altogether. But his early prose style is so rich and lyrical as to be almost hypnotic: the effect is to convince us effortlessly, whether we are dealing with ersatz religion or folklore (*The Gods of Pegana, Time and the Gods, The Sword of Welleran*) or parable (*Fifty-One Tales*). And yet, the parables of *Fifty-One Tales* in a way prefigure the later work: no one of course is expected to believe, in "The Prayer of the Flowers," that the flowers actually have feelings or that Pan actually speaks to them: everything here is symbol.

Dunsany's early novels convince by use of a simpler, less involved lyricism of style coupled with fantastic settings. The fantastic setting is then discarded, so that in *The Blessing of Pan* we are left wondering throughout the novel whether the source of Tommy Duffin's music is supernatural or not; but this question is of no especial importance, since we are really concerned only with the conflict of the old (symbolized by the music) and the new (represented by Anwrel). All this suggests that Dunsany is beginning to use fantasy or the supernatural as a prop or mechanism to convey his message, so that the interest in the supernatural event as such dissipates. This use of fantasy in a way makes Dunsany's repudiation or renunciation of fantasy in *The Story of Mona Sheehy* more explicable: if fantasy is merely a means to an end, then it makes no difference whether the fantasy is in someone's mind (as it is in Mona's) or whether it is actually postulated to exist in the world. Dunsany elaborates upon the *Mona Sheehy* technique in a late work, the novelette "The Man Who Ate the Phoenix." Again we are informed at the outset of the non-supernatural nature of the events: Paddy O'Hone has not killed and eaten a phoenix, but merely a pheasant; and when Paddy begins to tell tales of the creatures he has seen after eating the bird—ghosts, leprechauns, banshees, witches, the living dead—Dunsany is careful to imply natural causes for all these events. The whole tale is one of comic deflation.

This story provides a suitable transition to Dunsany's late works. We have seen how the comic element comes to dominate his writings of the 1940s and 1950s. It is here that Dunsany, at least in part, evades the whole question of belief in the supernatural events being narrated. A starting-point might be the avowedly humorous *My Talks with Dean Spanley*. Dunsany treads the line between belief and incredulity perfectly here, and does so by the use of what might be called the *significant detail*. This is different from what Lovecraft called "the maintenance of a careful realism in every phase of the story *except* that touching on the one given marvel"[35] because no laborious effort is made to build up this realism. It is simply that the dean's accounts of what he felt and thought as a dog are so perfectly consistent and so like what a dog might actually feel and think that they convince us willy-nilly. This tale is, for the reader, almost perverse in that we *know* Dunsany has his tongue in his cheek, and yet detail after detail hits home in an inimitable way.

This short novel's *editio major*, *The Strange Journeys of Colonel Polders*, carries the notion one step further. It is not merely that, like *Dean Spanley*, Polders's narrative is unfailingly accurate in recording the thoughts and feelings of the animals he has supposedly been; it is that Dunsany now uses a narrative technique that almost dares us to disbelieve him. This novel is written in that bare, flat, conversational style of Dunsany's late period; but, more than this, Polder announces each new incarnation in such a blunt way as repeatedly to take us aback: "In fact I was a dog" (Chapter 2); "I found that I was a fox" (Chapter 7); "the next thing that fellow did was to make me a moth" (Chapter 12); "I was a pig" (Chapter 13); "The damned fellow made me an eel" (Chapter 14); "Well, I was a tiger" (Chapter 15); and on and on and on. And yet, it is the significant detail that counts. When Polders is a cat he climbs up on a kitchen table to lap a jug of cream, but the cook repeatedly puts him back on the floor; nothing could capture the serene self-centeredness of a cat better than Polders's ingenuous statement at this point: "She can't have known what she was doing" (Chapter 18). Or there is the stupendous understatement in Polders's remark when, as a fox, he is being chased by hounds: "There is no other experience quite like it" (Chapter 11). But Dunsany is toying with us; and when Polders finally becomes a djinn, our unwilling credulity is strained to the breaking point.

One other means Dunsany uses to evade or undermine the question of belief is tacitly to deny the credibility of the narrators of the stories. This is something we find in both early and late stories: many of the stories in *The Last Book of Wonder* are tales told by various unreliable narrators, and we have seen how, in "The Long Porter's Tale," the narrator's deceitfulness is explicitly declared. The Jorkens tales make this technique a fine art, and again we tread the line between believing in the plausibility of what Jorkens is saying and the implausibility of his ever telling the truth. Indeed, it could be said that the one unifying feature in the stories included in both *The Man Who Ate the Phoenix* and *The Little Tales of Smethers* is the fact that nearly all of them are narrated indirectly—*i.e.*, through the voice of a character and not that of an omniscient narrator. Dunsany rarely states bluntly that we are to disbelieve these stories, but the use of the unreliable narrator absolves him from taking any stance whatever as to the veracity of what is being told.

I think it is worth discussing Dunsany as a science fiction writer in this context. Several works—the two Jorkens tales dealing with trips to Mars, "Our Distant Cousins" and "The Slugly Beast"; "The Possibility of Life on the Third Planet" (*The Man Who Ate the Phoenix*), about a radio message from Mars; *The Last Revolution*; and a few others—can be classified as science fiction by their subject-matter; but I hesitate to call Dunsany a real science fiction writer because he makes no especial effort to convince us of the probability of any of the events he is describing. This sense of intentional incredulity is dominant in the three short stories mentioned: the spaceship used to get to Mars is described in the most perfunctory way, as is the means by which the message from Mars reached a human radio operator and was translated by him. Dunsany is not interested in the mechanism but the effect: the effect of "Our Distant Cousins" is to portray a humanoid race that is *not* the dominant species on the planet; the effect of "The Possibility of Life on the Third Planet" is again the deflation of human self-importance, since the message speaks contemptuously of the great improbability of intelligent life existing on the Earth. In *The Last Revolution* the mechanism—intelligent machine life—is not ignored but simply presented bunglingly. Dunsany has no awareness of the stupendous complexity and difficulty of artificial intelligence, and this novel—like its antecedent, "The New Master" (*The Little Tales of Smethers and Other Stories*)—is simply unconvincing either in showing how machines could think independently or how they could come to gain the human emotions of jealousy, hatred, and ambition.

While we are at it we should discuss Dunsany as a detective writer. Here we are concerned with *The Little Tales of Smethers and Other Stories*, in particular the first nine stories in that collection, which form a cycle narrated by the travelling salesman Smethers. The interest in these tales, frankly, is not from the standpoint of detection—in this regard they are merely clever, and one ("The Shooting of Constable Slugger") uses the hoary device of the bullet made of ice that melts after inflicting the fatal injury—but rather from the standpoint of narrative technique. This is the first time in Dunsany's long career that he actually adopts another persona—that of the foolish and self-effacing Smethers—to narrate a tale. The result is interesting and amusing, but no more. Smethers constantly deprecates himself as a "small man," and stands in exaggerated awe of the detective powers of his friend Linley. The impression is that these tales are conscious parodies of the Holmes-Watson dichotomy, and perhaps we are to see the evil villain that runs through several of these tales, Steeger, as a pseudo-Moriarty. *The Little Tales of Smethers* contains several other detective tales, none especially notable; only the final tale, "The Shield of Athene," is supernatural, and it too is undistinguished.

The question of whether Dunsany is a horror writer is also worth some consideration. There are certainly horror elements all through his work: his early stories and plays hint of nameless fates for those who have offended the gods, although of course we get no Lovecraftian evocations of their reduction to "liquescent horror" or anything of the sort; and such a tale as "The Two Bottles of Relish," with its suggestion of cannibalism, is really quite revolting, and is intended to be so. One detects a smirk behind Dunsany's ostensibly self-deprecatory remark that "my literary agent was unable to get any man in England or America to touch it."[36] But this is a rare, perhaps solitary, instance of horror or gruesomeness for its own sake; Dunsany really only uses horror, as he does science fiction, as a means and not an end. The Jorkens tale "The Walk to Lingham" has all the brooding atmosphere of Machen, but the point of the tale is to suggest the poplars' tentative questioning of man's domination of the planet. Another tale, "The

Ghost in the Old Corridor,"[37] will illustrate the difference perfectly. This tale is a variant of "The Return," where the narrator at the end discovers that he himself is the ghost being discussed in the various places he visits along a lonely road (who cannot think of Lovecraft's "Outsider"?); but "The Ghost in the Old Corridor" is different in that the narrator, speaking to another man about the ghost, finds out that that man is the ghost. This is what the narrator says upon this discovery:

> I cannot say that he vanished when he ceased; for it was by now so dark that I only saw the outline of his face, and that no clearer than the will-o'-the-wisps that rose far off in the night. When his voice was silent there was nothing more to guide me to the direction in which he was, and I found my way home alone out of the marshes.

This calm, pensive ending would have been unimaginable to Lovecraft, whose narrators flee madly and precipitately from all contact with the supernatural: as defenders of reason face to face with the irrational, they can do nothing else. But Dunsany finds the situation one of pathos and not of horror; and all this points to a truth so obvious that many seem not to have realized it—that horror or fantasy is almost entirely a matter of approach rather than of subject-matter.

9. Conclusion

Throughout this paper I have discussed Dunsany's work chronologically, tracing themes, conceptions, and imagery from the beginning to the end of his career, because I think this is the only way to understand him. An honest reader of Dunsany must get beyond the early work, Siren's song as it is; one must explore what he chose to do in the nearly four decades of writing after *Tales of Three Hemispheres* (1919), and read this material with the expectation that it will be significantly different from—but not necessarily inferior to—the earlier work. I resolutely refuse to pass judgment on whether his earlier or his later writing is superior: there are times when I, like most readers, want to genuflect before *The Gods of Pegana* or *A Dreamer's Tales*, but I would never wish to part with *The Blessing of Pan*, *The Curse of the Wise Woman*, *The Story of Mona Sheehy*, or *The Strange Journeys of Colonel Polders*. But it is not a matter of likes or dislikes: Dunsany, quite simply, was always evolving as a writer. It is difficult to lay down any clear divisions in his work, especially with the recent discovery of a mass of uncollected fiction, early and late. Even the series of short-story collections from *The Gods of Pegana* to *Tales of Three*

LORD DUNSANY, by S. T. Joshi

Hemispheres cannot be regarded monolithically, since such things as *The Book of Wonder*, *The Last Book of Wonder*, and portions of *Tales of Three Hemispheres* represent a significantly different attitude to his work from that found in *Time and the Gods* or *The Sword of Welleran*. As I said earlier, the utter naiveté of the *Gods of Pegana* style was exhausted quite early on. The shift from short stories to novels with *Don Rodriguez* (1922) did not bring an immediate change of tone or style: of course, the novels as a whole are less intense and concentrated than the tales, but it would have been foolish—or at least risky—for Dunsany to have attempted to maintain the early short-story style in the novels. The real break comes, firstly, in the complete abandonment of archaism of both style and setting in *The Blessing of Pan*, then the use of his native Irish background in *The Curse of the Wise Woman*, and then the rejection of fantasy in *The Story of Mona Sheehy*. Overlapping this shift is the inclusion of overt humor, first with the Jorkens tales (the first one composed in 1925), then with *My Talks with Dean Spanley*, and finally the late stories and *The Strange Journeys of Colonel Polders*. In the plays the break is more straightforward, and the archaistic manner is abandoned almost completely after *Plays of Gods and Men* (1917). Lovecraft's comment is interesting in this regard: while he regarded Dunsany's comedies of manners (he must have been referring to the early *Lost Silk Hat* or to *Fame and the Poet*, since he was writing well before *Seven Modern Comedies* and the later plays) worthy of Sheridan, but he nonetheless regretted the change: "A reincarnated Sheridan is precious indeed, but the Dunsany of *A Dreamer's Tales* is a wonder twice as precious because it cannot be duplicated or even approached."[38] Much as I admire Lovecraft, it is precisely this attitude—this impatience with Dunsany's growth as a writer—that I am interested in combating.

In the end the career of Lord Dunsany is both unique and edifying. Let us by all means reverence the early work, the work we unconsciously designate when we use the adjective "Dunsanian"; but let us learn that the later work is just as Dunsanian because just as representative of his temperament at a later stage. Let us marvel at his seemingly effortless mastery of so many different forms—short story, novel, play, even essay and lecture—his unfailingly sound narrative sense, and the amazing consistency he maintained over a breathtakingly prolific output. Like Lovecraft, like Machen, Dunsany claimed aesthetic independence from his time and culture, became a sharp and unrelenting critic of the industrialism and plebeianism that were shattering the beauty both of literature and of the world, wrote works almost obtrusively and aggressively unpopular in tone and import, yet retained a surprising popularity—at least in terms of the sale of his work—through the whole of his career. The criticism of Dunsany is at an even more primitive level than that of Machen, Lovecraft, or M. R. James, and certainly more than that of Poe and Bierce. In part I think this is because many critics—and I will include myself in his number—find his early work so flawless of its kind as to be virtually uncriticizable, and most have not considered the later work at all. But it is also because Dunsany is seen by many simply as a *predecessor*: a dominant influence on Lovecraft, Tolkien, and others, to whom an obligatory tip of the hat and no more is necessary. Lovecraft died in 1937, the year *The Hobbit* was published; Dunsany continued to write for nearly two decades after this. I have done all I can to indicate the compelling interest in the whole of his work; later critics must continue the task of explication so that Lord Dunsany becomes more than just a hallowed name.

AUTHOR'S NOTE

I am grateful to Douglas A. Anderson, Ben Bass, Marie Claire Cebrian, Steven J. Mariconda, and Darrell Schweitzer for assistance in the writing of this paper.

II.

JAMES BRANCH CABELL

NO FIT EMPLOYMENT FOR A GROWN MAN

by Don D'Ammassa

James Branch Cabell was an aristocratic Virginian novelist and essayist whose peculiarly intellectual style caused his fantasy to be largely ignored when it was first published during the first half of the Twentieth Century. His most significant body of fantasy, a series of interrelated novels and other works running from twenty to twenty-five in number, depending upon one's individual interpretation of what should and should not be included, is generally referred to as *The Biography of Manuel*. Cabell spent so much effort working out the interrelationships of the characters in this universe that he eventually would release a genealogical history as a separate publication. Although he enjoyed a brief period of fame because of the banning of his most famous novel, *Jurgen*, his novels were almost unknown except to collectors until several were reprinted by Ballantine Books in the early years of the Adult Fantasy Series. At that time, with the exception of *Jurgen*, they had all been out of print for twenty to forty years. Why then did Lin Carter, editor of the Ballantine fantasy reprint series, refer to Cabell as the "single greatest fantasy novelist America has ever produced"? What special quality caused him to be singled out in this fashion from a company that included Howard Phillips Lovecraft, Edgar Allan Poe, Robert E. Howard, Clark Ashton Smith, A. Merritt, and others?

Cabell was in many ways this country's answer to Rabelais. There is an obvious sexual underlay to much of his fiction, often erupting into the genuinely ribald, although frequently cloaked in baroque symbolism. His novels are full of literary tricks, anagrams, references to mythical places, people, or events, or to the works of other authors. H. L. Mencken, Sinclair Lewis, Mark Twain, and others championed Cabell's fiction, and it is clear that Cabell himself felt that he was writing for a small circle of admirers rather than the general public. Indeed, the brief notoriety and popular appeal developed in much the same fashion as had that of one of his fictional characters,

Felix Kennaston. In *The Cream of the Jest* Kennaston writes a novel which becomes a commercial success only after it is decried as pornography, following which he is unable to approach writing in quite the same fashion, disillusioned as he is by circumstances. The obscure references habitually included in his novels, the intricately worked out relationships to be found in the various volumes of the *Biography*, and even the convoluted, highly intellectualized style, all point to Cabell's attitude toward writing in general, perhaps best summed up in his own words, from *The Cream of the Jest*: "...fiddling with pens and ink is, after all, no fit employment for a grown man." Even within the literary community of his time, Cabell had as many detractors as supporters, many of the former of whom considered his work frivolous, lacking respect for established institutions, or genuinely immoral.

Manuel, the central figure in Cabell's created universe, is a swineherd who becomes a knight in the mythical province of Poictesme, in thirteenth-century France, intent upon rescuing a fair maiden held in the power of the evil magician, Miramon Lluagor. Although he is the central character in only one book, *Figures of Earth*, which concerns itself primarily with the battle against Miramon and the consequences of Manuel's victory, there are numerous novels and a few shorter pieces dealing with Manuel's associates and descendants, even including some who live in the present-day town of Lichfield, probably in Virginia. After gathering together a group of followers and forming the Fellowship of the Silver Stallion, Manuel frees his homeland from invaders, then mysteriously disappears, giving rise to a cult following, the members of which expect him to someday return and redeem them from their many sins. Naturally, he never does.

Although there is much derring-do and adventure in Cabell's works, there is always the feeling that he never quite took the physical components of life seriously. He was uninterested in providing the details of a swordfight, but more interested in the motivations that led to the conflict. Rather, Cabell used the trappings and devices of fantasy to make statements about humanity's view of the world, of love, of religion, of government, and of just about anything else he felt inclined to comment upon. Carter's statement that Cabell was the greatest American fantasy writer of all time may be open to argument, but certainly it cannot be contested that he was the greatest satiric writer of fantasy in the Twentieth Century.

Cabell contended that there were three significant schools of thought about the proper attitude toward human existence, the chivalrous, the gallant, and the poetic. The chivalrous was what we might think of as a romantic point of view, in which the individual spends his life in pursuit of the goals of some higher idea—God, country, or perhaps the love of his life. The gallant viewpoint was more pragmatic. The world is pretty much as it is and we really can't change it, so we have to interpret what is going on and adapt our own actions to make the best possible use of what is offered to us. Finally, the poetic or artistic view considers the world as an unfolding drama which should be used as the source of inspiration for creative endeavor. Most of Cabell's works can be divided into these categories, depending upon the orientation of the protagonist.

Manuel's rise to fame and power is chronicled in *Figures of Earth*, but he promptly disappears at the outset of *The Silver Stallion*, which deals with the break-up of the Fellowship of the Silver Stallion and the scattering of its members, many to their ultimate doom. In his absence, Manuel's wife and a too fervent cleric combine to create a cult belief that one day he will return from Heaven to redeem the sins of his people. Manuel's supposed ascent to that high estate is reportedly witnessed by the young Jurgen, who visits an entirely different type of heaven in the volume of the same name, during his late adulthood.

The remainder of the volumes in the *Biography* deal generally with the descendants of Manuel, both in Europe and later as part of the family which migrated to the Western Hemisphere. His oldest daughter, Melicent, finds herself the pawn between two disparate men in *Domnei*, one a rebellious outlaw named Perion de la Foret, the other a pirate ruler named Demetrios, who coincidentally is the son of Miramon Lluagor, vanquished by Manuel with the aid of the enchanted sword, Flamberge. A second daughter, Ettarre, pops up in several places, being the mysterious love of a poet in "Music from Behind the Moon" and the forbidden dream lover of Felix Kennaston in *The Cream of the Jest*. Kennaston has a dream existence as Horvendile, but whenever Horvendile actually touches the woman he loves, he is immediately returned to the real world where he can never consummate his love.

Jurgen, the young boy who witnessed the ascension of Manuel, grows into a self-centered and basically unhappy middle-aged man by the time of the novel, *Jurgen*. Impressed by his defense of the existence of the Devil, a mysterious cloaked figure spirits off the wife about whom Jurgen expressed discontent, and then allows him to set off on a quest for his own perfect love, whom Jurgen believes to be Dorothy, Manuel's youngest daughter. But his adventures in a variety of worlds lead him to a quite different conclusion.

Cabell's two most common subjects are love in all its aspects and the institution of organized religion, toward the latter of which he appears to have held little respect. The religious implications of the life of Manuel the Redeemer are obvious. In *The Silver Stallion*, following his disappearance, an entire mythos arises surrounding his life, and his companions during those adventures discover that the common belief is in direct contradiction to their own particular memories of events; as time passes, they begin to edit their own lives to conform to the unfolding legend. The citizens of Poictesme become firmly convinced that one day their Redeemer will return and cleanse them of all their sins, and since this has been promised, naturally it is perfectly all right for them to go right on committing those sins until that day arrives. "It promises to gratify all their congenital desires, including cruelty. And, above all, it prevents their going mad to believe that somebody somewhere is looking out for them." The comparison with the Christian system of belief is too obvious to need explanation here. Ultimately, the cruelties inflicted in the name of Manuel's goodness become so great that the cleric who championed the legend acquires an evil power equal to and not dissimilar to that of the minions of Lucifer, who admits a grudging admiration for the man.

In *Jurgen*, the protagonist eventually makes his way to both Heaven and Hell in search of his love, and later his wife. Heaven, he discovers, did not exist until the death of grandmother, who was so upset with her discovery that the Christian God and afterlife did not exist, that she raised an uproar. Finally Koschei, the bureaucrat who really created the universe, brought into existence the Christian Heaven and God, borrowing him from Jewish mythology, just to keep her quiet. But Jurgen as he really is cannot measure up to grandmother's subjective opinion of him, and he finds Heaven not at all appealing. Conversely, Hell was created by egocentric humans who wanted to be punished on a scale consonant with their imagined sins.

The Roman Catholic Church in particular seems the target of Cabell's sharp satire in *The Silver Stallion*. A pagan named Hoprig becomes canonized simply because of the erosion of the lettering on the tomb of Horrig, the man who really should have become a saint. Since miracles have been regularly performed in the name of Hoprig, the non-believer, he decides to mend his ways and convert in order to justify people's faith in him once he discovers what has happened back on Earth. And there are frequent other references to the question of our creation: characters arguing about the nature of their author, Christ as a character "written" by God (*Cream of the Jest*), a roof that is built over the Earth when the world is at war so that no conflicting prayers will reach Heaven and present it with paradoxical situations (*Jurgen*). One of Manuel's followers is killed in a battle with a Viking, and due to a mix-up, he is carried to Valhalla while the Norseman is carried to the Christian Heaven, with comical results in both cases, as you might well imagine.

As a matter of fact, Cabell turns the idea of a Creator completely around by the very complexity of his constructed universe. God, as we know him, was created by a bureaucrat named Koschei, who really created our universe. But Koschei, we learn in *The Silver Stallion*, is a minor godling among the pantheon of Valhalla, which is ruled by Donander. Donander in turn is a character in a book written by Horvendile, the dream identity of Felix Kennaston, who may also be a character in a book by yet another character, who is one of the many descendants of Manuel of Poictesme.

JAMES BRANCH CABELL, by Don D'Ammassa

The other central theme in Cabell's work is the nature of love, both romantic and otherwise. The high sexual content of Cabell's work, although rarely expressed overtly, is a powerful theme. Many of his male characters devote their lives to the pursuit of a perfect love, only to discover for the most part that it was not quite what they had assumed. Considering the attempt to ban *Jurgen*, one might have expected that Cabell's views would be radical for his day and age, but they were in fact ultimately conservative.

For example, Jurgen takes advantage of the disappearance of his wife and the ability to leave the normal Earth to search for Dorothy, the woman he has loved from afar for most of his life. Along the way, he has affairs with a number of beautiful women, including the legendary Guenevere. But Guenevere turns out to be a disappointment, attractive but lacking in morals, and the rest of the beautiful women with whom he conducts liaisons have faults of one sort or another. Ultimately, he searches for Lisa, his wife, for despite all the conflict between them, their relationship is stable and basically they are fond of each other, an emotion which in the long term is far more worthwhile than a transitory romantic attachment.

The concept of a forbidden, remote beauty recurs frequently in Cabell's work, as well as the disappointment attendant upon acquiring what was thought to be beyond reach. In his dream identity as Horvendile, Felix Kennaston can look but not touch; whenever he actually physically contacts the lovely Ettarre, he is wrenched from that world and returned to the more mundane. In "The Delta at Rademonde," a man becomes enamored of a woman dead these thirteen hundred years, but immortalized in a painting. Through a magical device, he is able to restore her to life, but when she steps out of the painting, all of her human shortcomings become obvious and he is quickly disenchanted with the reality.

Prince Florian, protagonist of *The High Place*, finally realizes the goal of his youth when he is able to travel to the castle where the perfect woman remains forever separated from the world; he wins her love, but soon becomes disillusioned with her existence. Wars are fought and men's lives destroyed over Melicent in *Domnei*, and when she is finally rescued from Demetrios, her kidnapper, Perion realizes that she is no longer the young beauty he has sought after all of his life. Even more poignant is her own reaction to the eventual death of Demetrios, to whom she has been forcibly wed for most of her life, for now that she is to be separated from him, she discovers that the emotion she feels toward him is no longer hatred. Similar themes can be found in "The Thin Queen of Elfhame" and other titles.

In spite of the romantic ideal, Cabell generally concluded that we are better off taking a realistic view of human relationships. Despite all of the beautiful women whom he has known, Jurgen returns to his familiar wife. Manuel allows his unattractive lover to die in his place in *Figures of Earth*, but he remains loyal to her memory ever after, even while bedding a series of beautiful women, and eventually succeeds in bringing her back to life. Felix Kennaston discovers near the end of life that his wife in the real world is, in some mystical sense, the real Ettarre, and that he didn't need to enter the dream world in order to speak to her. Love, Cabell seems to feel, is a powerful force that is entirely separate from sexual attractiveness, though we may frequently confuse the two. In *Domnei*, we are told that "love may be a power so august as to bedwarf consideration of the man and woman it sways." And in *The Silver Stallion*, we are told that "it is love, not carelessness, that bids us forget our dead." For by so doing, we purify their memories and ignore their faults.

Cabell's rapier-like wit spared few targets. Jurgen at one point confronts the Master Philologist, a powerful entity whose control of language allows him to control all else. The Master Philologist is armed with his book of words, "a huge book wherein were the names of everything in the world, and justice was not among them." In *Jurgen* as well is a premonitive attack on those very forces which would hold up its publication and distribution for nearly two years: "...all the lewdness is in the insectival mind of him who itches to be calling these things by other names." It is perhaps interesting to note that in the favorable judgment which allowed the further publication of *Jurgen*, the judge decided in part because the symbolism in the book was so cleverly done that only the most sophisticated of readers would correctly interpret what was going on in any case. Perhaps reflecting on this entire situation, Cabell reflects in *Something About Eve* that "In American literature of a respectable cast, no human being has excretory functions."

Unfortunately, most of Cabell's work has once again been allowed to slip out of print. His novels are far too intellectual, his humor too subtle, his opinions too controversial to have much popular appeal. In *Something About Eve* his protagonist, Gerald Musgrave, is a novelist wrested from our familiar world when a being from an alternate reality offers to change places with him, so that he may go off and explore the world of legendry. Unfortunately, Musgrave becomes sidetracked, enchanted by a witch while almost in sight of his ultimate goal. It would have been easy for Cabell to have taken advantage of his transient fame to achieve a prominent position among writers of his time, by eschewing the erudite style he had affected in the past and catering to the public taste. But Cabell refused to be distracted, like Gerald Musgrave, from his course, and continued to write his own very special brand of fantasy, even when his name sank back into obscurity. He seemed to feel it was better to write for a select few who could appreciate what he was trying to say, even if that meant he could not count on material rewards. The result is a body of highly original work, unlike anything else of its or any subsequent time, although Cabell's influence can be found in the works of Jack Vance and other modern writers in the genre. But while his fiction is unlikely to ever achieve a wide distribution, it is equally unlikely to ever disappear entirely from the literary scene, and that is a form of literary immortality which Cabell would probably have found quite satisfying.

III.

MERVYN WALL

AND THE COMEDY OF DESPAIR

by Darrell Schweitzer

I got to see Charlie Chaplin's *Monsieur Verdoux* recently on the VCR. It's a rare and wonderful film, seldom seen because it is so out of step with the earlier Chaplin comedies, which still form the public image of the great comedian. I believe that *Monsieur Verdoux* was hastily swept under the rug when released in 1947, because the implications of it were so disturbing. (Also, the United States government was busily turning Chaplin into an unperson at that time.)

Monsieur Verdoux is the movie in which sweet, lovable Charlie Chaplin plays a mass-murderer—and remains sweet and lovable. It's a logical enough development from *The Great Dictator*, which, for all it caricatured Hitler, was essentially an *innocent* film, hopelessly naive even by the time of its release (1940). In *Monsieur Verdoux* the Tramp has lost his innocence. He isn't the Tramp anymore, but a worldly-wise Bluebeard, who is ruined in the Stock Market Crash of '29 and still has a crippled wife and a child to support. (One of those sentimental touches only Chaplin could make palatable.) So he turns to bigamy and murder, with great success. The film is sometimes like Chaplin's version of Alfred Hitchcock, complete with a wonderfully absurd sequence in which Charlie tries to arrange a drowning accident for the outrageously vulgar Martha Raye (she goes fishing in furs), only to be interrupted at the last minute by a company of yodellers. All the while, the self-absorbed victim has never suspects a thing.

The point of all this, why I am bringing it up just now, is the ending, which has a terrific impact on any sensitive viewer. Monsieur Verdoux is caught, and exposed as the monster he is. But our sympathies remain with him as he explains that by the standards of the world today, a few dozen murders are nothing. He is an amateur next to Hitler. And he goes to the guillotine in despair, not for himself, but for mankind.

Mervyn Wall, by Darrell Schweitzer

This blackest of black comedies works precisely because it *is* a comedy. As straight tragedy, it would seem too shrill. Only because we laugh are we able to accept its terrible vision at all.

There is one fantasy writer who has this ability—of presenting the terrible through laughter—and he is, to my mind, the best satirical fantasist in the world today. I have written about him briefly in *Fantasy Newsletter* once before. His name is Mervyn Wall, and he is alive and well and living near Dublin.

Wall is the author of those two marvellous, but sadly neglected fantasies, *The Unfortunate Fursey* and *The Return of Fursey* (originally published by Pilot Press in Britain in 1946 and 1948). Marvin Kaye first brought them to my attention in my interview with him and Parke Godwin (*Amazing*, March 1986, p. 66), referring to them as "two of the loveliest humorous fantasies I have ever read." Further investigation revealed a brief mention in the Tuck *Encyclopedia of Science Fiction and Fantasy* and a listing in Robert Reginald's all-inclusive bibliography, but that's about it, until very recently. The history of the field has otherwise been silent on Mervyn Wall. He has been completely missed by every reprint program of recent years—the Ballantine Adult Fantasy Series, Dover Books, the Newcastle Forgotten Fantasy Library, etc.

Happily the situation has changed a little bit. The admirable E. F. Bleiler gives Wall a glowing review in *The Guide to Supernatural Fiction*, referring to *The Unfortunate Fursey* as "a landmark book in the history of fantasy." Bleiler's *Supernatural Fiction Writers* has a whole chapter devoted to Wall, written by Robert Hogan, which, so far, is the best summary of the man and his work and his importance to the fantasy field that I have yet seen.

Nevertheless, the situation remains outrageous. That Wall remains out of print in this country, and almost totally unknown, even to fantasy writers, editors, and critics, is completely appalling.

I think you know that I am not prone to easy exaggeration, that I don't throw superlatives around at just anything that takes my fancy. But now is the time for a few superlatives: *The Unfortunate Fursey* and *The Return of Fursey* are not quaint esoterica for the specialist, folks, they are living *masterpieces*. They haven't dated slightly, and are as fresh and as powerful as when they were first written. If Terry Brooks and Piers Anthony are your standards of fantasy, then perhaps they are a bit too brainy, but for any thinking reader, they're completely accessible. They bear the same relationship to *The Sword of Shanarra* as, say, *Monsieur Verdoux* does to *The Beverly Hillbillies*. Wall and Brooks both write fantasy, but otherwise they have nothing in common. All to the better.

There are *not* a lot of lost and forgotten masterpieces out there. In some twenty years of fantasy reading, I have never made another discovery like this, and I'm not sure I ever will again. Sure, I know lots of good books that deserve reprinting. (Now that Celtic fantasies are so popular, why doesn't some brave editor reprint James Stephens's *In the Land of Youth* and *Deirdre*? They're infinitely preferable to Kenneth Flint.) But Wall is a special case.

To be blunt: he is without peer as a satirical fantasist, better than Cabell, who could be diffuse and repeated himself too much; better than de Camp and Pratt, delightful as they might have been (or de Camp still is today), because they lacked his underlying seriousness. The only writer he can be fairly compared with is T. H. White. The *Fursey* books outwardly lack the epic scope of *The Once and Future King*, since they aren't about the fall of an ideal kingdom, but about the adventures of one insignificant man. Yet they share the same sense of comedy and tragedy, intensely mingled together, and Wall has the same ability to encompass virtually all of life in a single story. His two books are, I think, a little bit better than *The Sword in the Stone*, or at least as good, for all they are a smaller achievement than the entire White tetrology.

As Bleiler points out in the entry on Wall in *The Guide to Supernatural Fiction*, the *Fursey* novels are difficult to summarize. But, briefly, they are the story of a lay brother in the Irish monastery of Clonmacnoise, circa A.D. 800. The monastery has been free of demonic invasion for a long time, but, one night, having been thoroughly pummelled by the prayers of the virtous monks, a band of devils and imps takes refuge in Brother Fursey's cell. Unfortunately, he is too slow of speech to utter the proper exorcisms in time, and the demons are able to remain. Clonmacnoise has been breached, and for Fursey, the trouble is just beginning.

He is thrown out of the monastery, spends the night in the cottage of an old hag called The Grey Mare, and then, for propriety's sake, is forced to marry her. (After all, they had spent a whole night under the same roof!) The Grey Mare is widely regarded as a virtuous woman, but actually she is a witch. When she is killed in a magic duel (which rivals White's famous one, of Merlin vs. Madame Mim), Fursey accidentally swallows her spirit, and becomes, once more, through no fault of his own, not merely a consorter with demons, but a sorcerer. He turns out to be a most incompetent sorcerer, whose sole trick is the ability to toss a rope over a branch or beam and pull down food. He woefully neglects Albert, his familiar, never letting him drink his blood in the approved fashion, and wants, more than anything else, merely to be readmitted to the monastery and put back to work in the kitchen.

But it is not to be, and Fursey spends the first book trying to prove its innocence and be reconciled with the Church. This doesn't work, and he is sure to be burnt, when the Devil himself (disguised as a Byzantine gentleman) takes an interest in the case, makes a deal with the Irish Church, and springs Fursey, who turns on his tormentors and, in front of them all, snatches up the woman he loves (she just pities him), and flies off to England on a broomstick, becoming "the first of many [Irish] exiles for whom a decent way of living was not to be had in their own country."

In *The Return of Fursey* he is extradited, but that is, again, just the beginning of the trouble. Fursey despairs of being a good Christian. After all, at the end of the first book, the Irish Church shockingly sold out to the Devil. He decides to become wicked, and goes into sorcery whole-heartedly. But this is no more successful, and he is disgraced at the Sabbat when poor Albert (who hasn't had a drop of blood all this time) misbehaves. His lady-love has married a soldier, and Fursey can't even work up enough wickedness to kill his rival.

This is very black comedy, filled with a wicked, barbed wit. You can find the most amazing one-liners on every page. When Fursey is asked by the Devil if his marriage with his sweetheart was ever consummated, he replies indignantly, "Certainly not. We both had a good Irish Catholic upbringing, and we don't know how." When the letter of extradition is delivered to the court of Mercia, Wall, who always has a wry word for bureaucrats, observes:

> The Civil Service of Mercia was a small, bald-headed man, whose administrative cares increased yearly as his warlike master pushed conquest further and further into the neighboring territories, but the Civil Service of Mercia was tenacious, and after three weeks study came to a full understanding of the document and of its implications.

In the first volume, the pseudo-Byzantine Devil presents Father Furiosus ("whose odor of sanctity" is "clearly discernable from his breath and person") and the Bishop of Cashel with a very special hound: a pointer which will prove helpful in the Church's "noble work in suppressing the hateful passion of love in this land" (*i.e.*, Ireland), because of its ability to point out lovers in doorways and ditches or wherever they hide.

The deal which the Devil offers to the Church of Ireland is that the Irish shall be immune to the temptations of the most heinous of all sins, *sex*, in exchange for which, "the clergy in their teaching would not in the future lay undue stress on the wickedness of simony, nepotism, drunkenness, perjury, and murder."

No wonder Fursey decides it's better to sell his soul, become wicked, and be done with it!

But, alas, the ending is like that of *Monsieur Verdoux*. Fursey has achieved a terrible enlightenment. Now that he has seen how the world works, he cannot return to the simplicity and safety of the monastery, for all he still wants this, more than anything else. So, too, with life. If we have bitter experiences, if we see the Great Darkness of the human soul, we can perhaps adjust, but we can't erase the memories and go back to the way we were before. You can't go home again after Auschwitz.

Chaplin's character is a lot smarter than Fursey, and becomes cynical, bitter, and reconciled to his own evil on the grounds that nothing matters. Perhaps nihilism is a comfort on the way to the guillotine. Fursey is merely crushed. There is no place left for him, either on the side of God, or of Satan.

We can accept such a conclusion only through laughter because we've had a delightful time getting there. Wall's humor, again, compares very favorably with T. H. White's. He uses the same kind of modern language to create deliberate, controlled anachronism, to reveal concerns ancient, modern, and eternal. There are moments of sheer delight, the encounter with George the Vampire, and the scene with the basilisk, but all of them have the cumulative effect of the best comedy, and build to something very serious indeed.

Like I said, *masterpieces*. It really is impossible to convey the full flavor of these books in a short column. Go read them and be converted.

I have had the privilege of corresponding with Mr. Wall for over a year now, and I have conducted what amounts to a brief interview through the mail. He has been very cooperative, and has told me much about himself and his work that I didn't know, and has even provided me with copies of some of his harder-to-find writings.

Remember, you read it all here first.

The basic biographical facts are available in reference works (notably the two by Bleiler, mentioned earlier), so I will briefly mention that Mr. Wall was "born in Dublin in 1908, educated at Belvedere College, Dublin, and in Bonn, Germany (two years residence there), in University College, Dublin, and a Batchelor of Arts degree from the National University of Ireland, 1928." He was in the Irish civil service, 1934-1948, was a Programme Officer for Radio Eireann from 1948 to 1957, and thereafter Chief Executive of the Irish Arts Council until 1975 when he retired. He was for ten years Honorary Secretary and Treasurer, and for two years president, of the Irish Academy of Letters (an organization founded by William Butler Yeats and George Bernard Shaw).

For all that he isn't well-known in America, he has apparently always been quite respected in Irish Literature, and in fact was the subject of a special issue of *The Journal of Irish Literature* (Vol XI, Nos. 1/2, Jan./May 1982). He started out as a playwright, then wrote the two Fursey books, followed by two novels about Ireland, *Leaves for the Burning* (1952) and *No Trophies Raise*, which were much acclaimed. *Leaves for the Burning* gave such an accurate picture of life in mid-century Ireland that it became required reading for British diplomats stationed there. More recently, another novel, *Hermitage*, has been published in Ireland (also serialized in *The Journal of Irish Literature*), and there is one collection of his stories, *A Flutter of Wings*, published by Talbot Press, Dublin, in 1974. Three of the stories in it are of some fantasy interest. There is also a fantasy novella in that special number of *The Journal of Irish Literature*, about which more later.

Our correspondence began with much talk of Fursey, including mention of the musical comedy version, staged in Dublin in 1962. It ran for six weeks, long for Dublin, but Wall reports that he "was dissatisfied with the treatment (Princess Margaret of Great Britain was outrageously introduced as a character), and so I refused permission to have the musical brought to the U.S.A."

More happily, he sold a film option to an Irish film producer, "being convinced of his ability, his concern to do a good artistic job, and to adhere closely to the original text."

And, another playwright has received permission to write a play based on *The Unfortunate Fursey*, and the entire book was read over Irish radio early in 1984.

Of course I asked him how he came to write about Fursey, and why he turned to fantasy when he did.

Mr. Wall replied: "I do not think that I am particularly attracted to fantasy fiction. I am considered a satirist who has used [in the *Fursey* books] fantasy for satirical purposes, as well as the pure fun of it. When young, I liked ghost stories. Recovering from a serious illness when I was 35, I was handed a book borrowed from a local library. It was an account of Continental (not Irish) witchcraft. The author was a French abbé and the book had been published in Paris in 1600. I was so amused by the extravagant language and beliefs of the time, that I just sat up in bed and began writing *The Unfortunate Fursey*, transferring European Continental beliefs to an Irish monastic setting. The extravagant use and love of words for their own sake is an Irish characteristic. Critics often write of 'Irish gigantism'—exaggeration just for the fun of it."

Actually, Fursey's travails began with a short story, which the author submitted to Sean O'Faolain, then editor of a literary magazine, *The Bell*. O'Faolain did not publish it, but a novelist friend, Francis MacManus, suggested it be expanded into a novel, and it duly was. The short story, which consisted of the first chapter of *The Unfortunate Fursey* with minor differences, was published in the British magazine *Argosy* in 1947 as "The Devil at Clonmacnoise." It ended, Wall says, "with Fursey's expulsion from the monastery, and he is shown desolate, with his only companions a horde of demons he would have preferred to do without."

The novel version followed in due course: "I wrote the novel without any prior planning. I just followed my instinct from page to page. Nor did I have to do any revising, other than improve the English. That I did each evening by going over what I had written the night before." Did he intend it to be a satire?

Wall: "I did not have satirical intent, but of course the book is a satire. I did not plan at all. I just wrote for the fun of it, and was quite surprised to read in reviews that I had used irony to good effect. Of course I did, but was not conscious of it when writing."

In the interview with him published in the Wall Number of *The Journal of Irish Literature*, he went on at great length about censorship problems in Ireland, particularly in the early years after independence. So it seemed likely that a book which depicted the Irish church striking a deal with the Devil would have run into some trouble.

Was he ever denounced from the pulpit?

Wall writes:

"I was told that *The Unfortunate Fursey* was submitted four times to the Irish Literary Censorship Board, but they could find nothing in it to justify banning. The Censorship Act, 1927, says that a book may be banned 'because it is in its general tendency indecent, or advocates birth control.' Over the years, until about 1960, when the position eased greatly, even one sentence, a reference which the censors thought improper, was enough to ban many good books. They could not find one such in *The Unfortunate Fursey*. I do not doubt that the Censorship Board would have liked to ban it. It was suggested to me that they might have been afraid of being laughed at if they did.

"However, the ecclesiastical censor for the Archdiocese of Dublin visited all the Dublin bookshops and asked them not to stock it. Most of them ignored his request. 'Denouncing from the pulpit' is not done nowadays, or indeed in my lifetime, and of course I never experienced anything so crude. I was in the civil service at the time...and shortly afterwards I was transferred to a remote part of the west coast. Some of my friends thought it was because of Fursey, but I have no reason to believe it was."

Has he read much other fantasy?

"I read Tolkien's *The Lord of the Rings* a few years ago. My son aged twenty recommended it to me. I liked it largely because of the maps which enabled me to follow the journeys of the characters."

What does he think a good fantasy novel should be? I asked.

His reply: "I doubt if I really know what a good fantasy novel should be. I suppose it should be wonderful rather than probable. I read James Branch Cabell many years ago with great pleasure. Fantasy should attract because of its strangeness and because of its promise of vicarious adventure. Legend used to attract me, ancient Irish epics, the *Morte d'Arthur*, German and Scandinavian myth. I liked James Stephens fifty years ago, but I would not think now of re-reading him. I would consider myself a very limited writer if I were only interested in fantasy."

MERVYN WALL, by Darrell Schweitzer

"The Garden of Echoes," the novella published for the first time in *The Journal of Irish Literature* in 1982, is the third major Wall fantasy. He wrote it about twenty-five years ago, but was unable to sell it. My own opinion is that this can be easily accounted for. First, the story is about 35,000 words, and is thus an awkward length for a book. Then, it is ostensibly a children's story, but it reads like a children's story written by Ambrose Bierce or Dean Swift. It is the blackest, bitterest children's story I have ever encountered. So, in a publishing sense, it fell between two stools, not quite a children's story, not quite adult, and the wrong length in any case.

This is not to say it isn't a fine piece of writing. But it isn't as much *fun* as the Fursey books. Much of the humor has evaporated, and the satire is, as *Monsieur Verdoux* would have been without the characteristic Chaplin antics, shrill.

The plot is a venerable one for children's fantasy. Two little girls, at home alone with a babysitter, go through a bookcase into a fantastic land, where they have a series of adventures. Meanwhile, the babysitter, a pretentious young student, follows them, intending to shoot Santa Claus. The girls race to find Santa first, and warn him.

The allegory is fairly obvious. The bookcase represents knowledge and education, and by going through that, the girls lose their innocence. Their adventures include a nasty school, greedy clerks in a store, and, in one of the best moments, an encounter with a king whose castle is filled with rats. He can't get rid of them because "they're the government."

"I thought of it originally as a satire on grownups from the point of view of children," Wall writes. "I now consider it to be mostly the writer's protest against the inevitable passing of childhood. While it has been enjoyed by children, it is primarily a book for adults who like children and their quaint ways."

One children's book editor "was shocked at the satirical note." An Irish literary publisher was interested, commissioned a frontispiece, and then sat on the manuscript for ten years. Wall's London agent's reaction was similar to that of the book editor.

Another editor suggested that if one of the characters were a boy, the book would have more commercial appeal. But Wall had based them on his two small daughters, and kept them that way.

He is not the sort of writer who slants things to a market.

"I regard myself as a literary writer, and would not wish to suit what I feel I must write to a popular audience in order to make money....I have always held that a good writer writes, *Firstly* for himself, *only at a second remove* for people of his own kind whom he would like to appreciate his work, and only *thirdly* for the general public. If [his work] is successful with them, money is earned, which is always very useful, but it is not the prime consideration of a good writer.

"I often quote a story which the Norwegian dramatist Henrik Ibsen told of himself. He kept a pet scorpion in a glass jar on his desk. As the week progressed, the scorpion would tend to sicken and become torpid. On the last day of the week Ibsen would drop a piece of pear into the jar. The scorpion would fall upon it and discharge its accumulated poison into the pear. Similarly, Ibsen would write a play every two years, thus discharging the poison from his system, and just as the scorpion after the discharge of its poison would be a happy little scorpion again, so also would Ibsen be again mentally at rest. Poison is a strong word. I would say that the writer by writing a book discharges his 'unrest'."

At this point I mentioned the distressing case of a promising young writer I know, who not only seems certain to cave in to the most overt sort of commercial pressure, but is determined to do it without the slightest resistance.

Wall commented: "I was depressed by the tale of the writer you speak of who sold his artistic soul for cash. I can only recommend that if he is of the Christian persuasion, you should emulate St. Ignatius Loyola, who saved St. Francis Xavier's soul by whispering in his ear every time they met: 'What does it profit a man if he gain the whole world and suffer the loss of his soul?' When you have whispered this in his ear fifty times, he will perhaps see the error of his ways and return to the true faith, that is to true artistic expression.

"It is my intention if I am ever honored by being presented to the President of the United States, to ask him: 'Sir, do you see this great country of yours as a great Christian nation?' I expect him to beam delightedly and answer, 'I do.' I shall then urge him to spread the Christian message far and wide by removing the words 'E pluribus unum' from underneath the American eagle, and substituting a line from the New Testament, the inspired words of St. Paul: 'The desire for money is the root of all evil'."

Mr. Wall sent me his delightful short-story collection, *A Flutter of Wings*. Three of the stories therein contain some element of fantasy. "The Demon Angler," which, he tells me, has recently been picked up for an anthology of Irish ghost stories, is not *quite* a ghost story, but about a vacationing would-be fisherman who can't catch a fish. He goes at it obsessively, losing job and family, spending his fortune on equipment and on books on the habits of trout. Still, incredibly, he can't catch anything. Finally, he is found face-down in a pond, with a twenty-pound trout on his hook, and thereafter there are rumors of the spot being haunted. We don't actually see any ghosts, but the character, of course, is someone who *deserves* to become a ghost. Perhaps he did.

"The Men Who Could Outstare Cobras" is a very funny piece about two master hypnotists, rivals, one a showman, the other a psychiatrist, who get into a hypnotic duel, and lock each other into rigidity. No one can snap them out of it, so they end up in a glass case.

Then there is "Cloonaturk," which reminds me of numerous later Lord Dunsany stories about Irish peasants who believe in supernatural things which, most probably, are just amusing delusions. In this case, the whole district of Cloonaturk is virtually soaked with illegal booze. Under the influence of such, a dead man is seen to walk again. But when the cops dig up all the stills,

> each time he manifested himself, he was paler and more shadowy. Ten days later he was seen for the last time. In that unearthly hour between twilight and nightfall Long Joe came on him sitting on the bridge lighting his pipe; but even before the pipe was well drawn, he had faded into nothingness, and Long Joe, gazing where he had been, could see nothing but the stream below the bridge spreading out across the sand as it lost itself in the grey Atlantic breakers.

The other stories in the book are gentle satires. There's one ("The Hogskin Gloves") about a down-and-out bureaucrat who saves all his money, and through great hardship, manages to afford a fine pair of gloves. Then, he must have a coat to go with the gloves, a hat, etc. This so bankrupts him hat he can't afford to go to the tavern with his old friends, and spends much time in the library. In time his superiors notice, take him for a gentleman and a scholar, for all he hasn't really improved, and promote him. The clothes have truly made the man. And there's another bureaucrat story ("They Also Serve") which Kafka might have written if he'd had a sense of humor. It's the story of a man who is looking for a job in government service. He doesn't actually get hired, but is left waiting in an office between two departments, with no one sure of what to do with him, until the various workers forget why he is there, and hand him papers to shuffle. He is completely forgotten, but issued a paycheck, and, though he has never been hired or given any useful work to do, at the end of the story he has been there seventeen years, and is hoping for a nice pension. Obviously Wall is putting his own experience with government bureaucracies to good use.

Will Mervyn Wall ever return to fantasy? Quite possibly he will. He mentions a work-in-progress, *The Odious Generation.* "It is to be a satire on the present-day world of threatened nuclear destruction," he says, "destruction of the environment, the selfishness of youth and all the horrors we live with. Fantasy will be introduced by the principle character's use of an hallucinatory drug. It will deal with the incredible stupidity of man and his imminent self-destruction. There will be a bit of *The Pilgrim's Progress* about it, and it will bear a

Christian message. I hope that I succeed in completing it. I have been working on it for nine years now (in August, 1984). I am up to my knees in notes and material collected. Advancing years, the cares of a household, and many distractions delay its progress. I get a great number of books for review from newspapers and journals, and I am frequently invited to give radio broadcasts. I have been doing radio work for forty-four years, and I suppose it is hard to break old habits. I also have been writing a radio column weekly for a Dublin newspaper since 1968. I know I could be spending my time to better advantage. I long for a spell in prison where I would have quiet and be free of distractions, and would thus be enabled to bring the novel to a satisfactory conclusion."

It's probably going to be a very bitter piece of satire. Wall sums up his satirical bent:

"I have a satirical element in my make-up because I think humanity is a failure, its history is of stupidity, illogicality, and doublethink, and it is inevitably doomed to nuclear destruction through that same stupidity. As is evident from the closing pages of *The Return of Fursey*, I regard human behavior, not only with humor, but with sadness."

Mervyn Wall's work has still not received the recognition it deserves. It's easy enough to explain why. He has never been typed as a fantasy writer, and for all *The Unfortunate Fursey* was published in the U.S. by Crown in 1947, it was not properly promoted, and the late '40s was not a period, in any case, notably favorable to fantasy.

So Mervyn Wall needs to be rediscovered. This has been the lot of virtually every major fantasist in the twentieth century. Think about it: only T. H. White found his audience immediately. All the others, Dunsany, Tolkien, Peake, Eddison, Evangeline Walton, etc. had to be rediscovered. Even when a writer continued to produce science fiction, and remained visible within the genre, frequently his *fantasy* languished in obscurity for decades before being recognized. Classic (in every sense of the term) examples: *The Dying Earth* by Jack Vance, *The Broken Sword* by Poul Anderson, *The Well of the Unicorn* by Fletcher Pratt.

In this country, we are simply waiting for some editor to be bold enough to reprint the two *Fursey* books in mass-market paperback as fantasy. They are brilliant books, far better than anything being written in the field today. Readers will be endlessly grateful. They do not follow the strict rules of today's commercial genre, but, I hasten to point out, today's commercial fantasy genre is based entirely on books (like *The Lord of the Rings*) which were striking and original, and didn't follow any rules either.

I bet the *Fursey* books would even be quite commercial.

MERVYN WALL, by Darrell Schweitzer

If anyone is interested, inquire. I have the address of Wall's agent. Meanwhile, Wolfhound Press of Dublin has published a two-in-one volume, *The Complete Fursey*, to much acclaim in Ireland. Some enterprising fantasy dealer would do well to import them.

A truly marvellous reading experience awaits you.

IV.

JOHN COLLIER

FANTASTIC MINIATURIST

by Alan Warren

"Without mincing words," reads the Introduction in *The Playboy Book of Horror and the Supernatural*, "we are going to come right out and say that the reason John Collier is opening this book...is because, in this difficult and demanding genre, he is the undisputed champion, nonpareil and king. He is a consummate artisan, a wicked wit, a superb storyteller and a proud stylist who polishes his phrases like precious gems."

Although Collier could be horrifying on occasion, he is essentially a fantasist. His stories are peopled with genies, demons, angels, and witches, yet for the most part they are told with a smirk, a gentle nudge, and an eerie precision with words that render them almost unique in English literature. As Clifton Fadiman noted, "he has the genuine *soufflé* touch."

John Henry Noyes Collier was born in London in 1901 and privately educated by his uncle, Vincent Collier, a sometime novelist. He became a poet, and in 1922 received a prize from a literary magazine, *This Quarter*; yet he was to publish but one slim volume of poetry, *Gemini*, in 1931. By then he was already a novelist.

Collier's first novel, *His Monkey Wife* (1930), can only tangentially be considered fantasy. It is basically a reasonable facsimile of a Victorian novel, featuring a hero, his cold fiancée, and Emily, the long-suffering heroine who loves him. The distinction is in the species of the heroine: Emily is an ape. The story is set in the Upper Congo, where Fatigay, the hero, is a schoolteacher. Emily is his best pupil, able to read and write, and single-minded in her devotion to her instructor. Fatigay, the archetypal thick-headed Englishman abroad, is unaware of Emily's affections and plans to marry Amy, who does not love him. Emily takes matters into her own hands by threatening Amy with a knife (and a copy of "Murders in the Rue Morgue"), and forces her to act as bridesmaid while she is married to Fatigay herself. By the story's end Fatigay realizes it is Emily he loves. And:

Into the depths of those all-dark lustrous eyes, his spirit slid with no sound of splash. She uttered a few low words, rapidly, in her native tongue. The candle, guttering beside the bed, was strangled in the grasp of a prehensile foot, and darkness received, like a ripple in velvet, the final happy sigh.[1]

His Monkey Wife is written in an extravagantly full-blown style that Collier was later at pains to restrain. It is notable for its allusiveness: Collier makes no secret of his erudition, and *His Monkey Wife* is replete with references to Donne, Shakespeare, and Milton, among others. It is a unique performance, and remains Collier's most widely read novel.

Collier published two more novels, *Tom's a-Cold* (published in America as *Full Circle*) in 1933, and *Defy the Foul Fiend* in 1934. The first is an uncharacteristically serious utopian science fiction, the other a comic, partly autobiographical novel. Neither book is now generally available, although two chapters from *Defy the Foul Fiend* are reprinted in the 1972 collection, *The John Collier Reader*.

Collier found himself at a dead end as a novelist. In *Ten Contemporaries* (1933), edited by John Gawsworth, Collier distinguishes between impressionistic prose,

"...in which you give yourself up to the subject," and the other kind, "in which you hold your puppet subject at arm's length, give it a jerk or two, then laying it down, you lean across the table, and with smile or leer address your ideal auditor direct, as one good fellow to another...[this] other sort is capable of quite a lot of development, and anyway I like it best. I wonder if, supposing I work hard for ten years, I shall find myself at forty in a position to write it well. That would be worth doing."

It was "this other sort" that was to occupy Collier's attention over the next forty-seven years. He had begun writing short stories in 1926 with surprising ease: "Out of nowhere came this writer who wrote these stories, and it was me," he later recalled. To these stories he brought the poet's love of language and an obsession with style. At the same time his novels were appearing he began publishing slim volumes containing a single story—*Green Thoughts* (1932), *Variation on a Theme* (1935), and *Witch's Money* (1940). These stories, slightly rewritten, appeared in later Collier collections. One story, however, has not been reprinted since its initial publication in 1931.

No Traveler Returns is a longish short story concerning one Professor Wilkinson, the embodiment of all that Collier finds objectionable about science. He finds the lip of an excavation pouting up from under-earth, goes to investigate, and "descended promptly into the grotto, whence he also never came up." He has trod upon "a mathematical banana skin," and stumbled upon a different time sphere coexisting with this world, one in which no women exist, synthetic foods are offered, scientists have come to figure as music-hall buffoons, and the denizens feed on human flesh. The Professor is kidnaped and held in a cage along with other men. After failing to entertain spectators with an exhortation of science, he is selected to be eaten. He is laid on a slab. "And as his spirit flickered up, and failed, he saw out of the tail of his eye, a scullion take from out of a basket, and hold in readiness—a lemon."

No Traveler Returns is a curious work, told in the extravagant style of *His Monkey Wife*, heavy-laden with satiric jibes at contemporary figures (metamorphosed into Professor J*l**n H*xl*y, Lord B**v*rbr**k, M*x B**rb*hm, and Messrs. Ch*st*rt*n and B*ll*c), and ripe with disdain for science—"By Newton!" one character exclaims. It was suppressed by Collier, probably because of the heavy-handedness of its satire, and remains one of his most elusive works. The flavor of its satire is set forth in "The Apology" which precedes the story proper, in which Collier lays bare his scorn for science and scientists as the apostles of a new, illusory, creed:

> ...these emigrationists of that undiscovered country, from which not only no traveler returns, but for which not a man-jack of them all has ever set forth, have so bemused the vulgar, that there is no doubt we must all henceforward proceed as by the Davy Lamp of science, and strike a course into the mines and caverns of snoring comfort, if only that its beams may show to better advantage than among the shining positive pleasures of our upper earth. This is not my lot, and if my descendants choose to ignore the precepts of their dad, they may tunnel to Hell for all I care, and be as heartily damned at the end of their laborious journey, as if they had got there by a simple and pleasant short cut, which I might, but will not, prescribe.

The definitive Collier short story collection, *Fancies and Goodnights*, published in 1951, contains fifty of his cleverest and most carefully wrought "fantastic miniatures," some no more than four or five pages. Most of these can be divided into groups: the Faustian stories, featuring demons, succubi, and occasionally the Devil himself; the Hollywood stories, in which wealthy film producers are as Machiavellian as the otherworldly tempters; and the stories about murder, usually in a domestic setting. Clifton Fadiman considers these "the cream of

Collier." They are masterpieces of concision, compression, and deftness of style, of which the best known are "Midnight Blue," "Little Memento," "De Mortuis," "Back for Christmas," "Wet Saturday" and, perhaps most memorable of all, "The Touch of Nutmeg Makes It," which critic Damon Knight termed "the finest short murder mystery ever written."

Collier's triumph in these tales is to make art seem effortless. In part, this is due to his experience as a screenwriter: he worked on the screenplays of *Sylvia Scarlett*, *Elephant Boy*, *Deception*, *I Am a Camera*, and *The War Lord* among others, not always harmoniously. "I couldn't have had a better guide than [director George] Cukor," he later told interviewer Tom Milne, "but I wasn't in the mood to learn." He looked upon his screenwriting as frankly commercial, done under financial pressure; yet he later reversed himself by adapting Milton's *Paradise Lost* for the screen. And there was an additional, unexpected benefit: as Anthony Burgess perceptively points out in his Introduction to *The John Collier Reader*, Collier "is a master of the scriptwriter's craft. Read his short stories and you will see all the scriptwriter's virtues—intense economy, characterization through speech, the sharp camera-eye of observation."[2] There was also a dry wit, a mocking impudence, and a mastery of understatement that make his opening lines so memorable:

> As soon as Einstein declared that space was finite, the price of building sites, both in Heaven and Hell, soared outrageously.[3]

> There was a young man who was invariably spurned by the girls, not because he smelt at all bad, but because he happened to be as ugly as a monkey.[4]

> Louis Thurlow, having decided to take his own life, felt that at least he might take his own time also.[5]

> In Hell, as in other places we know of, conditions are damnably disagreeable.[6]

"Evening Primrose" is one of Collier's most accomplished stories. Betty Richardson, in her full-length critical study *John Collier*, considers it "probably Collier's most perfect story, flawless and unique." It is narrated by a poet, and found "In a pad of Highlife Bond, bought by Miss Sadie Brodribb at Bracey's for 25¢." In order to escape the bourgeois world, the poet has taken up residence in a large department store, only to find others living there, posing as mannequins. The caste system they practice is no different than the one he is trying to escape. He falls in love with a young girl, Ella, who unfortunately is in love with the night watchman. When the others find out, Ella is taken to the Surgical Department to be permanently transformed into a mannequin. The poet, along with the night watchman, sets out to save her, leaving behind his story as a testament should he fail. Fearing that possibility, he exhorts the reader:

> Look for three new figures: two men, one rather
> sensitive-looking, and a girl. She has blue eyes, like
> periwinkle flowers, and her upper lip is lifted a little.
> Look for us.
> Smoke them out! Obliterate them! Avenge us![7]

Collier is sometimes criticized for maintaining too rigorous a distance between himself and his characters, the witty, dispassionate tone masking the absence of any serious intent. But "Evening Primrose," while nominally a fantasy, is a hauntingly wistful story that takes a more jaundiced view of humankind than would be possible told "straight," and it concludes with an affecting *cri de coeur*. Here the distance between author and character is reduced to negligibility.

Other stories show Collier, the diabolic jester, at his most grimly sardonic. In "The Right Side," Philip Westwick, about to jump from Westminster Bridge, is dissuaded by an older man, who happens to be The Devil. He offers Westwick a cigarette.

> "I suppose it's not doped?" inquired Philip,
> sniffing it suspiciously.
> "Oh, come!" said the Devil with a sneer. "Do
> you think I need resort to such measures as that, to
> overcome you? I have *reason* on my side. Will you
> have a light?" Without pausing for a reply, he ex-
> tended his middle finger, the tip of which immediately
> ignited the cigarette.[8]

"Fallen Star" is the witty tale of a lovely young she-angel sent down to Earth by an "elderly, fat and most unprepossessing devil" by the name of Tom Truncheontail in hopes that she will sin so that her soul will be his. She is found *sans* clothes and memory in Central Park, and taken to the office of a handsome young psychoanalyst, who decides she is experiencing counter-transference. He decides on some unorthodox treatment. "We will draw a veil over the scene that followed," the storyteller says, "for the secrets of the psychoanalytic couch are as those of the confessional, only more interesting."[9] The psychoanalyst marries the angel, but she is constantly visited by the devil in visible form. On one such visit the psychoanalyst detains him and proceeds to psychoanalyze him, with the result that the devil, now tailless, becomes engaged to one of the psychoanalyst's patients. In the end he becomes a model citizen and goes on "to Wall Street, where he did so extremely well that he was soon able to endow a superb clinic for the young psychoanalyst."[10]

"Halfway to Hell" recounts the adventure of a young man, Louis Thurlow, who decides to commit suicide because of a young woman, Celia, in love with someone else. He takes an overdose of veronal tablets, but rather than dying he awakes to a kind of half-life in which he looks down at his own corpse lying in bed. He realizes he is invisible, and goes out to enjoy London nightlife, only to run into a fiend, who has been waiting for him and has caught a nasty cold. The fiend explains that they will travel down to Hell on an escalator located in the subway. But before they go Louis suggests a cure for the fiend's cold, a drink that tastes like liquid fire. When the fiend is quite drunk they go into the subway, where Louis spots his rival taking a late train home. Louis tricks the fiend into taking the rival instead, and they jump onto the escalator, "whose terrific acceleration seemed even more marked and more admirable than before." Louis thinks about going to see Celia, but thinks better of it, "and, in fact, did not go at all, but went to Paris for the autumn, which shows that girls should not play fast and loose with the affections of small men with blue eyes, or they may find themselves left in the lurch."[11]

Other stories (such as "Sleeping Beauty" and "The Frog Prince") are revisionist versions of fairy tales; some are literary borrowings ("Without Benefit of Galsworthy," "Another American Tragedy"). "The Lady on the Gray" is an updating of the Circe legend, set in Ireland; "Thus I Refute Beelzy" is a deliberate rewrite of Saki's "Sredni Vashtar." And the immortal "The Chaser," one of Collier's most frequently anthologized tales, deals with a young man seeking a love potion, and relies for its impact upon its memorable closing line. "Bottle Party" is a typically Collierian updating of the genie-in-a-bottle fable. Its protagonist, Franklin Fletcher, dreams of women but is unable to obtain one for himself. "At thirty-five he gave up, and decided he must console himself with a hobby, which is a very miserable second best." He buys a bottle containing a genie in one of those little shops so plentiful in fantasy fiction, takes it home, and pulls out the stopper. "Out flowed a prodigious quantity of greasy smoke, which immediately solidified into the figure of a gross and fleshy Oriental, six feet six in height, with rolls of fat, a hook nose, a wicked white to his eye, vast double chins, altogether like a film producer, only larger."[12] The genie grants Franklin's request for beautiful women, but Franklin overreaches himself, with the result that he winds up inside a bottle himself, which is bought by some sailors. "When they unstoppered him at sea and found it was only poor Frank, their disappointment knew no bounds, and they used him with the utmost barbarity."[13]

Collier was to go on writing such stories for many years for such publications as *Playboy*, *Ellery Queen's Mystery Magazine*, and

The Magazine of Fantasy & Science Fiction. His last major work, however, was in quite a different vein: a grandiose and probably impossible undertaking: *Milton's Paradise Lost*, "A Screenplay for Cinema of the Mind" (1973). "No clue is offered...," John Updike wrote in his review of the book, "as to what possessed John Collier to turn John Milton's *Paradise Lost* into a screenplay." Ironically, one answer appears in Updike's own speech, "The Future of the Novel," reprinted in his *Picked-Up Pieces*: "Artistically, this century has belonged to the eye." Underscoring this, the jacket flap of Collier's book informs us that "The twentieth century here salutes the seventeenth; the master fantasist, Collier, uses the characteristic medium of our time to bring us closer to the greatest art of another epoch."

In one sense, *Milton's Paradise Lost* is the epic Collier had been working toward throughout his entire career. The loftiness of his ambition, combined with the visual appearance of the book itself—described by Updike as "a kind of Loew's Orpheum Art Deco"—led some critics to dismiss it as a stunt or an aberration. Collier's own view of Milton was curiously ambivalent: though he recognized the subject as the greatest imaginable, he felt that Milton's epic was flawed and badly constructed. There is another profound schism: Collier was an atheist. As he notes:

> The ideas in *Paradise Lost* arise out of profound scholarship, but they are not profound in themselves, being a magnificent but quite orthodox expression of the religious beliefs of three hundred years ago. I do not share these beliefs, and I have substituted other ideas, also not profound in themselves, but which are more in accord with those commonly held today.[14]

In addition, Collier sympathizes with Satan: "...the prisoner was paroled in order that he might commit fresh crimes and incur a yet heavier sentence. Man, at the cost of death to all and damnation to many, was to serve as bait in this outrageous trap."[15]

Collier's epic begins with a dazzling light show: "THE BLUE NIGHT OF INFINITE SPACE. We are moving upward into a region where the blue is lighter and clearer."[16] We see millions of angels falling into a lake of fire. From the lake rises Satan:

> His resplendent beauty is blasted, but it is all the more appealing for that. Whatever perfection of form has been lost is compensated for by new elements born of his defeat and suffering. We shall see that courage, gentleness, sweetness, understanding, sensitivity are all raised to a level which makes him almost irresistible. Lifting his face, he inhales the sul-

phurous air. He feels it to be charged with a mysterious force. He is strangely exhilarated. He wrenches
an exultant cry out of what perhaps began as a groan
of agony."[17]

Satan has become the center of Collier's epic, from which
Collier has omitted God and heaven: "Heaven might be adequately expressed in music and even to some extent in words, if they are Milton's
words," Collier notes in his Apology. "Unfortunately any attempt to
conjure up a definite picture results in something more fit for the calendar than for eternity."[18]

This shift of emphasis dangerously overbalances Collier's epic.
Adam becomes a farmer, and Eve a sensualist. It is left to Satan, whom
Collier likens to the rebel against the Establishment, to perform heroic
actions, such as the creation of magic—a noble act because it is handed
down to the creative artist. And in the end we are left with something
dangerously close to the calendar art Collier warned against.

Milton's Paradise Lost, Collier's most ambitious undertaking,
was also his last. Critics, galvanized by Updike's unfavorable review,
inveighed against Collier's revisionist epic. Collier, disheartened, produced little work afterward; at the time of his death in 1980 he was
working on a still-unpublished novel, *Finding Ernie*. Today he is best
remembered as a purveyor of satiric fantasy, whose leer did not obscure
his essentially pessimistic nature, so at home in the company of genie
and devils.

V.

A. MERRITT

A REAPPRAISAL

by Ben P. Indick

He was dubbed "Lord of Fantasy," and his works of adventure and fantastic romance have endured three lifetimes already: first in their original printings, from 1917 through 1934; again in reprint during the 1940s in the pulp magazine *Famous Fantastic Mysteries*; and, currently, as they continue to appear in paperback reprintings. The popularity of A. Merritt will surely survive to delight and amaze future generations.

During much of the quarter century which encompassed his fiction writing career, Abraham Merritt was the editor of *The American Weekly*, a Hearst newspaper chain Sunday supplement. Born in Beverly, New Jersey on January 20, 1884, Merritt grew up hoping to study law, and actually matriculated in the University of Pennsylvania. Unfortunately, family finances prevented his continuing, and at the age of eighteen he became a reporter for the *Philadelphia Inquirer*. Here, as he wrote later in a biography for *Argosy* and again for *Famous Fantastic Mysteries*, "it happened he saw one day something that made it awkward to have him within reach of the witness stand. The result was that he spent a happy year at no expense to himself wandering around Central America, getting in and out of tight places and acquiring a taste for archeology."[1] Indeed, the wonders he saw in those exotic climes became integral to his thinking and writing. Folklore and legend would be a lifetime preoccupation. Returning home, "reluctantly," he found that his talent for graphic expression brought him a position as night city editor, and, in 1912, a position with the far-flung Hearst Enterprises. Eventually he became assistant editor and finally full editor of *The American Weekly*. This was no simple rotogravure section in the manner of the times, but a full, newspaper-sized magazine with a widely varied content, a fair amount being pseudo-scientific articles and even fiction. John Hawkins's science fiction novel, *The Ark of Fire*, appeared serially here, illustrated by an artist Merritt liked, the young

A. Merritt, by Ben P. Indick

Virgil Finlay. Merritt surely produced pseudonymous writing of his own, some of which has been uncovered, as will be discussed below.

His busy schedule left little enough time for writing fiction, but, perhaps to allow his fertile imagination room to roam, Merritt wrote as often as time and energy would allow. If his total accomplishment was relatively small, it was compensated for by the fanatical devotion of a legion of readers. All of his novels would reach hardcover publication during his lifetime with one exception published posthumously.

A half-century later, fantasy and science fiction publishing has become a major sales category, Tolkien, Howard, and Lovecraft have achieved incredible international popularity, and the sensuality which fascinated Merritt (but which he could not freely express) has become an accepted part of modern fiction. How does the corpus of Merritt's work stand up in this new situation? To better understand the man and his work, we shall examine all of his fiction in some detail, to perceive if his unique qualities still survive intact, and if, in fact, within his own niche, Abraham Merritt remains The Lord of Fantasy.

"Through the Dragon Glass," which appeared in the Frank A. Munsey Co.'s *All-Story Weekly* in 1917, was his first published story, and in it he was already delineating the type of romantic adventure he would exploit in his later work: a brave hero, a beautiful heroine, a fantastic world, and an ornate, adjectival prose incorporating references to obscure and esoteric legends. To lend the story relevance, it is narrated from within a New York City apartment. This would become one of the author's favorite devices; time after time, as in *The Ship of Ishtar*, *Burn Witch Burn!*, *Seven Footprints to Satan*, and *Creep, Shadow!*, he compares by inference the reality of New York (and it sparkles for later readers with the Art Deco glitter of photographs of yesteryear, with our image of a gay, glamorous city) with his ornate fantasy worlds.

A mixture of beautiful fantasy and frightening horror, "Dragon Glass" employs an Alice-like prop in which the hero steps through a dissolving jade mirror, ringed by bejeweled dragons, into a mysterious Oriental world, pursuing an exotically lovely woman he has seen within it. As was common in magazine fiction of the day, and as he would often do in later work, Merritt paved the way for a sequel, although in this instance, it never appeared. The mystery of the world behind that enchanting mirror remains untold.[2] Still, this is an enticing bit of *chinoiserie*, indebted to a degree to the works of Robert W. Chambers, the then-popular writer of historical romances and several works of extraordinary fantasy, including *The King in Yellow* and *The Maker of Moons*. (Chambers's influence would be felt later as well in "Three Lines of Old French" and *Creep, Shadow!*) "Dragon Glass" was a great success with editor and readers, and the promise of the author's debut was amply fulfilled in his second story, "The People of the Pit," which appeared in 1918.

This remarkable horror tale, set in an Alaskan chasm and dealing with the desire by men for gold, presages several of Merritt's later novels, *The Face in the Abyss* and *Dwellers in the Mirage*. It is a wholly gripping story of an explorer held hostage by and finally escaping from non-human, tentacled, god-like creatures. Quite possibly the story influenced the as yet non-professionally published H. P. Lovecraft, an *Argosy* reader and admirer of Merritt; indeed, the two writers would eventually meet, as we shall see.

Fans of the magazine by now were well aware of Merritt, but his next story would exceed each of the preceding in popularity, and would rival that of another comparatively new writer, Edgar Rice Burroughs. In his first *Argosy* novel, *Under the Moons of Mars*, and in his spectacularly successful next novel, *Tarzan of the Apes*, Burroughs had essentially mined the field so ably exploited by H. Rider Haggard in his adventure romances of faraway and mysterious lands. Merritt's "The Moon Pool" (1918), a novelette, was an instant success, and has remained one of his most popular stories. By quickly enlarging the original with its novel-length sequel, "The Conquest of the Moon Pool" (1919), the author set a pattern for much of his later work, creating a lost race in an exotic, unexplored setting, with a beautiful heroine plus an equally beautiful villainess, as well as a non-human being of vast power who is controlled by the latter. To one degree or another, this same cast of characters would also appear in *The Ship of Ishtar*, "The Snake Mother," *Dwellers in the Mirage*, and *Creep, Shadow!* A supplementary cast of imaginative characters would include: frog men, ancient semi-godlike beings, invisible serpents, etc. The debt to Burroughs and his early Martian novels is clear, and even the narrative style is similar, the action swinging back and forth from one character to another in continual movement.

Today, the novel is betrayed by its period. One may forgive the dependence of a wholly non-human creature upon a woman; the Shining One seems almost to be a *pet* of Yolara, just as in a later novel the Metal Emperor dotes on his human Norhala. (But we have our pets too, dogs and cats, and may be uncertain which of us *is* the pet!) And we may smile at the stereotypical Irish hero and German villain (in the book version the latter became a Russian as the author expressed his distaste for things Bolshevik!). However, the characterization is shallow and dependent on authorial *dicta* rather than true development. There is no shading, no growth. Lakla is wholly "good" and Yolara entirely "evil." In the post-Victorian sensibility "evil" was likely to mean power-lust or sexual desire. In this context, true, unselfish Love could finally suffice to weaken an enemy to its destruction—which is, indeed, the climax of the novel.

A. MERRITT, by Ben P. Indick

If the novel does not have our contemporary hero, with his self-doubts in a hostile universe, there is nevertheless a hint of it—an element characteristic of many of his climaxes. The villain is rarely defeated directly by the hero himself; for all his grit and daring, the latter is more often a bystander at that moment, while other agencies as fantastic as the villain perform the task. Thus, the grieving Silent Ones in *The Moon Pool*, the dwarf Sri in *Dwellers in the Mirage*, a short circuit in *The Metal Monster*, the Snake Mother in *The Face in the Abyss*, a stubborn doll in *Burn Witch Burn!*, the elemental powers of the sea in *Creep, Shadow!*, all prove the undoing of evil. One wonders at the reluctance of the author, having brought his hero through numerous episodes of personal bravery and danger, to include the final element of the pulp adventure hero. It is as though no man is capable of completely dominating his circumstances, and must ultimately need help from some outside agency. Underlying this, the climaxes often have tragic elements: the hero and the heroine have vanished at the end of *The Moon Pool*; all the beloved friends of the hero of *Dwellers in the Mirage* are lost, and he must return home alone; the hero of *The Ship of Ishtar*, at the moment of his triumph, is found dead. Even when the protagonist escapes death, the "happy ending" of fairy tales is absent; for example, their experiences have irreparably singed the heroes of *Creep, Shadow!* and "The Woman of the Wood." Thus, if there is depth and development in Merritt's characterization, it is at the climax of the story, and can be found in the character of the hero alone.

A wistful World War I romance, "Three Lines of Old French," appeared after the Moon Pool stories in 1919. It champions love as salvation from despair, a sentimental balm to those who had suffered loss in the war, but still a poignant theme in Merritt's hands.

Merritt now turned to a difficult new idea in a novel which would became his least popular, and which would bedevil him over many years through several rewritings. It must have taken courage for the editor of *Argosy*, Bob Davis, a knowledgeable man who had developed an all-star stable of writers, to print the nearly abstract novel, *The Metal Monster*, in 1920. The tale is almost wholly expository, with the protagonists witnessing rather than causing the climactic events. Whatever happens directly to them, such as a kidnapping by latter-day descendants of Alexander the Great's Macedonian troops, is incidental, and obviously inserted to provide *some* action, however desultory. Nevertheless, if the reader will forego the author's usual mannerisms, he will find a remarkable attempt to describe an utterly non-human, non-hydrogen-based form of life. The story opens in an uncharacteristically leisurely manner, as Merritt philosophizes for several pages about the possibilities of other forms of life evolving simultaneously with our own. His interest in popular science perhaps led to this theme; indeed, he prided himself on his scientific accuracy (even if it was of the journalistic sort), and he was never loath to stop the action altogether to discuss, if only in a footnote, a reference to a text or to an article which will lend credence to a fantastic event.

Merritt was certainly not financially dependent on the small checks of pulp magazines,[3] and was quite sensitive to reader response. If his science fictional novel of living metal received brickbats and cries of dismay, he returned emphatically to his *métier* in a novella, "The Face in the Abyss" (1923). In the mountains of Peru a group of greedy adventurers discover a lusciously beautiful heroine from a nearly hidden, hitherto unknown land (which would only appear later in the sequel), and, among an array of fantastical creatures, even encounter some pint-sized dinosaurs. (It should be noted that a decade earlier A. Conan Doyle had placed full-sized dinosaurs in South America in *The Lost World*.) Merritt's heroine is occasionally threatened with that "fate worse than death"' so familiar to Burroughs's heroines; spider-men and invisible flying serpents which emit "elfin" sounds also lend a tingling quality to the mysterious atmosphere.[4] The story is no mere romp, however; the elements are very well tied together and lead to a climax which is at the heart of Merritt's message: all must test their moral strength against their basic instincts of greed and lust. Nowhere in his writing is the test more direct than when his explorers, good and bad, behold the awesome Face across the hidden valley, promising all their desires. Significantly, none passes the test, although the hero is saved by the all-powerful Snake Mother, who is half snake, but also half woman. Like "The Moon Pool," the story is designed for a sequel; Merritt provided it, but he made his readers wait seven more years for the follow-up.

"The Snake Mother" first appeared in 1930 as a full-fledged novel. Apart from the original subsidiary characters, who had long since flowed as golden droplets into the Abyss, the story maintains the same leads, plus a host of new characters. "Snake" moves the hearty group of adventurers directly and immediately into the lost land only hinted at previously. Soon they find an immortal people who spend their days living in dreams, creatures which have been genetically engineered by men into half-beast/half-human caricatures, with hints of extra-terrestrial origins for the serpent people, of whom the Snake Mother is the last, mysterious super-machinery, and a culture which, in spite of its scientific advancements, is partial to amphitheatre entertainments like those of ancient Rome.[5]

"The Snake Mother" is a robust adventure, its elements neatly meshed. The morality of the novella is fully elaborated in Merritt's superb shadow-villain, Nimir, the very incarnation of power-lusting evil. The scenes in which Nimir attempts to wheedle the loan of his body from Graydon, the hero, are among the author's finest. In contrast, Adana the serpent-woman possesses the sweetness of a gentle grandmother, the firmness of a wise schoolmarm, and, in spite of her scaly body and a face that is closer to a cobra's than a woman's, a sensuality

A. MERRITT, by Ben P. Indick

more affecting than that of the lissome heroine. (It should be noted that the latter's ivory body, like those in other Merritt novels and those of his fellow pulpsters, never hides any of its voluptuous charms amid the clinging gossamer robes which she and her legion of sisters invariably wore, with the authors constantly reminding us of that fact.) A slam-bang ending is only partially vitiated by pseudo-scientific explanations, and a fine bellicose attitude of the hero toward the outside world he has renounced is regretably eliminated in the hardcover version of the book (the two novellas were published together as *The Face in the Abyss*).

While readers were impatiently awaiting this sequel, the author produced another novel, one which would later be voted the finest fantasy published in *Argosy*'s long history. *The Ship of Ishtar* (1924) is as brilliant as the jewels the author continually uses as a metaphor, its episodes dazzlingly creative as hero John Kenton veers back and forth between the reality of New York and the poetic beauty of a ship suspended in time.

Merritt uses the Burroughsian device of having his hero *wish* himself back in space and time to the deck of a ship which, sculpture-like, rests on a block of stone in his apartment. In later novels the author has his heroes move into previous incarnations, but here Kenton skips back and forth between our reality and the suspended eternity of the ship, often moving against his will, manipulated by the gods who control its (and our) destiny, with only one rather feeble attempt by the author to provide a "scientific" explanation for his journeys. Since the ship is already immersed in Babylonian mythology, there is no mention to legends of other origins, as is common in Merritt's work. The writing is quasi-poetic, at times approaching the level of an epic:

> Said the Phrygian, low...

> Forward they ran...

> Sigurd, Trygg's son, I...

> Kenton, my name...

> Of green upon it there was none...

Much of the novel is set on the isolated ship floating on an endless, apparently empty ocean, peopled by a group of well-depicted if two-dimensional characters (having lived together for thousands of years, they can hardly be expected to change!). In one of his most famous scenes, Merritt counters the evil god's action of bringing up a multitude of armed soldiers in bubbles on the sea by having the kindly Ishtar produce an equal effervescence of beautiful women within bubbles. The women embrace the soldiers to their mutual doom. Ultimately, the author leaves the ship for the action ashore, but his invention is such that the pace never flags. And for once the romance of the lovers, consummated aboard the ship, has the warmth and tenderness of genuine love. For many devotees the tale of the precious ship, embedded forever in its sea of lapis lazuli, is the essence of fantasy itself, one which makes this work one of the favorites in Merritt's canon.

The author turned in 1927 to straight mystery, and made an Arabian Nights of New York in *Seven Footprints to Satan*, which was popular not only in book form, but also as a silent film. The tale owes much to Sax Rohmer, copying the latter's crisp writing style and his bent for creating evil, larger-than-life villains. Merritt's villain, who presumptuously calls himself Satan, lacks the ethnic bias so common to this period. The conceit of the seven glowing footprints of Buddha, which offer the challenger either wealth or servitude, is one of the author's most intriguing; however, all of the characters, without exception, from the Cockney friend of the hero to the pretty sweetheart (the intended mother of Satan's children, naturally), and even the astonished hero himself, are no more than clichés. The story is far-fetched but fun, no more or less substantial than many of the mysteries of its era.

Following publication of "The Snake Mother" in 1930, *Argosy* next published Merritt's *Dwellers in the Mirage* a year later. One of the author's most popular novels, it exploits not only reincarnation, but has an extra-terrestrial monster-god. Merritt's earlier story, "The People of the Pit," has been mentioned as a possible influence on H. P. Lovecraft, but here it seems Merritt may have returned the favor. Lovecraft's "The Call of Cthulhu," the first clear expression of his so-called Mythos, had appeared in *Weird Tales* in 1928, and his subsequent work would involve powerful creatures from outer space or the depths of time who might be summoned by humans through various rituals. Lovecraft uses mythical ancient books as the sources of such hazardous knowledge; Merritt offers no such explanation, nor is his Kraken-god Khalk'ru precisely the equivalent of Cthulhu, despite a certain etymological debt.

Apart from its image of the terrifying Kraken, the novel is not at all Lovecraftian or even weird. *Dwellers* features the usual Merritt mix of a swaggering if uncertain hero, beautiful women, and exotic locales, from the distant Gobi desert to a lush valley hidden in a perpetual mirage-like fog in Alaska.

Four decades after its writing, the novel offers a blend of the author's best and worst work. Here the good and evil aspects of the human psyche are again personified in the author's depiction of women, but his feelings have now become more ambivalent than in *The Moon Pool*, and Lur, the darker vision (if lighter in complexion than the angelic Evalie) is not the cardboard figure of Yolara. She is real enough that we must regret the conventions of the time that prevented the author from developing her further. Warrior and witch, Lur is suspicious

A. MERRITT, by Ben P. Indick

and selfish yet generous; her very name betrays Merritt's attitude toward her. Lur! Beloved Lur! An older reader remembers her even over these vanished years, and all that she seemed to promise. But if Lur can never grow older, we must. We discover her to be rooted in adventure fantasy of the old tradition, a creation of the pulp thirties; and one can see her, hair braided in Valkyrie coif, scarlet lips set in a "square" of hatred, "uptilted breast" bare (but was breast ever so unmoving?).

She offers the hero love and gives it, although in his pride he believes he has taken it; but in this finest, if flawed, depiction of his tragic heroines, Merritt is still restricted by the conventions of the time. How we would like to find within her the deep hunger and even lonely fear which her stereotyped hunting companions cannot satisfy. Something of this emotion escapes in her pensive love for the haunting Lake of the Ghosts, more is revealed as she lies dying. Leif Dwayanu, the hero torn between his modern self and a millennia-old incarnation, a man loving two women, turns to her: "The Witch-Woman looked up at me. Her eyes were soft and her mouth had lost all cruelty. It was tender. She smiled at me. 'I wish You had never come, Yellow-Hair!'" We recall Edward Arlington Robinson's Tristram and his two Iseults, and his passion and despair; such is needed here, rather than facile description and trite bravado.

Perhaps it is the voracious nature of the reader to demand *all*, yet a writer can hardly satisfy all tastes, nor can he predict the tastes of generations yet to come—or readers grown too old. Ultimately, and as Merritt often averred, he must write to please himself first.

He had also to please his editor. Merritt, who wrote rather little considering his certain and well-compensated salability, was chagrined when his editor demanded a happy ending to the novel, in opposition to his own conception. He accomodated the wish, and the hardcover version of the book, with a slight change of wording, followed suit: Lur must die, and something in the hero with her, but Evalie could live—to follow her lover out of the Mirage—only to become a docile housewife?

The final word was the author's. More than a decade later, in the *Fantastic Novels* magazine reprint, Merritt at last had his own way, and the novel transcended its own weaknesses. The hero must lose both visions of Woman simultaneously. Love dies but is not forgotten. In his beautiful and memorable final paragraph, Leif/Dwayanu, leaving the hidden land with bitterness in his heart, recalls: "Ai! Dark Evalie of the Little People! Ai! Lur—Witch-Woman! I see you lying there, smiling with lips grown tender—the white wolf's head upon your breast! And Dwayanu lives still within me!"

In an abrupt switch, Merritt employed for the first time in his fantasy the unadorned style of his *Seven Footprints to Satan*, making it in fact even leaner, in *Burn Witch Burn!* (1932). Narrated by a physician, this story is both spare and direct, so tightly constructed that the author does not have to introduce his villainess until three quarters of the way through the novel.

When he does, however, she is unique. Grossly fat, with hair growing upon her lip, repellent but magnetizing, she shows her evil personality lurking within her brilliant eyes (*all* of Merritt's characters speak volumes with their eyes). Madame Mandilip is an unlikely but worthy successor to Merritt's gallery of female characters, and, in fact, he hints that, should she so desire, she could as easily appear ravishingly beautiful.6 The story is a *tour de force* marred only by some stage-Irish accents that he gives his 1932 Irish policeman.

There had been several other short stories published in the intervening years. Unaccountably, *Argosy* had rejected "The Woman of the Wood"; he thereupon sold what he would later term his only "perfect" story to *Weird Tales*. It is an excellent tale, somewhat in the pensive post-World War I mood of "Three Lines of Old French," with a strong feeling for the beauty and mystery of Nature.

In the early thirties, Merritt generously wrote two stories for fan publications, which he subsequently revised and sold to *Thrilling Wonder Stories*. One, "The Last Poet and the Robots," which he would retitle "Rhythm of the Spheres," appeared as part of a round-robin effort by major writers, each contributing a chapter, barely related, to an effort called *Cosmos* for *Fantasy Magazine*. His ability to write in this length is considerable, and one regrets that he did not do more. It has been established by George Wetzel and Sam Moskowitz that Merritt also published at least one pseudonymous story, "The Pool of the Stone God," as by W. Fenimore, in *The American Weekly* in 1923, and it does bear some relationship to certain aspects of "The Moon Pool."7 Quite possibly other examples of his work may eventually be discovered buried in periodicals of this kind.

Merritt left behind a number of unfinished works after his death. Several were mere fragments, including "The White Road"2 and "When Old Gods Wake."8 Two, however, were more complete as they stood, and of sufficient length to warrant being completed by other hands. The task was attempted, with only fair results, by the late artist Hannes Bok; the longer piece, "The Fox Woman" reads well enough in its original state, whereas "The Black Wheel" is too fragmentary.9 It is clear that the originals were all in rudimentary form, far from the finished work, either in plot and character, that a careful writer would submit for publishing.

Always a busy man, finicky about his fiction, Merritt was a man of many hats, and when writing and editing proved trying, he could gladly duck down to a second home in Florida. Here he shared some twenty acres with "pelicans, cranes and herons, porpoises, sharks, cardinals and mocking birds and extremely large and hairy spiders." His favorite hobby was raising bees.10 Because he found it so hard to

A. MERRITT, by Ben P. Indick

please himself, the author said, he wrote very little. However, to the end he toyed with the idea of "grabbing family and typewriter under arms and migrating to the key and writing again."[1]

Creep, Shadow!, Merritt's final novel, appeared in *Argosy* in 1934. Interestingly, while working on the novel he met the great horror story writer, H. P. Lovecraft, already a mainstay of *Weird Tales* magazine, during Lovecraft's several-year stay in New York City.

In a letter to his protégé, Robert H. Barlow, in January 1934, Lovecraft wrote: "It seems he had long known my work and held a very kindly opinion of it. Hearing of my presence in NY he took steps to get in touch with me, and finally invited me to dinner at his club..."[11]

As stated earlier, Lovecraft had admired Merritt's work from afar for many years. "The People of the Pit" possibly influenced his own "Dagon," in which a shipwrecked sailor is thrust upon a volcanic island recently spewed up from the depths. Somewhat like Merritt's prospector, he discovers within a crater a monolith depicting an unearthly monster-god. Lovecraft would also express his admiration for Merritt's novel, *The Metal Monster*. In a letter he enthusiastically wrote: "It contains the most remarkable presentation of the utterly alien and non-human that I have ever seen. The human characters are commonplace and wooden—just pulp hokum—but the *scenes and phenomena*....oh boy!"[12]

Lovecraft also reported that Merritt had told him he was working on "a sequel to *Burn Witch Burn!*" That book, which would be called *Creep, Shadow!*, would have a monstrous creature as something of a tool to be used in ritual acts, as he did in *Dwellers in the Mirage*. If these unearthly beings somehow resemble Lovecraft's own, as in "The Call of Cthulhu" and "The Dunwich Horror," there are differences. Lovecraft's are entities in their own right and individuality, while Merritt's may be worshipped by humans desirous of using their powers; but the author, haunted by the need to emphasize a scientific basis for his stories, considers them as aspects of the Universe itself, the ultimate Chaos which destroys Life, a sort of barely controllable entropy. Thus, the shape in which the Being appears is likely to be dictated by the choice of the human worshippers, rather than being indicative of some actual form. The shape of the kraken, seen by Merritt on his archeological expeditions, is very different from that of The Gatherer in the Cairn in *Creep, Shadow!*, which is more amorphous, an enveloping mist. The usage varies as well. Merritt's formula of voluptuous women and dashing heroes utilizes the horror as part of the adventure plot; for Lovecraft, the horror itself and its ultimate effect upon the hero is the pivot.

Creep, Shadow! appeared in *Argosy* in 1934. Merritt could not know it would be his final novel, but in some ways it is a summation of his career. There is something of the full fantasy style of his earlier career, yet, free of the signature trademarks of that era, the story moves swiftly, with characters both contemporary and ancient. It has a few hold-over individuals from *Burn Witch Burn!*, but is quite dissimilar to the lean style of that novel. As in *Dwellers in the Mirage*, reincarnation is vital to *Creep*'s plot; however, the hero's sense of a prior life is shared here by the evil heroine, the brilliant Dahut, the Demoiselle de Keredal D'Ys and her father as well! Dahut lacks something of the fiery intensity of Lur, but she is a most realistic witch, whether over cocktails in a New York apartment or on a Long Island estate converted to a representation of ancient Ys on the shore of Brittany. At either end of the millennial bridge, Dahut is a credible snarer of the shadows of men. Merritt, a poet of some skill, paints her in "the old Breton song," remembered by the hero from the long-gone past:

> Fisher! Fisher! Have you seen
> White Dahut the Shadows' Queen?
> Riding on her stallion black,
> At her heels her shadow pack—
> Have you seen Dahut ride by,
> Swift as cloudy shadows fly
> O'er the moon in stormy sky,
> On her stallion black as night—
> Shadows' Queen—Dahut the White?"

Other tantalizing couplets occur in the text, almost as though to contrast the gangsters and the horrors which are also on hand.

Unlike Lur, Dahut is saddled with an aggressive and ambitious father, and a past in which they, and the hero, mingle tragically; as in Greek drama, they are fated to relive their roles. Merritt employs a Lovecraftian monster-god, The Gatherer in the Cairn, which would appear to be more susceptible to human ambition, since its father, with its powerful aid, plans to rule the Earth. The novel is swiftly paced, and White Dahut is a worthy finale to the portrait gallery of women good and evil whom the author loved.

It is more than half a century since Herndon vanished into the Dragon Glass, but Merritt's work continues to be read, returning regularly to print and to the discovery of new readers. *Books in Print* lists six of his titles as currently available, including even the two collaborations.

We cannot bring back the emotion of the past, with all it gave us to dream on: bold women, clinging heroines, daring heroes, scenes of bold fantasy. We recall the sheer daring of the prose, bursting with color and the glory of dreams we ourselves could not dream; but, rereading, older now, we sense exasperation with over-stylized tricks, cliff-hanging pulp jumps, endless pace-killing references to legends which no longer seem exotically beautiful, scientific references that

A. Merritt, by Ben P. Indick

were dubious even at the time, women whose beauty is as dated as the beauties of Mucha, Gibson, and Fiagg, dark, sneering villains, and heroes who were incapable of dealing successfully with their own period. There is not the dramatic intensity and crushing beauty of a Tolkien, nor the fragmented, grotesque vision of a Peake, nor the cold and epic grandeur of an Eddison.

What can we make of this writer who created such visions for us? Shall we relegate him to the legion of new young readers who continually rediscover him? Is the fault our own, for having had to leave Never-Never Land in the guise of Nan-Metal in the South Pacific, a mirage-laden valley in Alaska, shadow-shrouded Ys, and all those other places of mystery and glory? Four decades ago, the writer of this essay, then a boy, wrote a plaintive letter to beloved A. Merritt—a name of sheer magic—imploring him to do more writing. He still treasures the courteous reply on *American Weekly* stationary, in which the author hopes he would be able to devote himself to completing two stories, "one of them (he considered) as probably the best of any."

The letter was written April 25, 1943; on August 20 of that same year, Merritt died in Florida, aged fifty-nine.

Whatsoever the faults, his, ours or Time's, he left behind him a body of stories unique, and for their own particular qualities, unrivaled in Fantasy. We remain indebted. Ai Evalie! Ai Dahut! Ai Santhu! Ai Adana! Ai Lur! And A. Merritt is still the Lord of Fantasy!

VI.

VILLAINS OF NECESSITY

THE WORKS OF E. R. EDDISON

by Don D'Ammassa

Eric R. Eddison was born in 1882 and spent most of his adult life working as a civil servant, specifically as a member of the British Board of Trade. Eddison early conceived a fascination and respect for the aristocracy, which he saw as almost a superior breed of human being, with a moral responsibility that exceeded that of the common man. He was also unhappy with the time in which he found himself living, and admired more primitive times, which resulted in the Viking novel, *Styrbiorn the Strong*. But Eddison's literary career really started with the 1922 publication of his fantasy novel, *The Worm Ouroboros*.

The Worm Ouroboros deals with the epic struggle of two powerful sets of characters: on the one hand, the Lords of Demonland and their allies, on the other, King Gorice of Witchland and his lieutenants and tributary nations. Through magical artifice, Gorice conjures up a supernatural being which kidnaps one of the Demon lords and spirits him off to a far land, and much of the energy of his enemies is diverted to repeated attempts to rescue him. Eventually their efforts are successful, and they return in time to repel the invaders of their homeland and bring the war home to the Witches. Ultimately triumphant, the Demons realize that without an enemy, their lives are empty and pointless, and a sympathetic goddess solves their problem by twisting time so that they are suddenly back in the opening chapter.

This solution obviously made it difficult for Eddison to write a sequel, so his next novel, *Mistress of Mistresses*, is ostensibly set in the heaven of the world of Ouroboros, Zimiamvia, as are the remaining two novels Eddison wrote. This conceit really doesn't work all that well, since Zimiamvia is a land much like any other, but the author doesn't dwell on the situation and it does not detract from the novels themselves.

The Zimiamvian trilogy consists of *Mistress of Mistresses* (1935), *A Fish Dinner in Memison* (1941), and *The Mezentian Gate* (1958), published thirteen years after Eddison's death. This posthu-

E. R. EDDISON, by Don D'Ammassa

mous novel was not completed at the time of his death, but Eddison left detailed summaries of the missing chapters, and it is coherent enough not to detract appreciably from the narrative. The sequence of events in the three novels is chronologically almost the reverse of the order in which they were written and published. *The Mezentian Gate* and *Mistress of Mistresses* form a straightforward story, with *A Fish Dinner in Memison* more of an embellishment and explanation of some of the events which take place in the other two novels, even though it was written first.

The Mezentian Gate starts with the events surrounding the murder of the current King of Fingiswold. Fingiswold is the most powerful kingdom in Zimiamvia. It is bordered on the north by the primitive land of Akkama, founded by malcontents and fugitives from Fingiswold itself. Far to the south is Meszria, a small kingdom ruled by a weak family. Centrally located is Rerek, a collection of self contained states, the scene for constant battles and intrigues as the minor powers jockey for position.

The death of the king creates a power vacuum. In Rerek, the Parry family is perhaps the most adept at intrigues, but its two leaders, Supervius and Emmius Parry, disagree on the best course of action to pursue, with the latter, a canny politician, finally prevailing for patience. The result is not entirely to his liking, because the infant king eventually matures into a strongminded and competent ruler who extends his authority into Rerek to quiet the constant turmoil that disturbs that land. Emmius Parry contents himself with the placement of his daughter Rosma in Meszria, where she marries into the royal family, and quickly murders and intrigues herself into a position where she is sole ruler of that nation. Most of the novel consists of the conflict between King Mezentius and the Parry family, first Emmius, later the more skillful and persistent Horius Parry, who becomes Vicar of Rerek, surviving despite his occasional treason. Mezentius marries Rosma, an act of state rather than love, and conquers Akkama, effectively bringing the entire world under his rule. The book ends with his own murder.

Mistress of Mistresses takes up the story at that point. The heir to the throne, King Styllis, is murdered almost immediately, due to the machinations of Horius Parry. Meszria and Rerek were split into a number of smaller holdings under the terms of Mezentius's will, but Parry moves to consolidate his own power, and Duke Barganax abrogates the will himself, seizing control of Meszria and placing himself in opposition to the Parry family. Several conflicts result, with Parry's chief lieutenant, Lessingham, acting as a moderating influence, trying to advance his patron's situation without doing injustice to any other party, often risking his own life in search of what he considers a higher principle. The novel ends with the climactic confrontation between the two forces.

A Fish Dinner in Memison is almost parallel to the plot of the other two. It provides a more detailed look at some of the conflicts between Mezentius and Horius, but the centerpiece of the novel is a special feast with the principle characters all present. They discuss at length the nature of reality, God, and their own persons, speculating that perhaps in some fashion they are gods and goddesses themselves. They attempt to create a world, and in fact a spherical object appears, a representation of our own world, which we are shown glimpses of as some of the characters flit back and forth from one reality to the other. As further proof of their power, one of the dinner guests pricks the bubble, destroying the entire created universe in which we live.

This exalted view of the aristocracy is obvious in all of Eddison's works. In *The Mezentian Gate*, for example, he asserts that "weak natures can attain to greatness in nothing, neither to great good nor to great evil." When Gabriel Flores, the conniving aid to Horius Parry and one of the very few weak characters to appear anywhere in Eddison's fiction, speaks disparagingly of Duke Barganax in *Mistress of Mistresses*, Lessingham rebukes him: "When you speak to me of great men...speak with respect, be it friend or unfriend."

C. P. Manlove, in *The Impulse of Fantasy Literature*, characterized Eddison's fantasies as "anaemic," that is, the characters were so one-dimensional that they lacked verisimilitude. In Manlove's view, the irreality of this kind of fantasy destroys its effectiveness as fiction, reducing it forever to a kind of fairy tale. But Eddison would have been outraged to be classified as an allegorical writer. In *A Fish Dinner in Memison* he tells the reader that "It is the defect of allegory and symbolism to set up the general above the individual, the abstract above the concrete, the idea above the person."

Nor is Manlove the only writer to cite Eddison as lacking in the ability to create credible characters. Franz Rottensteiner, in *The Fantasy Book*, claims that "there is not really...all that much in the way of difference between Gorice and his enemies." Lin Carter wrote in *Imaginary Worlds* that the characters in *The Worm Ouroboros* were "two groups of heroic and magnificent warriors unfortunately pitted against each other by Fate." Even James Stephens, in his introduction to *Mistress of Mistresses*, says that "even his varlets are tremendous." None of these writers shows any evidence that he recognizes that there is a fundamental difference in the way Eddison treats his heroes as characters and the way he treats his villains as characters.

Heroes on the side of good are constrained by their very natures to perform in certain specified fashions; they literally cannot make decisions because they have to do what is right and honorable. There is no such restriction on the actions of the villain, who can be good, bad, or indifferent, serious or capricious, limited only by his or her will and circumstances. Villains are necessarily more interesting, deeper characters than their opponents.

E. R. EDDISON, by Don D'Ammassa

The Worm Ouroboros features the four Demon lords, Juss, Spitfire, Brandoch Daha, and Goldry Bluszco. These four characters are so interchangeable that it is impossible to distinguish among them. Indeed, Keith Henderson's illustration in the original edition show four identical men standing in a row. When the vow is made to rescue Goldry Bluszco, the others must do so, even if it means leaving their homeland virtually undefended. They cannot do otherwise, because the code of honor dictates what they must do. Each man is brilliant in war, brave, honorable, intelligent, and completely uninteresting as a character, simply because we always know in advance what he will do in a given situation.

Not so Gorice and his court, and the most interesting scenes in the novel are generally those concerned with the intriguing and other events that take place in Witchland. Gorice himself is the least interesting of the villains, secretive, engaged in sorcerous pursuits, but still recognizing the needs of his subordinates. When one of his generals disobeys him, causing a serious early reversal, he refrains from carrying out his original threat, and endeavors to find a way for the man to save face and regain his place of honor.

The three generals of Witchland are more interesting. Corinius and Corsus, for example, are strange combinations of strength and weakness. Corinius is young, brash, fearless, and a brilliant tactician. As the novel progresses, he begins to mature and gain control of his tendency to fly off the handle. Corsus, on the other hand, has crossed the boundary between courage and cowardice as he enters middle age, and although he is frequently brilliant in his military skills, he ignores the advice of his associates, murdering one of them in a rage, and brutally subjugates the local population, causing greater unrest against the invading force. Ultimately, there is a serious question about the man's sanity, and his final act is to turn against his own allies.

Corund is the third of Gorice's generals, the most skillful, and arguably the most noble and admirable character in the entire novel. Corund is torn by opposing forces, for he considers Gorice's war unjust and perhaps unwise, yet refuses to abrogate his allegiance to the throne, showing respect for the institution if not for the man seated there. Personal ambition is beneath him, but he is thrust by events into an ever more important role in the unfolding war. His wife, Prezmyra, adds to his problems, and is a genuine villain in her own right. The sister of La Fireez, ruler of the tributary nation of Pixyland, she is incensed against the demons, partly because she hopes that the war will increase the stature of her husband. Indeed, she becomes Queen of Impland when Corund conquers that nation. It appears as well that she is personally opposed to the Demons, and at least part of this results from the fact that her brother runs afoul of Gorice early in the novel when he repays an old debt to the Demon lords by rescuing them from Gorice's clutches.

The last major villain in the novel is the Lord Gro, a renegade from Goblinland, now in the service of King Gorice, functioning as his adviser. Gro tries to manipulate Gorice and the others, assuming that with the reduction of Demonland, he will be able to establish himself as one of the most powerful men in the world. But during the invasion, he falls in love with a local woman, and abandons his former allies, joining the Demons for the final battle. Tragically, he reverses himself again as the result of a taunt, and is cut down for his perfidy. Gro is probably the most complex character in the novel, torn by internal conflicts, never certain where his place in the world should be, where his true loyalties might lie.

Manlove's label of "anaemic" would seem to apply even less to the Zimiamvian books, which are such a collection of Machiavellian plots and counterplots that no character, with the possible exception of Lessingham, comes across as entirely admirable. And once again, although the "heroes" of the books are probably King Mezentius and Lessingham, the most powerfully drawn characters are certainly the villains, specifically the Parry family.

Horius Parry, the Vicar of Rerek, dominates *Mistress of Mistresses*, and to a lesser extent, *The Mezentian Gate*. King Mezentius is so fascinated by his powerful personality and absolute talent for intrigues that he forgives him his many treasons and disloyalties, even against the advice of his closest advisers and friends. Parry might be seen as a classic villain, but he is at the same time capable of recognizing and appreciating the nobility of character of his opponents, when they deserve it, and expresses considerable family loyalty as well.

Another major character is Rosma, daughter of Horius Parry, who marries the King of Meszria and murders him with the connivance of his brother on their wedding night. Taking the new king as her husband, she then arranges his murder shortly afterward, followed by the murder of one lover and the exile of another. Now safely ensconced as the sole ruler of Meszria, she attempts to have her own child murdered, but is secretly thwarted. When King Mezentius comes courting her for reasons of state policy, she coerces him into the conquest of Akkama in order to put off the wedding. Later she attempts to murder another of her children.

Superficially, this description would make Rosma seem a typical shallowly depicted villain, unwilling to stop at any excess. But as the novel progresses, Eddison allows her character to mature, so that she raises children with genuine affection, regrets some—but not all—of her earlier acts, and becomes almost a sympathetic character at times.

The only significant villain in all of Eddison's work to be portrayed in a superficial and "anaemic" fashion is Gabriel Flores, flunky to Horius Parry. Flores is a weak-willed, mean-spirited man forever conniving against his betters, but not intelligent enough to fool anyone, let alone the wily Horius Parry, who uses him as nothing more than a tool. But Flores is a weak man, with no courage or force of character. Recalling Eddison's comments on weak natures, it is clear that Flores could never even have hoped to succeed at greatness.

The inclination to assume that Eddison's characters are invariably shallow caricatures rather than full blown personalities is probably attributable to the natural inclination to identify with the "good" characters, the heroes. But to judge Eddison's works on that basis is to do them a major injustice. Heroes do not make decisions, and it is in the deciding of courses of action that characters become realistic and of interest to the reader as personalities. Villains have many more options available to them, and it is characters like Lord Gro, Corund, and Rosma Parry who will remain in our memory long after the book is closed.

VII.

SUBTLE PERCEPTIONS

THE FANTASY NOVELS OF ALGERNON BLACKWOOD

by Jeffrey Goddin

Imagine a man well over six feet tall, lean and elegant of manner, with a long face lined by over eighty years of living, and the open air of a dozen countries of two continents. Even in the photograph, taken near the end of his life, the dreaming mischievousness of his pale eyes is inescapable. He could be a tired emperor, the wisest of priests, or an actor who plays Prospero. He is, in fact, Algernon Blackwood, one of the most unusual fantasy writers of the century.

Blackwood is best known for his supernatural tales—"The Willows," "The Wendigo," "The Empty House," and "Ancient Sorceries" are among the most frequently anthologized. The supernatural tales are characterized by a superb evocation of atmosphere, especially that of wild natural places, and by subtle insights into human psychology. Blackwood's fantasy novels are today less well known, if not downright obscure. One which I obtained from a southern library to complete my researches had last been checked out in 1964.

A variety of influences can be found in Blackwood's fantasy: an early, avid interest in theosophy and Eastern religion; the love of nature that inspired so much of his supernatural fiction; the intensely religious environment of Blackwood's childhood, which, though in Blackwood quite pagan, could be a valid attribution. Blackwood was not one to imitate others, but rather to adopt a diversity of ideas to his particular purposes.

The themes of the fantasy novels are relatively consistent, if varied in development: Karma, as in the broad sense of reincarnate fate; the potential of certain individuals to escape the petty, deadening demands of a materialistic social world and develop a higher consciousness; the *challenge* of living true to one's best spiritual fate or potential; and nature and children as loci, mediums, and doors to that truer and happier world of eternal and timeless feelings, perceptions, and forms.

ALGERNON BLACKWOOD, by Jeffrey Goddin

Blackwood's ideas of underlying forms and, to a certain extent, beings, should not be interpreted in a purely Platonic sense. Rather, there is something more akin to alchemy, or high ceremonial magical thought, in Blackwood's thematic developments. He was for a time a member of The Golden Dawn, that strange and idealistic magical organization that at one time or another attracted Aleister Crowley, William Butler Yeats, and Arthur Machen. Blackwood knew his magic, though it is fair to say that his interpretation of occult lore, unlike that of, say, Aleister Crowley, was always of a spiritual bent.

1. Past Lives

Reincarnation, particularly the concept of living through the patterns of past lives in the present, and perhaps resolving unfinished spiritual business, was a theme that fascinated Blackwood. He often gave the theme a specific paradigm: the dynamic interrelation between two men and a woman. One might oversimplify and say that the men usually symbolize a more idealistic, or spiritual, yet weaker element, and the women a more primal, less spiritually focused, oceanic element. You could place this interpretation loosely on some of Blackwood's novels, but this would not quite do them justice. Blackwood rarely used symbolism unambiguously, and his characters can be quite complex spiritually.

Three works in which this paradigm occurs, of greater or lesser importance to the plots, are *The Wave: An Egyptian Aftermath*, *Karma: A Reincarnation Play*, and *Julius LeVallon*.

The Wave: An Egyptian Aftermath (1916) is a mystery play. From childhood, the protagonist has been haunted by three images, or rather, psychic sensations: the wave, the "whiff," and a pair of beautiful dark eyes. The wave is a psychic image of a wave, mysterious of form and nature, and somewhat menacing in its impending, cresting nature. The "whiff" is a very unusual smell, and the eyes are feminine eyes. The onset of these sensations always precedes a crucially important moment of consciousness, or of perception.

This is subtle stuff. The conceit is developed and extended through the protagonist's years of success and failure, and a fated meeting in mysterious Egypt with implications of reincarnation. The connection between the owner of the dark eyes and the protagonist is oblique, frustrating, and spiritual, as is often the case in Blackwood's description of adult male/female interactions. It also contains the reincarnate triad of two men and a woman, working out the fate of their past lives, which occurs so prominently in *Julius LeVallon*.

The Wave is an oddly romantic novel, and a case of spiritual *caveat emptor*. Let future readers judge its effectiveness for themselves.

Though conceived as a dramatic piece in collaboration with Violet Pearn, *Karma: A Reincarnation Play* (1918), deserves mention in a discussion of Blackwood's novels because of its consistency of theme with *The Wave* and *Julius LeVallon*.

In *Karma*, a reincarnated triad of two men and a woman trace a pattern through various historical periods. The milieux include the banks of the Nile in a pharaonic period of 2000 B.C., fourth century Greece at the time of Alexander the Great's consolidation of power, and the fifteenth century Italy of the Medicis. The vignettes are historically ambitious, to say the least.

In each of these settings, until the conclusion of the play, a similar scenario is enacted. Through the selfish, but well-meaning love of a woman, a man abandons his ideals or is somehow undone. Although the drama is of necessity quite brief, the sketching of the historical scenes is nevertheless interesting, and does indeed build suspense regarding what the final outcome of this pattern will be in the present. It would be fascinating to see modern actors attempt a production of *Karma*.

The final novel in this group is *Julius LeVallon* (1916). Along with *The Bright Messenger* and *The Human Chord*, *Julius LeVallon* clearly shows the influence of Blackwood's theosophical and Golden Dawn researches.

The title character, of the same name as the indirect protagonist of *The Bright Messenger*, is a mystical lad who leads the narrator into perilous glimpses through the veil of reality, not unlike that those of some of Arthur Machen's tales, though in Blackwood such adventures are usually more benign, and often linked to past lives. The glimpse behind the veil afforded by LeVallon may be direct, or it may be almost too subtle to perceive, and only reflected in the actions of others, or of animals, as in a scene when a herd of sheep are stampeded by unknown forces.

As the narrator and LeVallon's friendship progresses, it becomes more and more difficult for the narrator to keep up with the spiritual pace. One of the weirdest passages of Blackwood's novels occurs in this work, describing a partially successful experiment in necromancy.

The narrator and LeVallon must part company, only to experience a fated reunion. By this time, the triad which formed their past lives is completed in the person of LeVallon's wife, a young, initially unprepossessing "peasant" woman, who proves to be one of Blackwood's more unusual personality sketches. Together the three must work out the ill they did in the distant past, through the path of transcendental magic.

2. A Variety of Themes

The Bright Messenger (1921) seems at first to have a very accessible plot, and is to a certain extent a sequel to *Julius LeVallon*. The book is not altogether unlike a Tarzan adventure, or "boy-raised-by-wolves" novel in overall premise and structure, though the differences between Julius LeVallon and other people are far more subtle than a mere bestial/civilized dichotomy.

LeVallon is a product of the peculiar mating of a reclusive artist and a very unusual woman—just how unusual becomes clear as the plot develops. He is associated with the element of fire (Blackwood often uses air and fire imagery in his writing), and is capable of unusual sensitivity—and radical rudeness—in the presence of other people. He also communes with "forces," which may become apparent to others during the boy's communion.

A reciprocal mentor relationship develops between a doctor and LeVallon at the home, or institute, at which the boy is staying. Even as LeVallon develops a grudging tolerance of some human ways, combined with a painful nostalgia for his old life, the doctor is tempted more and more into sharing LeVallon's unusual ways of perception.

There is a strong element of the supernatural, or the deistic pagan, about LeVallon. It is as if Blackwood were trying to describe a spirit, or deity, and a person at once, and the effect is suitably weird, as is the mood created by the novel as a whole. By the end of *Julius LeVallon* the reader can hardly but share the boy's yearning for a more intense world of dynamic, elemental forms behind the dross of daily interaction.

The Human Chord (1910) is Blackwood's most occult novel, in the sense of the ritual occultism practiced by members of The Golden Dawn—or by Aleister Crowley. The carrier for the plot is simple adventure. An unfocused young man of dreamy disposition, Spinrobin, answers an ad for a person of peculiar talents. He travels to a secluded country house where he meets the bearded Mr. Skale, who has been seeking someone whose voice has the perfect pitch necessary to supplement the voices of himself, his daughter, and his housekeeper to create a perfect chord. By making this chord, Skale hopes to invoke forces of the Hebraic (Cabalistic) names of power.

The operation is, needless to say, somewhat perilous, and in the rarefied atmosphere of the secluded house love blossoms between Spinrobin and Miriam, the daughter, as we knew it would. The action develops into a conflict between "good" and "evil," though in more ab-

97

stract and spiritual terms than those one finds in most novels. *The Human Chord* is a perilous balancing act between a somewhat Faustian quest for subtle magical discovery and the equally magical power of young love.

The Promise of Air (1918) is a strange novel by any account. The entire work is a kind of extended metaphor on birdlike qualities, in a symbolic, romanticized sense—of being free, happy, unfettered, divorced from mundane materialistic thoughts and desires.

This work is also somewhat poignant in that the Promise, which was present in the unlikely mating of Joseph Wimble, a chemist's son with a university education, and the daughter of a Norfolk cornchandler, dies out in their romance, only to be reborn in the character of their daughter Joan, with whom her father has a deep affinity.

The Promise of Air touches on a variety of themes of human interaction through a symbolic, and sometimes mystical metaphor: how the hopes and dreams one has may be crushed by experience, and how they can be reborn through one's child; the dichotomy of the spiritual and emotional versus materialistic values; the joy and liberating power of deep personal affinity.

Significant dramatic action is slight in this novel. It is primarily a work of spiritual and emotional perceptions, a flight of fancy grounded in the interactions of a rather unusual family.

The Centaur (1911) may present Blackwood's most coherent mystical perception in novel length, and it is one of his most unified works. While traveling around the Mediterranean, the narrator, O'Malley, who has a touch of mystical sight from his portion of Celtic blood, encounters a very strange man and his son. The pair are physically odd in their massiveness of build, but there are other qualities about them that intrigue O'Malley, and gradually draw him into a friendship with them.

The man and the boy, it develops, are of a rare type, a type that hearkens back to the planet's childhood:

> There have been projections of the Earth's great consciousness—direct expressions of her cosmic life—Cosmic Beings. And of these distant and primitive manifestations, it is conceivable that one or two may still—here and there in places humanity has never stained—actually survive. This man is one of them.[1]

Gradually O'Malley, through his association with his new friends, is drawn into a perception of the *Urwelt*. As his consciousness expands, he experiences visions of the earth's childhood, the primal days, which are among Blackwood's most extravagant lyric passages:

> The Spirit of the Earth, yes, whispered in his ears as he waited covered by the night and stars. She called him, as though across all the forests on her breast the long sweet winds went whispering his name. Lying there upon the coils of thick and tarry rope, the *Urwelt* caught him back with her splendid passion. Currents of Earth life, quasi-deific, gentle as the hands of little children, tugged softly at this loosening portion of his Self, urging his very lips, as it were, once more to the mighty Mother's breasts.[2]

The novel progresses to a triumphantly pagan series of visions in the Caucasus, which are almost religious in spiritual beauty. *The Centaur* is a novel of dual journey, distantly akin to Conrad's tales in that the protagonist is not only taking a physical voyage, but is also traveling into unexplored regions of perception and knowledge.

3. Through a Child's Eyes

Most of Blackwood's later fantasy novels can be classed as children's fiction—or as fiction written for both children and adults.

Jimbo: A Fantasy (1909) is a very nicely paced children's tale. Here we have a solidly British country milieu. The father is a retired Colonel who loves horses, dogs, guns, and riding whips—and his children. There is a troup of whimsy children, including a Nixie, a fey female child who may appear again in another guise in *The Education of Uncle Paul.*

The protagonist, James (Jimbo), is a dreaming lad who imagines pictures in the fire and talks to furniture. His father, somewhat disturbed by his son's otherworldliness, hires a pragmatic governess for the children, thus creating the conflict. She tells the children a cautionary tale of being trapped in The Empty House, and, through the liveliness of childhood imaginations, creates a real fantasy of terror.

Jimbo contains delicate descriptions of childhood perceptions, that "original" way of thinking, as in this revery of Jimbo:

> It was difficult to understand why the sea of white moonlight that covered the lawn should fill him with such joy, and at the same time bring a lump into his throat. It made him feel as if he were swelling out into something very much greater than the actual limits of his little person. And the sensation was one of mingled pain and delight, too intense for him to feel for very long. The unhappiness passed gradually away, he always noticed, and the happiness merged

after a while into a kind of dreamy ecstasy in which he neither thought nor wished much, but was conscious of one single unmanageable yearning.[3]

A Prisoner in Fairyland (1913) was made into a stage piece called *The Starlight Express*, with music by Sir Edward Elgar. Though much concerned with childhood perceptions, this is not really a children's tale. A very successful man takes a sentimental journey to the village of his childhood. There he encounters the third-class railway carriage which his father had set out as a place for him to play, and which our hero called "the starlight express."

Once again the carriage exerts a potent spell, and in it, the protagonist does indeed take a journey back into childhood, and the wonder of childhood perceptions, traveling to such places as the Star Cave, where the lost starlight gathers. *A Prisoner in Fairyland* is a sweet, nostalgic story, with some of Blackwood's most delightful pastoral imagery:

> The flowers seemed alive and walking. There was a voice of beauty. Some lilac bud was singing in its sleep. Sirius had dropped a ray across its lips of blue and coaxed it out to dance.[4]

The Extra Day (1915) is more purely a tale for children. In this book the personification of the youthful heroes is somewhat alchemical. Judy, the eldest, is associated with air, Tim, the middle child, is associated with earth, and Maria, the youngest, manifests a higher spiritual level altogether:

> Maria's passions were unknown. Though suspected of being universal, since she manifested no deliberate likes or dislikes, approving all things with a kind of majestic and indifferent omnipotence, they remained quiescent and undeclared. She probably just loved the universe. She felt at home in it. To Maria, the entire universe belonged, because she sat still and with absolute conviction—claimed it.[5]

The Extra Day is both whimsical and occasionally penetrating in describing the elaborate conceits with which childhood faces reality—and also the conflicts which occur when the world of fantasy and reality clash. It is a rambling fantasy of the world of the imagination, and sometimes very dreamy, as the question the children ask themselves in sleep: "Why God has put blue dust upon the body of a dragon-fly?"[6] [sic].

ALGERNON BLACKWOOD, by Jeffrey Goddin

Dudley and Gilderoy has long been one of Blackwood's most popular books. It is a straightforward fantasy of the experiences of a parrot (Dudley) and a cat (Gilderoy) as they seek adventure in London after escaping from their country home. They are a classic pair, Dudley philosophical and reflective and Gilderoy more the mischievous wanderer. As often with personification, the animals are sometimes quite human, especially Dudley. This book is of note for book collectors in that some shortened editions contain beautifully whimsical illustrations by F. Rojankovsky.

The Fruit Stoners (1934) is almost a fairy tale. In young Maria's fantasy world, a group of men she's imagined as being represented by fruit stones (as per the old nursery rhyme) have come to life in the abandonned wing of the huge family home.

Though somewhat puzzled and frightened by the sinister Man Who Wound the Clocks, Maria, guided by her black cat, Judas, gains entrance into this world of "alternate reality." The happenings here are both enchanting and disturbing, for the characters can only be precisely as she has imagined them, and some of them complain of their lacks. *The Fruit Stoners* lacks the wit and narrative power of some of the other "children's works, such as *The Education of Uncle Paul*, but it is perhaps in some ways more coherent. Blackwood details the psychology of fantasy-come-to-life, and of escalating fantasy, as when Maria's own body changes into that of a young woman, with a deft touch. The novel works fairly well as a simple adventure with psychological overtones, a flight into a carefully structured gap in time.

Blackwood's writing, which in his novels always demonstrates a certain measure of a subjective and spiritual nature, is of a kind to generate personal favorites. Mine among the fantasy novels is *The Education of Uncle Paul* (1909). Ostensibly a child's story, they can be read by adults as well, and has some magnificent flights of truly original fantasy.

The thesis of the novel seems to be that a person who is truly of the magical breed, who is capable of seeing through the shallow details of everyday existence into the true world of forms, fantasy, and magic cannot really escape his fate—to (at least partly) live in this world and join with and help those who are also of this breed.

Paul Rivers, "Uncle Paul," has spent twenty years surveying timber in the forests of North America, a profession he has chosen to be free of the clinging distractions of an over-civilized life. He longs to be close to nature—and to his dreams.

He responds to a request from his sister-in-law to come and visit her and her children in England. His brother, who was somewhat similar to him in his dreaming nature, has died, but Paul feels both a kind of curiosity and obligation to visit his late brother's family.

101

He determines to be what he appears to most people, a vaguely rugged man in his mid-forties with simple ideas. But the children, who have a huge menagerie of pets, are of the magical breed, and have marvelous games and rituals and insights into this and other worlds.

Paul tries to remain conventional, but you can't fool children about your true nature—especially not Nixie, a half-wild waif of exquisite perception:

> The eldest and most formidable of his tormentors, standing a little in advance of the rest, was Margarite Christina, shortened by her father (who, indeed, had been responsible for all the nicknames) into Nixie. And the name fitted her like a skin, for she was the true figure of a sprite, and looked as if she had just stepped out of the water and her hair had stolen the yellow of the sand. Her eyes ran about the room like sunshine from the surface of a stream, and her movements instantly made Paul think of water gliding over pebbles, or ribbed sand with easy and gentle undulations. Flashlike he saw her in a clearing of his lonely woods, a creature of the elements.[7]

Before long Uncle Paul is drawn deeply into the children's world of special perceptions of nature and imagination, and becomes a willing participant in these visions. One of the most fascinating episodes occurs when he and Nixie fall asleep side by side on the lawn and go to the place where the winds sleep. In a shared dream, Paul and Nixie venture into the depths of the forest:

> It was very wonderful. No words can describe adequately the still splendor of that vast forest as they stood there, waiting for the sunrise. Nothing stirred. The trees were carved out of some marvelous dreamstuff, motionless, yet conveying the impression of life. Paul knew it and recognized it. All primeval woods possess that quality—trees that know nothing of men and have never heard the ringing of the axe. The silence was of death, yet a sense of life that is far beyond death pulsed through it. Cisterns of quiet, gigantic, primitive life lay somewhere hidden in these shadowed glades. It seemed the counterpart of a man's soul before rude passion and power have stirred it into activity. Here all slept potentially, as in a human soul.[8]

ALGERNON BLACKWOOD, by Jeffrey Goddin

The narrative develops into an actual vision of the gossamer winds hanging in hidden places waiting to be awakened by the sun's first rays. These passages must be read in their entirety to be fully appreciated.

If you are one of those who still recall with pleasure those childhood days when a fantasy was no sooner imagined than true, when the fall of a flower petal was a symbol and pets had motive intention, this is your book. It also finally resolves the knotty question of the distinction between beetles, beedles, and beeties.

Algernon Blackwood, whose friends included Rilke, Hilaire Belloc, Elgar, and Lord Dunsany, enjoyed a real surge of popularity in England and Europe during his later years. His fantasy novels offer a rare reading experience to those who can track them down. Blackwood was a writer whose experiences indeed formed part of his *oeuvre*. From a long life of observing his fellow men, of travel, adventure, and broad eclectic reading, and of wandering in the wilderness places he so loved, he culled unique insights into the human spirit.

Blackwood persistently and consistently rejected the life of trivial friendships and material aspirations that guide the paths of so many people. He held to an ideal of a beautiful, mystical world, overlapping and underlying the world of experience, often visible to the eyes of children, and to those rare adults with the sensibility to perceive it. He did his best, in his novels, plays, and short stories, to present glimpses of this world of lasting beauty and primal forms and patterns. In passages from The *Education of Uncle Paul*, *The Centaur*, or other of his novels and tales, his writing is, in the truest sense, both spiritual and mystical. These are, indeed, subtle perceptions.

VIII.

DAVID LINDSAY

AND THE QUEST FOR MUSPEL-FIRE

by Galad Elflandsson

In the long tradition of fantasy, it is inconceivable that there has been so tragic a tale as the life and literary career of David Lindsay, author of *A Voyage to Arcturus* and six other, lesser known works. As one is literally swept through *Arcturus,* and then led through the awkward, oftentimes labyrinthine novels that followed it from Lindsay's pen, it is difficult to accept such a statement without some reservation; however, the tragedy cannot be fully comprehended until one has gained insight into the life and motivations of this strange and sadly neglected visionary. *Arcturus,* for all its rampant wealth of imagery and thought, is but a germinal seed from whence was sprung an entire evolution of spiritual questing. Arguably, it is Lindsay's best work. Unquestionably, it is the one and singular product of his career in which his limited capacities as a writer were outweighed by the sheer intensity of his vision.

1. The Life of Lindsay

Lindsay was born in Scotland on March 3, 1878. Reared and educated in Blackheath, he grew into adulthood as a shy, solitary young man who found his greatest pleasures in long walks among the lonely Highland hills, the music of Beethoven, and in books, *i.e.,* Norse sagas, the novels of George MacDonald, and the philosophical works of Schopenhauer and Nietzsche. Though he won a scholarship to university, a family decree sent him into the business world as a clerk with Lloyd's of London. Dissatisfied as he must have been with such mundane employment, his stern, Scottish Calvinist upbringing yet made of him a conscientious worker, so much so that he was offered a directorship with the firm before he reached forty years of age.

DAVID LINDSAY, by Galad Elflandsson

Despite family opposition on both sides, Lindsay married in 1916, and with his wife's support, declined the offered directorship in favor of taking up literature. In 1919 they moved to St. Columb Minor in North Cornwall and Lindsay began work on *Arcturus*. It appeared in the following year, and though Gollancz accepted it for publication immediately, it was with the stipulation that it be cut to a shorter length. Fifteen thousand words of the original were excised and are now irrevocably lost; and so began the tragedy of David Lindsay's career. The stroke of luck that whirled *Arcturus* into print after one submission would never be repeated and his successive novels (see Bibliography) were rejected time and time again before finding publishers. *The Violet Apple* and *The Witch* remained unpublished until thirty-one years after his death. He wrote in his notebooks:

> Disagreeable accidents should always be examined to see if they cannot be turned to account... Just as the remedy for fear is not courage, but daring; so the remedy for worry is not relief, but invention; the transformation of an evil into an advantage.

Lindsay strove to apply this to himself by writing furiously, even in the face of his constant rejections. But he was a writer at heart, and wished to be recognized for his work. Not one of his novels, *Arcturus* included, ever sold out its first printing or gained him widespread acclaim. In 1928 he moved to Ferring in Sussex with his wife and two daughters, and from 1932 until his death on June 6, 1945, he published nothing. Unable to support his family through writing, Lindsay finally succumbed to frustration and bitterness. In his final years, he grew silent, reclusive, and careless of his health. In fact, his fatalism grew so great that he actually died from blood poisoning caused by the neglect of his rotting teeth!

2. The Mysticism of Muspel

A Voyage to Arcturus begins with a séance attended by a group of fashionable and very superficial people, including Maskull and his curiously distracted friend, Nightspore. They witness the materialization of a hauntingly beautiful, cryptically smiling youth; and then the abrupt intrusion of a wild-looking man called Krag, who breaks the apparition's neck with his bare hands. Horrified, those assembled see the dead apparition's mysterious smile transformed into a "vulgar, sordid, bestial grin, which cast a shadow of moral nastiness into every heart." Krag, Maskull, and Nightspore then depart. In the street, Krag informs Maskull that he is to accompany him and Nightspore to the planet Tormance, which revolves around the double-star of Arcturus. The trio assembles in a deserted observatory in Scotland, and from there, Krag transports them to Tormance. Maskull awakens to find himself alone, and begins his odyssey.

In his opening section of *The Strange Genius of David Lindsay*, J. B. Pick states emphatically that *A Voyage to Arcturus* "is not to be taken as a problem for solution, but as a vision to be seen." It is valid statement, for *Arcturus* is *not* an allegory to be puzzled out; rather, it is *a* simple narrative containing characters and events of clearly defined significance. In Chapter 2, just after leaving the séance, Krag advises Maskull, "You are looking for mysteries...so naturally you are finding them. Try and simplify your ideas, my friend. The affair is plain and serious." Such advice is helpful when reading *Arcturus*. Its simplicity is deceptively hidden if the reader approaches it with preconceived notions of good and evil, or is too willing to place faith in outward appearances. A brief summary of Lindsayan philosophy, coupled with a general application to *Arcturus* itself, should eliminate some of the confusion one would normally find upon reading it "cold."

David Lindsay was a mystic, intuitively aware of what he felt to be the absolute truths of existence. In the simplest of terms, his mysticism was centered on the contention that life as we live it is an illusion, a battleground between *real* reality and the snaring, evil deceit of beauty that masquerades as goodness; that all our actions and social interactions are motivated by a false or non-aware sense of the true nature of reality. *Arcturus* is the journey of one soul (Maskull) back to an awareness of Lindsay's "sublime" reality—the sublime reality that he called Muspel, postulating further that every living being bears a spark of Muspel-fire within it, but that the spark has long been submerged and perverted by illusions of false beauty.

Arcturus is seemingly filled with contradictions, and though Lindsay does not *seek* to confuse us, neither does he intend that we have an easy time of it. Maskull's confusion *must* be our confusion, unless we are quick enough to recognize the one symbol in *Arcturus* that will allow us to discard illusion as we encounter it. Loren Eiseley, in his much maligned introduction to the Ballantine edition of *Arcturus*, failed to grasp this symbol's full significance, and so was unable to interpret the book as anything more than a fragmentary *mélange* of Lindsay's perceptions,

Lindsay's indicator is the "vulgar, sordid, bestial grin" seen on the face of the apparition Krag has "murdered." Before leaving for Tormance, Maskull is told that is "Crystalman's grin," but whenever it appears on the face of a dead being of Tormance, Lindsay is symbolically rejecting the beliefs and morality of that being's life. Though Maskull meets almost two dozen inhabitants on his trek across Tormance, each of them has been deceived by Crystalman, and in some manner, has lived his or her life blinded by one of his illusions.

One other point that should be clarified is that Maskull assumes Krag to be evil because of the latter's aggression during the séance. By association, he also condemns Surtur, who is said to be "Krag's chief"; however, scarce has Maskull set foot on Tormance when he learns that the natives have three interchangeably used names for their seemingly beneficent deity—Crystalman, Shaping, *and* Surtur! It is yet another deception, for Crystalman is *not* Surtur, though he often masquerades as him. Maskull falls into the deception because, with few exceptions, everyone else on Tormance has already done so. They have all mistakenly associated Crystalman with Surtur, and like Maskull, they have condemned Krag as *the* evil one solely on the face value of his actions. In effect, Lindsay has mirrored a very human failing—the inability to separate that which is truly good for us from that which is not. In the end, we find that Krag is the *real* Surtur of Muspel, whose name on Earth is Pain; that he would be recognized as such if we were not swayed by beauty, pleasure, or the outward appearance of both. Similarly, the beings of Tormance all seek unconsciously to re-attain Muspel, but they are unable to see the way clearly because their beliefs and motivations are nothing more than empty, Crystalman illusions of duty, morality, power, or self-sacrifice.

Lindsay is saying that Muspel (or perhaps, Nirvana, in the Buddhistic sense) can be reached only by undergoing a ritual of fire, suffering the soul to cast off the trivial, social values that are used so often to reassure ourselves that our lives are meaningful and worthwhile. Maskull must be deceived over and over again, he must suffer the confusion and the nothingness of being stripped of his earthly values before he can begin to understand the vision of Muspel shown to him by Krag (or Surtur) in the final chapter of *Arcturus*.

What exactly is Muspel? Lindsay himself had no clear conception of its exact nature when he wrote *A Voyage to Arcturus*. Intuitively, he felt its reality and so he sought to isolate its positive existence by illustrating negative existence, exposing the true, selfish motivations of human behavior. In this sense, *Arcturus* is a scathing lesson in psychology. But it is only in his later works that Muspel evolves into something less cryptic and abstract. Speculatively, I see Lindsay's "sublime" as a form of archetypal, ancestral memory—the spark of Muspel-fire within us that ever seeks to find its way through our illusion-fraught perceptions, back to Infinite awareness, the Beginning of Life itself.

3. Lindsay as a Writer

Earlier, I stated that *A Voyage to Arcturus* was the one product of David Lindsay's career in which his limited capacities as a writer were outweighed by the intensity of his vision. The fact is, *Arcturus* succeeds by its very strangeness, being unique in concept and execution. Pent up inside of Lindsay for over twenty years, it exploded outward and flowed torrentially from start to finish. Tormance was so *alien* a selling that Lindsay was able to dispense with all earthly convention and plunge directly into the philosophical exchanges between his characters. He was in his element, thus his literary eccentricities and lack of characterization may be overlooked, if noticed at all. To illustrate: looking back on *Arcturus,* I personally cannot see Maskull, the protagonist, as anything more than a hulking, bearded figure. In reading again, one finds that he possesses very little character or emotion beyond what the author has chosen to *tell* us about him. He lacks human-ness, and this fault seems to run through the gamut of Lindsay's players, in *Arcturus* right through *The Haunted Woman, Devil's Tor, Sphinx, The Violet Apple,* and *The Witch.*

In his introduction to *The Violet Apple and The Witch,* Colin Wilson observes that "Lindsay's style is awkward and amateurish; he writes like a retired maiden lady. An extremely introverted, reserved man, he could never bring himself to write easily and naturally...Lindsay is...a truly original genius...also a genuinely incompetent writer... There have been few major writers on whom the gods have played such an apparently malicious trick: to grant such a profound vision, without the powers to convey it to other people."

Wilson immediately qualifies this last statement by saying it was an initial thought after writing his first long essay on Lindsay in 1968. Having gone back to the novels that followed *Arcturus,* he found them more and more satisfying at each sitting. While I can wholeheartedly echo this (indeed, having read *The Haunted Woman* for the second time and *The Violet Apple* for the first, I cannot remember ever having been so exhilarated by mere words upon a page), there is still no denying that Lindsay's prose leaves much to be desired. In reading the above-mentioned novels, it is immediately evident that Lindsay is moving wooden figures through the motions of being human. The dialogue is usually stiff, archaic, and affected, as if excerpted from a grade two primer. In many instances, *Lindsay's* queer verbiage and misplaced modifiers force you to backtrack over entire pages to find out who or what he has been talking about, and yet (and I write these two words with a note of profound awe ringing in my head), when his story moves into realm of the experience and sensation of inspired revelation, one can only sit back and start looking for angels, burning bushes, and the nearest re-run of *The Ten Commandments.*

Arcturus poured from Lindsay's brain like molten lava, but when it was time to follow it up, he found no other milieu at disposal besides the conventional novel. Somehow, his vision would not conform to such trappings. Its utter transcendence of terrestrial concerns sat uncomfortably at tea parties or in polite conversation in social clubs—but Lindsay drove himself to force the harmony and brilliance that produced *Arcturus*; more often, he plodded along, struggling to get through the necessary, logical progressions of plot and character interaction, until reaching the next point where he might give utterance to his mysticism. One could analogize Lindsay's efforts to express his thoughts in novel form with trying to put a Pierre Cardin suit on Conan of Cimmeria. As the horizon of his career shrank in upon him, Lindsay withdrew more deeply into himself, away from the companionship of others. This, coupled with the essential pessimism of his philosophy, made the portrayal of humanity that much harder.

4. Imagery and Symbolism

Arcturus is such a riot of color and anomalous creation that it would be impossible to go through it here, chapter by chapter, to examine all of its imagery and symbolism. What I shall seek to do is outline major influences upon Lindsay and their respective manifestations in his writings, those symbols that will significantly aid in elucidating *Arcturus* further.

In moments throughout the book Maskull hears a sound "like the beating of a drum...very faint, but quite distinct...in four-four time, with the third beat slightly accented... that seemed to belong to a different world." Eventually, we learn that the drum-beat is the sound of Maskull's heart, the spark of Muspel-fire within him that drives him to seek Muspel with its "music." This theme of music, long stately chords of ethereal sound, songs held within the mere fragments of a song, was to occur and recur throughout Lindsay's work until in *The Witch,* his words seem to echo with the ponderous, agonizing strains of some utterly cosmic symphony. Indeed, Lindsay was exceedingly *pleased* by the music of Beethoven, Brahms, and Mozart. He found Muspel-fire in their music, and his visions of the sublime were consequently filled with observations of a musical tenor, in an attempt to recreate the tingling sensation that often attacks one's flesh when listening to the symphonies of the classical masters.

Whatever deep, personal experience wrenched the "Ode to Joy" from Beethoven's tortured soul, it is interesting to note that Maskull's aural perception of the drum-beat of his heart, and his visual perception of Muspel-fire, are often preceded by periods of intense physical/mental stimulation, *i.e.*, confusion, primitive emotion, anticipation. It is the hyperactive body state, when our metabolism is doing double time and we are lifted from the normal quiescence and relative lethargy of the commonplace, that expands our perception and allows us glimpses of the Infinite. After leaving Earth, Maskull is in a state of hyper-stimulation while on Tormance, yet he must be super-stimulated there before he may transcend its hyperstimulate reality; thus, it is comparable to Maskull having transcended 2+ levels of "consciousness" had he remained on Earth.

It would seem likely that Lindsay first heard the beat of his own heart during his boyhood, whilst tramping through the somber majesty of the Scottish Highlands; that his introspective nature delighted in the wide open spaces unfolding before him, and the sights, smells, and sounds of the shadowy crags and valleys that he visited. It was in the hills, away from the trivial, empty striving of his fellow man that he glimpsed the duality of existence, saw through even his own sensual delight to the metaphysical wonder of Muspel; and as the wonders of the Scottish Highlands were naught but illusions masking a higher reality, so too are the imposing natures of the Ifdawn Marest and Lichstorm Mountains intended to distract us (and Maskull) from the serious business at hand. Life, on Earth and on Tormance, is a duality. Unlike the Roman god Janus, Man may look in only one of two directions—to the satiation of his sensual appetites, or through the pain of rejecting them to Muspel. It is not without reason that Lindsay transformed Arcturus into a *double* star.

He also used a series of tangible symbols that were often instrumental in awakening his protagonists to the existence of a higher reality, or, simply, as markers delineating the extent of their awareness. His favorite images were of stairways leading upwards and windows looking out over super-normal vistas. In *The Haunted Woman*, these two symbols form the crux of his story, but in *Arcturus*, they are logically presented to illustrate Maskull's evolution towards Muspel. In Chapter 4 of *Arcturus*, he ventures to climb the stairway of the tower from whence he shall depart Earth, but finds that "Hardly had he mounted a half dozen steps...before he was compelled to pause, to gain breath. He seemed to be carrying upstairs not one Maskull but three. As he proceeded, the sensation of crushing weight grew worse and worse. It was nearly physically impossible to go on." But Maskull does go on, *struggling* in order to reach the first of six windows in the side of the Starkness observatory tower; and for his suffering, he is allowed to see through that window a telescopic vision of the double sun Arcturus and the tiny, glowing sphere that is Tormance. It is not until Krag bleeds Maskull that the latter may ascend to the top of the tower, but by then the windows have lost their other-worldly properties.

Outwardly, it is explained that Tormantian gravity has supplanted Earth gravity in the tower, but Lindsay's intention is clear—a simple act of blood-letting is not enough of a sacrifice. Maskull must suffer spiritually for his enlightenment, and his ascension to the first window entitles him only to his ticket to Arcturus. In the final chapter, another tower is utilized, a tower that the protagonist ascends easily. He has not gained to Muspel, but he has awakened to its existence and so is able to view clearly (through another window) the hideous effect of Crystalman's illusions on the pure sparks of Muspel-fire emanating forth from Creation. The ritual of purification is done, and a clear-sighted war upon illusion is now possible. It is here as well that the full significance of Nightspore's cryptic relationship to Maskull is made plain.

Lindsay's most striking bit of imagery is undoubtedly Maskull's sprouting of Tormantian sense organs upon arriving on Tormance and their subsequent metamorphoses as Maskull progresses across the planet. While these organs (the *breve, poign,* and *magn*) each have their own respective properties that correspond and illustrate Maskull's changing philosophical attitudes, collectively they serve to idealize Lindsay's own contention that our sense perceptions commit terrible distortions upon our spiritual perception. Maskull is all too eager to change his outlook in concert with the new influence of a new sensory organ. No sooner has he learned the selfless love that is instilled in him by his *magn*, then he is become brutal and power-seeking by its trans-formation into a third arm—but even Lindsay was not immune to the influence of beauty and its illusion. Perversely, it awakened his scorn while haunting him, perhaps causing more unhappiness in his life than the failure of his work to bring him rccognition as a literary figure.

5. Paradox and Tragedy

In *The Haunted Woman* Isbel Loment, the main character, first realizes the depth of her inner being when she sees her reflection in a "magic" mirror. David Lindsay never did find the mirror that would give him an accurate reflection of his true self, and so he remained as stiff and awkward as the people he wrote about; however, in reading *Arcturus,* one finds that in spite of his inability to draw convincing characters, Lindsay does seem to brighten up considerably when por-traying his *female* charactors. They begin to come alive with emotion, depth, and physical contour, and then Maskull treats them as just so much refuse to be cast aside when they have outlived their usefulness to him. It is this curious ambivalence towards his female characters that points to the paradox within David Lindsay, the paradox that may have been the ultimate reason for his failure to achieve recognition.

Though Maskull treats such vibrant females as Joiwind and Sullenbode abominably, one can sense that underlying Maskull's cal-lousness is a tenderness that is coming from deep inside David Lindsay, a tenderness born out of respect for and fascination with all things feminine. It is imperative to point out that every male character who dies in the pages of *Arcturus* wears the Crystalman grin at his moment of death; however, Lindsay does not allow Joiwind to die, nor do we actually see (through Maskull) the "grin" on the faces of Oceaxe, Ty-domin, or Sullenbode! Lindsay contrived to hide it from us, unwilling (subconsciously or otherwise) to utterly dismiss their lives as worthless just because they had succumbed to Crystalman's illusions. Strange as it may seem, noble-minded and highly moral David Lindsay was also a sensualist, and *very* susceptible to any and all forms of the illusory beauty that he has Maskull consistently reject in Arcturus. It is unlikely that Lindsay ever gave in to what he considered his failing, but it is a certainty that it tormented him throughout his life and was a constant source of self-deprecation.

In The *Strange Genius of David Lindsay*, E. H. Visiak states that Lindsay, in spite of his morality, "was one of those idealists who are tortured by sexual beauty...he condemned eroticism in any form whatsoever...His reaction from sex impetuously impelled him, while his mystic concept of sublimity drew him on." Lindsay recognized this in himself and wrote in his notebooks:

> Women are small wholes: men are large parts. Hence the nature of the first is harmony, of the second emphasized tendency...The sense of beauty which ought to be diffused in our hearts over the whole of nature, is drawn down to earth by the lightning-conductor. Woman, and henceforward we have eyes for nothing but the vulgar prettiness of petticoats.

Knowing that feminine beauty exercised such power over him, Lindsay fought against it, denied and condemned it. In essence, the above quote is a lament, for Lindsay felt the feminine spirit to be natively closer to Muspel, more intuitively tuned to Muspel, than the masculine spirit. It was difficult for him to reconcile this belief with the fact of his distraction by femininity; indeed, *Arcturus* might have been the beginning and the end of his career as a writer had it not been for this ever-present contradiction in himself. Each of the novels that followed *Arcturus* held a woman in the main role, and Lindsay sought for the rest of his life to find the proper relationship between himself and "Woman" and his concept of Muspel. It is doubtful that he ever found it, though Muspel eventually evolved into something that loosely resembles the "Great Mother" concept of creation and existence.

Aside from the definite lack of writing skill that made the conveyance of his ideas to others so difficult, the greatest tragedy of Lindsay's life must surely be that he found himself to be, in Nietzsche's words, "Human, all too Human," in spite of awesome magnitude of his mysticism.

IX.

CLASSIC AMERICAN FAIRY TALES

THE FANTASIES OF L. FRANK BAUM

by Neal Wilgus

At first glance it may seem strange to see L. Frank Baum of *The Wizard of Oz* fame included among masters of classic fantasy such as Lord Dunsany, A. Merritt, and Clark Ashton Smith. But a survey of his fantasy fiction will reveal that Baum himself was one of the greatest masters of the form in the first half of this century. That most of his work consisted of fairy tales and other children's books hardly detracts from this, for many of his fantasies are still in print, he has at last gained critical recognition, and each new generation of American readers (and movie and TV viewers) is guaranteed to be exposed to some of his work.

Lyman Frank Baum (1856-1919) was born in Chittenango, New York, to a large, well-to-do family, and was educated mostly at home, which perhaps contributed to his becoming a great writer of the imagination. Described as a solitary child and an avid reader, young Frank became interested in printing and journalism as a teenager, when his father gave him a printing press for his birthday. In the late decades of the nineteenth century, Baum worked as a chicken breeder, a salesman, a reporter, actor and playwright, a theatre manager, a store manager, and finally editor and publisher of several publications—with varying success.

By 1891 Baum had settled in Chicago with his wife and four sons, and was at last successful as a china and glassware salesman and later as publisher of a magazine devoted to store window display. With an audience of four boys to entertain, Baum began to make up stories about the traditional Mother Goose characters and about some whimsical characters of his own who dwelt in a place called Phunnyland. At the urging of his mother-in-law, Baum began writing his stories down, and by the end of the decade (and century) his true career began to emerge.

Technically, Baum's first book was *The Book of the Hamburgs*, a treatise on chicken breeding and exhibiting, but his elaborations on Mother Goose that made up his first children's book to see print, *Mother Goose in Prose* (1897), illustrated by Maxfield Parrish, was moderately successful, although it is said to have done more for Parrish's reputation than for Baum's.

A collection of nonsense verse, *Father Goose: His Book* (1899), was Baum's first collaboration with artist William Wallace Denslow, and it was a top-selling children's book for the year, establishing the reputations of both men in juvenile literature. In 1900 Baum followed through with *The Songs of Father Goose*, which was nothing more than some of the *Father Goose* poems set to music, and with two additional verse collections, *The Army Alphabet* and *The Navy Alphabet*, both of which were quickly forgotten. But 1900 also saw the publication of two other Baum fantasies —*The Wonderful Wizard of Oz* in September of that year, and *A New Wonderland* in October.

A New Wonderland was actually Baum's first children's book, for it was written in 1896 and scheduled for publication in 1898 under the title *The King of Phunnyland*.

Baum's original publisher went out of business, and a second publisher put the project on hold; it was not until 1899 that a third publisher got serious about the book and arranged for it to be illustrated by William Francis Ver Beck, an artist who specialized in comic animal drawings. Following the success of *The Wizard of Oz*, Baum brought out a revised edition of *Phunnyland/Wonderland* in 1903, with additional Ver Beck illustrations, and the title changed to *The Magical Monarch of Mo*—an attempt to capitalize on the alliteration of *Wonderful Wizard* and the popularity of a two-letter word for a magical kingdom.

The Magical Monarch of Mo is one of the four non-Oz books by Baum still kept in print by Dover Publications, and, like the other three, it has an introduction by Martin Gardner, the well-known science writer and an expert on Baum's work. Gardner points out many similarities between Mo and Oz, both being enchanted lands where no one grows old or dies, where animals can talk, there is no such thing as money, and many useful items such as swords, bicycles, and lunch pails grow on trees. Gardner notes that references to Mo occur in a couple of later Oz books, and that some of the ideas and incidents in Mo were later to turn up not only in Baum's work, but in fantasies by other writers as well. Surprisingly, Gardner fails to mention that one of the Mo stories, "Timtom and the Princess Pattycake," is something of a prototype, with Timtom going in search of the sorceress Maëtta in order to find a cure for Pattycake's foul temper. Timtom encounters a spider, a bird, and a rabbit, each of whom help him along the way, but make a request of a special gift from the sorceress in return—surely a forerunner of Dorothy's search for the Wizard in the company of the Scarecrow, the Tin Woodman, and the Cowardly Lion.

HALF PRICE BOOKS

2036 Shattuck Ave.
Berkeley, CA 94704-1117
510-526-6080

12/09/08 07:50 PM
#00037/AC037/00002

CUSTOMER: 0000000000
SALE: 0000828753

1	@9.98	DVDD	9.98
	588040-Sir Lancelot (3-DVD)		
1	@0.98	PB	0.98
	5787-(Paperbacks at half price)		
1	@4.98	UN	4.98
	5799-(Used books at low prices)		
1	@8.98	BTU	8.98
	5759-(Used books-on-tape)		

SHIP/HAND	0.00
TAX (8.75% on $24.92)	2.18
TOTAL	27.10

PAYMENT TYPE

CHECK (7147/APPROVAL:3829)	27.10

PAYMENT TOTAL	$	27.10
CHANGE DUE	$	0.00

THANK YOU!

We buy books, music, movies and more!

END OF TRANSACTION

- We cannot guarantee receipt.
- We obey all copyright laws.

The Personal information you provide is confidential and will not be used by Half Price Books or sold, rented or disclosed to a third party for commercial purposes.

 # REFUND POLICY

Cash refunds and charge card credits on all merchandise* are available within 7 days of purchase with receipt. Merchandise charged to a credit card will be credited to your account. Exchange or store credit will be issued for merchandise returned within 30 days with receipt. Cash refunds for purchases made by check are available after twelve (12) business days and are then subject to the time limitations stated above. Please include original packaging and price tag when making a return. Proper I.D. and phone number may be required. We reserve the right to limit or decline refunds.

*Gift cards cannot be returned for cash.
*Software Policy: Returns accepted within one month with receipt for store credit only.

- We cannot guarantee receipt.
- We obey all copyright laws.

The Personal information you provide is confidential and will not be used by Half Price Books or sold, rented or disclosed to a third party for commercial purposes.

 # REFUND POLICY

Cash refunds and charge card credits on all merchandise* are available within 7 days of purchase with receipt. Merchandise charged to a credit card will be credited to your account. Exchange or store credit will be issued for merchandise returned within 30 days with receipt. Cash refunds for purchases made by check are available after twelve (12) business days and are then subject to the time limitations stated above. Please include original packaging and price tag when making a return. Proper I.D. and phone number may be required. We reserve the right to limit or decline refunds.

L. Frank Baum, by Neal Wilgus

The Wonderful Wizard of Oz, which was retitled *The New Wizard of Oz* for the 1903 edition, was Baum's masterpiece. It spawned a series of Oz books by Baum himself, as well as a continuation of the series by Ruth Plumly Thompson and a host of others—plus countless radio, movie, TV, and comic book adaptations as well. The familiar story of Dorothy Gale being swept away to Oz by a Kansas cyclone, of her joining forces with the Scarecrow, Tin Man, and Lion, and of their common search for their most desired goals struck a responsive chord in the American imagination. With classic illustrations by W. W. Denslow and innovative use of color and design, *Oz* sold over 20,000 copies by 1901—a respectable number for its day.

Baum's imaginative genius may also have extended to his later accounts of how it all came about, as the reader will discover in a piece titled "The Creation of Oz" in *Brainstorms and Thunderbolts: How Creative Genius Works* by Carol Orsag Madigan and Ann Elwood (1983). According to Madigan and Elwood, Baum's story that he named the land "Oz" in 1898 while looking at a file cabinet labeled "O-Z" may itself be a fabrication, since the first submitted manuscript of the story was titled *The Emerald City*, and "Oz" was not the name of the land, but of the ruler, the Wizard Oz. Madigan and Elwood suggest at least four alternative possibilities—that Baum altered Charles Dickens's pseudonym "Boz," that Oz is an adaptation of the biblical land of Uz, that Baum claimed a good story should elicit "Ohs" and "Ahs," which can both be spelled "Oz," or that Baum merely went through a series of two-letter combinations until he found a pleasing sound.

Whatever the inspiration of "Oz" may have been, Madigan and Elwood suggest that the origins of the Scarecrow and the Tin Woodman are on more solid ground. They quote Russell MacFall to the effect that the strawman came from a dream in which Baum was chased by a malicious scarecrow, and they cite an *Indianapolis Times* story claiming that the Tin Man was inspired by a hardware store window display that Baum created using a washboiler torso, stovepipe legs and arms, saucepan face, and a funnel hat. Madigan and Elwood also quote a friend of Baum's, poet Eunice Tietjens, as saying in her autobiography, *The World at My Shoulder*, that Baum "had come to the place where he could honestly not tell the difference between what he had done and what he had imagined." The success of *The Wizard of Oz*, as the title eventually became, encouraged Baum to push forward with many more projects, including a stage adaptation of *Oz* which opened in Chicago in 1902, followed by a Broadway production in 1903 which introduced the comedy team of Fred Stone and David Montgomery to stardom, and ran 293 performances—phenomenal for that time. The year 1901 also saw publication of Baum's second book-length fantasy and final collaboration with Denslow, *Tot in Merryland*—plus his only science-fiction title, *The Master Key*, and his *American Fairy Tales*, which ran first in several eastern newspapers and were then collected into book form with illustrations by Ike Morgan, Harry Kennedy, N. P. Hall, and Ralph Fletcher Seymour. *Dot and Tot* and *The Master Key* did not fare well and are no longer in print, but *American Fairy Tales*, despite its prosaic setting in urban America, has retained its appeal and is still available from Dover with additional illustrations by cartoonist George Kerr from the 1908 edition, and a new introduction by Martin Gardner.

Baum's 1902 book-length fantasy, *The Life and Adventures of Santa Claus*, illustrated by Mary Cowles Clark, is also available from Dover with a Gardner introduction, and it has the distinction of having been revived for modern audiences as a 1985 TV Special from Rankin/Bass, Inc. Using their "animagic" technique with clay models, Rankin/Bass followed a simplified plot line of the Baum novel in which the wood-nymph Necile begs the Great Ak, Master Woodsman, to allow her to keep a babe who has been discovered in the magic forest of Burzee. The babe, of course, grows up to become Santa Claus, who battles with the evil Awgwas when they seek to hinder his efforts to take presents to the world's children at Christmas time.

In 1903 Baum published a book-length fantasy called *The Enchanted Island of Yew*, and in 1904 another fantasy, *Queen Zixi of Ix*, began serialization in the children's magazine *St. Nicholas*, with illustrations by Frederick Richardson. Meanwhile, pressure had been growing on him to write a sequel to *The Wizard of Oz*, and in 1904 he published *The Marvelous Land of Oz* (now known simply as *The Land of Oz*), which recounts the further adventures of the Scarecrow and the Tin Woodman after Dorothy and the Wizard had fled. The book introduced a number of new characters such as Jack Pumpkinhead, the Sawhorse, the Witch Mombi, the Wogglebug—and the boy Tip, who at the end of the story is magically transformed into the rightful ruler of Oz, the fairy princess Ozma.

Baum had always been fortunate in his choice of illustrators, but with *The Land of Oz* he teemed up with one of the best fantasy artists of the twentieth century, John R. Neill, and it was Neill who illustrated the rest of the Baum Oz books, as well as several non-Oz titles by Baum, nineteen Oz books by Ruth Plumly Thompson, and three Oz titles written by Neill himself. Taking Denslow's quaint, almost dwarfish models from *The Wizard*, Neill stretched them out to more realistic looking figures who took on a life of their own. Neill's brightly colored covers have delighted generations of readers and helped sell millions of Oz books, and his black and white drawings continue to be reprinted—most recently in the Del Rey paperback reissues of Baum and Thompson.

In 1905 *Queen Zixi of Ix* came out in book form, and it is generally considered Baum's best work after *The Wizard of Ox*. Martin Gardner, in his introduction to the Dover edition, calls *Queen Zixi* "the most classical in form of all Baum's book-length fairy tales," and quotes critic Edward Wagenknecht as praising it as "one of the best

L. Frank Baum, by Neal Wilgus

fairy tales ever written by anyone." *Queen Zixi*, which concerns a magic cloak and how it is misused by a series of foolish characters, is typical of Baum's storytelling—short on actual plot, but long on inventiveness, word play, and sheer fun.

Meanwhile, Baum was busy with various other projects. In 1905 he published a series of fairy tales in a magazine called *The Delineator* which were intended to be published as a book the next year, but which didn't actually see print until the International Wizard of Oz Club brought it out in 1989 as *Animal Fairy Tales*. In another 1905 project Baum tried a second stage play, this one an adaptation of *The Land of Oz* titled *The Woggle-Bug*, but it closed in only one month. And in 1906 he produced a series of fairy tales for very young readers called *The Twinkle Tales*, which have never been collected in book form.

Baum's *John Dough and the Cherub*, another Oz-like fantasy, was also published in 1906, and in the same year he began producing books aimed at teenaged readers under a number of pseudonyms. As Edith van Dyne, Baum published ten titles in the *Aunt Jane's Nieces* series between 1906 and 1914; in 1906 and 1907 he published two *Sam Steele's Adventures* books under the name Captain Hugh Fitzgerald; and in 1908 he started the six-book *Boy Fortune Hunters* series as Floyd Akers. He also used the van Dyne name for a series of five *Mary Louise* books, wrote additional children's stories as Laura Bancroft and Suzanne Metcalf, and wrote several adult novels as Schuyler Staunton. Other adult novels include his spoof on his neighbors at a summer resort on Lake Michigan, *Tamawaca Folks: A Summer Comedy*, originally published under the name John Estes Cooke in 1907, and an adult thriller, *The Last Egyptian*, published anonymously in 1908. Baum resumed the Oz series in 1907 with *Ozma of Oz*, in which Dorothy joins forces with Ozma and a party from Oz which has come to the kingdom of Ev to confront the mischief-making Nome King—a delightful underground villain who was to return in a number of later Oz titles. Another full-length fantasy, *Policeman Bluejay*, also appeared in 1907, and in the same year Baum undertook a unique project to promote his three Oz titles—film "travelogues" of Oz which he narrated, and in which he appeared briefly to give the introductions. Baum himself financed these *Fairylogue and Radio-Plays* and they were popular, but his costs were too great and in 1908 the show was forced to close.

In the next three Oz books it was clear that Baum was trying to bring the series to an end. In *Dorothy and the Wizard in Oz* (1908), the Wizard is allowed to return to the magic kingdom and become a permanent resident; in *The Road to Oz* (1909) Dorothy and Toto return to Oz with such major new characters as The Shaggy Man, Polychrome, and Button-Bright; and in *The Emerald City of Oz* (1910) Dorothy herself, along with Aunt Em and Uncle Henry, also become permanent residents of Ozma's realm. At the end of *The Emerald City* Baum informed his readers that Ozma had decided to cut Oz off from the rest of the world by making it invisible. Since Oz was already surrounded by impassable deserts on all sides, this meant that Baum's readers "will never hear anything more about Oz..."

These three Oz titles had been completed while Baum and his wife Maud spent their winters in California, and in 1910, using money that Maud had inherited, they built a house they called Ozcot in Hollywood, just as the movie industry there was beginning. At Ozcot Baum wrote two additional book-length children's fantasies, *The Sea Fairies* (1911) and *Sky Island* (1912), but despite his prolific output he fell into bankruptcy in 1911, and was forced to turn again to the Oz series to earn a living. He tried first for a stage success with *The Tik-Tok Man of Oz*, and in 1913 he published a series of booklets titled *The Little Wizard Stories of Oz* and the seventh Oz novel, *The Patchwork Girl of Oz*, explaining in the latter that he had established contact with the magic land by "wireless telegraph."

In 1910 the Selig Polyscope Company in Chicago had released four one-reel Oz films with moderate success, and it was perhaps inevitable that Baum would be drawn to the film industry that was springing up around him. He soon started the Oz Film Manufacturing Company, and in 1914 the organization produced film versions of *The Patchwork Girl of Oz*, *The Magic Cloak of Oz* (an adaptation of *Queen Zixi of Ix*), *His Majesty, the Scarecrow of Oz*, and *The Last Egyptian*—all of which bombed at the box office, as did the 1915 release *The Gray Nun of Belgium*. Oz critic Allen Eyles describes the surviving films as primitive even for their day, but gives them relatively high marks for costuming and some of the special effects.

Following these setbacks, Baum turned back to his most popular series, the Oz books, publishing an additional volume each year until his death in May, 1919. The remaining Oz titles are: *Tik-Tok of Oz* (1914), in which the Wind-Up Man confronts the Nome King; *The Scarecrow of Oz* (1915), in which the title character plays a relatively minor role compared with newcomers Trot and Cap'n Bill; *Rinkitink in Oz* (1916), which takes place outside of Oz until the very end; *The Lost Princess of Oz* (1917), in which Ozma is "stolen"; *The Tin Woodman of Oz* (1918), in which the Tin Man meets the Tin Soldier; *The Magic of Oz* (1919), which concerns the Nome King's attempt to subvert Oz with a magic word; and *Glinda of Oz* (1920), which brings a fitting end to the series with the triumph of Ozma and Glinda, the Good Witch from the original story.

This was far from the end, however, for the series was continued by Ruth Plumly Thompson, who published a book every year from 1921 through 1939—and wrote two more for the Wizard of Oz Club in the 1970s. Numerous other writers and artists have published additional novels, short stories, and artwork situated in the Oz realm, and there have been a great variety of new intrepretations of Oz on radio

L. FRANK BAUM, by Neal Wilgus

and TV, on stage, and in film—the most widely known being the classic 1939 movie of *The Wizard of Oz* and the 1978 Black version, *The Wiz* (not to mention another box office Baum, *Return to Oz*, in 1985). The best single source of information on all aspects of the multimedia universe of Oz is *The World of Oz* by Allen Eyles (1985), which includes a splendid selection of art and pictures from all the books and most of the stage and film versions, in addition to an excellent text.

Despite his continuing popularity with readers of all ages and audiences of all kinds, Baum's work was for a long time disapproved of and largely ignored by literary critics, teachers, and librarians. That situation began to change somewhat with the publication in 1929 of Edward Wagenknecht's booklet *Utopia Americana*, a critical study of Baum's books, and much later by the formation of the International Wizard of Oz Club and publication of *The Wizard of Oz and Who He Was* by Martin Gardner and Russel B. Nye in 1957, and by the 1961 biograghy of L. Frank Baum, *To Please a Child* by Frank Joslyn Baum and Russell P. MacFall. Today *The Wizard of Oz* is generally recognized as an American classic, and Baum's imaginative genius is no longer in serious dispute. Now over 2000 strong, the International Wlzard of Oz Club, Inc. holds yearly conventions and publishes new Oz material, as well as its thrice-yearly journal, *The Baum Bugle*—a first-rate semi-professional magazine devoted to Baum's life and works.

One interpretation of *The Wizard of Oz* which has proven unpopular in the Oz Club, however, is the political allegory theory put forward by Henry M. Littlefield in a 1964 essay in *American Quarterly*. According to this populist interpretation, the Scarecrow represents the American farmer, the Tin Woodman stands for the industrial worker, and Dorothy is a symbol of Everyman/woman searching for the truth—while the Lion is populist William Jennings Bryan, and the Wizard sybolizes the deceitful President (a humbug). The Yellow Brick Road to the Emerald City thus stands for the gold standard (measured in ounces, abbreviated "oz.") which leads to Washington, and the Wicked Witch of the East is the Power Elite who took advantage of the little "munchkins" and caused the Tin Man to cut himself apart and become mechanized in her service.

This interpretation is not necessary to enjoy *The Wizard of Oz*, of course, and it may or may not have been Baum's conscious intention. But support for this view can be found in such things as the influence on Baum of Lewis Carroll's *Alice in Wonderland* with its political references, in Baum's rather cynical moral lessons in such works as *American Fairy Tales*, *Animal Fairy Tales*, and *The Master Key*, among others—and in the continued use of *Wizard of Oz* themes in political cartoons today. It's worth noting that as recently as May, 1985, a political interpretation of the 1939 movie version of *The Wizard of Oz* is to be found in Lynette Carpenter's article in *Film and History* entitled

"'There's No Place Like Home': *The Wizard of Oz* and American Isolationism."

It's generally conceded that L. Frank Baum was no great stylist. His stories are told in a simple, almost reportorial manner which is always clear and concise, but which has few flourishes and rarely rises to great heights. Martin Gardner has written that "Baum's style is sometimes pedestrian," and that carelessness was often his hallmark, but Gardner also notes that "his narratives move along briskly, seldom flagging in interest and...invention." And, in fact, Baum's stylistic strengths are in the realm of vivid imagery, word play, and sometimes surrealistic twists of the imagination, rather than the more conventional "literary style."

Something similar can be said for his plotting. In his introduction to a 1976 collection of Baum's stories, *The Purple Dragon and Other Fantasies*, editor David L. Greene remarks that "many of his books are rambling and episodic," and in *The World of Oz* Allen Eyles points out that it was "of no consequence to him how much coincidence, contrivance or damage to pace was caused by his bright idea." A typical Baum plot is to have his characters go on a trip and to simply keep adding side trips and diversions from the main goal until the story has reached book length—at which point the situation is often resolved by someone largely divorced from the earlier action. In *Queen Zixi* there is no plot in the usual unifying sense at all, only the central device of the magic cloak and three subsequent episodes involving the same main characters.

Amazingly, Baum gets away with it. Over and over thoughtful Oz critics such as Gardner and Eyles turn to a single word—inventiveness—to describe what is best, and most magic, in Baum's fantasies. Baum didn't just invent Oz, he invented Mo and Oz and Ix and Ev and the Nome Kingdom and Sky Island and countless other fantasy lands, each vividly realized. As Eyles points out, there are 220 Baum Oz characters listed in Jack Snow's *Who's Who in Oz* (1954), and while many of them only appear briefly, a great number return repeatedly, and quite a few become—again—vividly realized.

Eyles also refers to C. Warren Hollister's essay "Oz and the Fifth Criterion" in *The Baum Bugle*, in which Hollister acknowledges Baum's weaknesses in theme, characterization, plot, and style, but points to what he calls a "three-dimensionality" which translates into strong reader appeal, transcending all such lapses. "You not only suspend disbelief in Oz," Hollister says, "you not only positively ardently believe in Oz; you are there!" And it is, of course, this vividness, this inventiveness, this—yes—magic, that makes up (and then some) for whatever other failings a critic might detect.

And because of this magic, Baum deserves to be included as one of the masters of fantasy of the twentieth century. So move over, you writers of weird tales and heroic adventures, you sword-'n'-sorcerers, you movers-'n'-shakers of the castle and graveyard and other-dimensional realm. Make room, in the waxwork museum of the mind, for the Royal Historian of Oz—Mr. L. Frank Baum.

X.

HENRY KUTTNER

MAN OF MANY VOICES

by Don D'Ammassa

Henry Kuttner (1915-1958) was one of the most prolific writers of all time, using over a dozen pseudonyms during his short career, establishing himself as one of the major writers in the science fiction genre as well as contributing significantly to the mystery field and to both fantasy and dark fantasy. Part of the explanation of his enormous output is undoubtedly attributable to his marriage and literary partnership with Catherine L. Moore, who was a writer of considerable talent in her own right, although she seemed content to exist in the shadow of her husband's reputation for most of her own career. Their very informal approach to writing makes it difficult to evaluate Kuttner alone in the years following 1940, as in many cases even the authors themselves were unable to recall afterward their individual contributions to specific stories. It is quite probable, however, given her own "Jirel of Joiry" stories and others, that Moore contributed more substantially to Kuttner's heroic fantasies than his others in this genre.

Kuttner's debut in *Weird Tales* was an auspicious one: "The Graveyard Rats," a claustrophobic short about an evil gravedigger and his ironic encounter with a horde of rats in the tunnels under a graveyard. Kuttner became a member of the Lovecraft circle, corresponding with Robert Bloch, Fritz Leiber, and others, and some of his subsequent stories show the influence of this association.

The enormous popularity of Robert E. Howard's "Conan" stories led to two attempts by Kuttner to write in the same manner. The Elak stories were set in Atlantis, and featured an incognito prince roaming the countryside. "Spawn of Dagon," the first in the series, is undoubtedly the best, and certainly the most imitative of Howard. Elak is tricked into attacking a wizard in his lair by a group of monsters masquerading as human. Subsequent adventures such as "Thunder in the Dawn," "Beyond the Phoenix," and "Dragon Moon" were more concerned with his involuntary return to protect the throne of his homeland. Only two stories appeared in the Prince Raynor series, which were published in the short lived *Strange Tales*. "Cursed Be the City" showed considerable promise, with an ancient god released to destroy a fated city, but the second, "Citadel of Darkness," was standard fantasy fare.

A series of short novels began appearing about this time, most of them with rational scientific explanations for their fantastic events, even though narratively they often owed much to the works of A. Merritt and other writers of the Lost Race novel. *Beyond Earth's Gates*, *The Time Axis*, and *Well of the Worlds* fall into this category, but two others are straightforward fantasy. *The Dark World* is one of Kuttner's best efforts, featuring a man who is translated between realities, replacing his twin in that world where the creatures of fantasy actually exist as mutations of normal beings. The conflict between brutal overlords and the suffering masses is mirrored in the protagonist, who discovers that something of both personalities remains within him, so that he must resolve the inner struggle before he can deal with the greater one. The other novel, *The Mask of Circe*, is quite unlike anything else Kuttner wrote in this genre, a very straightforward retelling of ancient myths.

Where Kuttner really excelled was when he wrote in what has been called the "*Unknown*" style of fantasy, so-called because of the association of this type of story with *Unknown Worlds* magazine. "A Gnome There Was" has long been regarded as one of the classic tales of this type, wherein a man lost in a mine meets and is transformed into a gnome. The light, good-humored approach was a perfect expression of Kuttner's talents, and much of the best of his science fiction, such as the "Hogben" and "Gallagher" series, were to similarly employ absurdity and fun in their narrative approach. "The Misguided Halo" is similar in this regard, featuring a man who suddenly discovers he has acquired a halo, and the consequences when he appears in public. Kuttner was less successful in "Wet Magic." Following a plane crash, the protagonist discovers himself in a magical world under a lake, ruled by Morgan le Fay, but while the setting is evocative, the humor generally misfires. Far more successful, and rather more serious, was "Housing Problem," one of Kuttner's half dozen best shorts. In return for good luck, a man builds a house for a pair of pixies. But when their privacy is invaded, they look for other accommodations, with predictable consequences for their landlord.

As mentioned, Kuttner worked in dark fantasy as well, sometimes in the mode of H. P. Lovecraft, in such stories as "It Walks by Night," "The Salem Horror," and "The Black Kiss," the lattermost in collaboration with Robert Bloch. He even wrote at least three "deals with the Devil" stories. "By These Presents" and "Threshold" are the usual twisted plots resulting in the defeat of the human being; "The Devil We Know" revealed to the reader that, just as demons prey on human beings, so there is another order of entities which demons fear.

As Kuttner's talents progressed, his approach altered, however, and the results were generally quite entertaining. In "Compliments of the Author," the murderer of a magician steals a book which magically contains the solution to every possible question. It appears that this will make him the most powerful man in the world, but as a matter of fact, events conspire to trap and destroy him despite his use of the book. A very strange and not entirely successful story is "Before I Wake," a moody piece about an unhappy boy who rescues a toad and then dreams of fabulous lands full of exotic people and events.

The sympathetic vampire so common in modern horror fiction appears in a Kuttner short, "I, the Vampire." For the most part, this is the traditional tale of a beautiful young woman falling under the influence of a mysterious man who never travels about during daytime, until the hero can recognize what is taking place and effect her rescue. Instead, the protagonist fails, but the vampire himself is torn in two directions by his love for his intended prey, and his revulsion for the thing he has become; ultimately, he sacrifices himself rather than transform her into one of the undead. Kuttner played with the same theme in "Masquerade," in which stranded travellers find themselves staying in a house run by a band of murderers. The tables are turned when the visitors reveal themselves to be vampires, and the reader is left to wonder which is the more evil creature, human or vampire.

"Time to Kill" is another story with a twist in the tail. A man with a telepathic link to a psychopathic killer tries to convince his roommate that he is not imagining things, that he can see through the killer's eyes even if he doesn't know the man's identity. The killer, of course, is the roommate himself. Kuttner's best short story in any area is the last to be considered here, "Call Him Demon." A new uncle shows up to visit a family, and only the children realize that he is not a real person at all, and did not even exist prior to his arrival. Now they propitiate him through an elaborate ritual in the attic. Kuttner manages to accomplish more in this short piece than most modern horror writers manage in an entire novel—full characterization, a unique menace, suspense, hints of greater complexity and horror beyond the imagination.

Henry Kuttner was greatly influenced by other writers with whose works he was familiar, most notably Robert E. Howard, H. P. Lovecraft, and A. Merritt. Since much of his output stylistically and thematically resembled that of other writers, he has been criticized at times as imitative. Sam Moskowitz asserts that while Kuttner may have wanted to be an original writer, he "seemed unable to bring to bear any qualities that were fundamentally his own."[1] He sees Kuttner as a literary magpie, delving through the works of better writers, then using their ideas and style to produce basically mediocre imitations. R. E. Briney had these charges in mind when he defended Kuttner, saying that while there is no question that Kuttner drew from the works of others, they were "all filtered through his own sensibility, and emerged transmuted."[2]

The charge that Kuttner was unoriginal and overrated is easy to understand but difficult to justify. Robert E. Howard may have created the sword-and-sorcery story in many ways, and certainly set the standard for stories of this type, but his work in no way diminishes the later efforts of such writers as L. Sprague de Camp, Poul Anderson, or Robert Jordan, who contributed at a later date to the Conan series. Karel Capek's creation of the robot in *R.U.R.* does not mean that the works of Isaac Asimov and others are lacking in qualities of their own. It is true that Kuttner did not create a body of work which in itself went on to inspire significant and obvious imitations, but then few writers do, and Moskowitz does not make similar complaints about the other writers on whom he has written.

The very fact that Henry Kuttner's name remains as prominent as it has, even decades after his death, indicates that there was some quality in his work which separates it from the other magazine writers of the day who have lapsed into obscurity. Anthony Boucher referred to Kuttner as "literate and intelligent,"[3] and there is no question that the prose quality of Kuttner's work was much higher than most of his contemporaries. Like all good writers, Kuttner reached out into the world around him and chose those elements which would enable him to become a successful writer, and those elements necessarily contained elements of the literary environment in which he worked. Because he attempted so many different styles and themes, there *is* in fact a lack of clear focus to his work. It is perhaps his very versatility, therefore, that resulted in the appearance that Kuttner had nothing to say that was unique to himself. A failure to recognize the enormous talent of the man and the enduring quality of his work is a failure of perception rather than an inherent fault in the stories. R. E. Briney perceived this when he wrote that Kuttner "did, in fact, speak in many voices, but they were all his own."[4]

And he will continue to speak to generations to come.

XI.

OF THE MASTER, MERLIN,

AND H. WARNER MUNN

by Don Herron

In the letters column of *Weird Tales* for March, 1924, Howard Phillips Lovecraft inadvertently launched a young man on a literary career which would span more than half of our century. Questioning the originality and *true* weirdness of stories that superficially might pass as "weird tales," Lovecraft asked: "Take a werewolf story, for instance— who ever wrote a story from the point of view of the wolf, and sympathising strongly with the devil to whom he has sold himself?"

Who indeed? This query addressed to the readers of *Weird Tales*, then only starting its second year on the newstands, had a profound influence on Harold Warner Munn of Athol, Massachusetts. Born November 5, 1903, Munn was barely into his twenties, at work in a factory. His imagination was seized by this concept, so idly tossed off by Lovecraft in the course of a larger argument. Why not write a story from the viewpoint of the lycanthrope?

In spare moments at a desk in the factory Munn began composing the tale of "The Werewolf of Ponkert." His memoir on "Writing for *Weird Tales*" recalls how

> I entered the mind of my protagonist. I lived and suffered with him.... It was easy to describe his adventures. I had not the slightest doubt that *Weird Tales* would accept the story. It did. I was not even surprised. I was only pleased to accept the check for $65.00....

Munn adds that he also got a note of congratulations from Lovecraft, but undoubtedly that came before the story itself saw print. In the letters column for March 1925 Munn wrote: "I am delighted that Lovecraft is to be a steady contributor. *Weird Tales* discovered him, I believe; and if it had never done anything else, that would be sufficient

H. WARNER MUNN, by Don Herron

reason for its continued existence." Munn's admiration for H. P. Lovecraft came to the attention of W. Paul Cook, a printer and publisher residing in Athol, who knew Lovecraft through amateur journalism. Cook asked if Munn would care to meet his idol, and they were off to Providence, Rhode Island.

Munn recounted this first meeting in "HPL: A Reminiscence," which appeared in *Whispers* #1, and was continued in #13-14. He wrote:

> I felt myself an inarticulate clod. This brilliant man! This *author!*... Could I ever write like him? Would anything I wrote be saleable? Oh, sure! I had already written "The Werewolf of Ponkert" and sold it to Farnsworth Wright, but this had been suggested by the man who sat near me, talking to Cook.... I had merely worked up *his* thought. Wright might realize his mistake at any time. My story was not yet published.

More of Munn's anxiety over his first story's future comes out here than in the memoir concerning *Weird Tales*, and his youthful nervousness in the presence of his first real author neatly sums up the universal experience of would-be writers at the feet of the great.

With *Weird Tales* for July 1925 Munn joined the company of published writers. "The Werewolf of Ponkert" appeared as the lead story in an issue that also included the first published story of another young writer, "Spear and Fang" by Robert E. Howard. The lycanthrope's tale opens as an American stops at a favorite inn some thirty miles outside Paris. For two pages of this framing device he engages the innkeeper in talk over wine, but far into the night he hears a disquieting story from the man's ancestral history which he presses his host to *prove* by light of day.

> The proof was a book, bound in hand-tooled leather, and locked by a silver clasp. When open it proved to be written in a crabbed hand in old Latin on what was apparently parchment, now yellow with age, but must, when new, have been remarkably white.
>
> It comprised only four leaves, each a foot square, and glued or cemented to a thin wooden backing. They were written on only one side and completely covered with this close, crabbed Latin.
>
> On the back of the book were two iron staples, and hanging from each, several links of heavy, rusted chain. Evidently, like most valuable books which

were available to the public in the past, it had been chained fast to something immovable to prevent theft.

The unnamed American ends the tale's prologue by stating that this book "remains without dispute the only authentic document known of a werewolf's experiences, dictated by himself."

Researchers worrying through stacks of *Weird Tales* for references to invented arcane volumes have made little of Munn's invented book. Clark Ashton Smith's *The Book of Eibon* and Robert E. Howard's *Nameless Cults* of Von Junzt garner frequent attention, but not this leather-and-chain-bound volume. "The Werewolf of Ponkert," if we may call it that, in fact is a significant creation for a twenty-two-year-old, first-time author, writing before the rules of the game for invented volumes of eldritch lore were made clear. The most famous of all such invented books, Lovecraft's *The Necronomicon*, received its first casual mention by HPL in "The Festival," whose year of composition scholars date as 1923. "The Festival," bearing the name of *The Necronomicon* to the world, saw print in *Weird Tales* for January 1925, only five months before Munn's debut, and it would be another year before "The Call of Cthulhu" elaborated on that suppressed book's properties—the majority of Lovecraft's Cthulhu Mythos tales would not see print in *Weird Tales* until 1928 and after.

The yellowed pages of Latin recount the story of Wladislaw Brenryk, a jeweler and peddler of the village of Ponkert, in Hungary. Homeward-bound in his horse-drawn sleigh one evening, he is pursued by a wolf pack along a frozen river. Cornered, Brenryk sees that they are not true wolves, but tailless and hairless beasts, gray in color, with red pig-like eyes and "long and misshapen hind quarters, which lent them a rabbit lope when they ran." The black wolf leader alone adopted the size and shape of a true wolf.

Brenryk slays one of the things in his defense before the pack surges over him and taps the vein inside his elbow. The peddler sinks into delirium. When discovered by villagers, he raves of "wolves which were not wolves, and a black fiend with eyes like embers." Later, when he is well again, the memory of that night struggling to be forgotten, he hears a wolf howl—and is drawn into the forest.

He is met by "the master," the leader of the werewolves, who puts to him this offer: join the pack, replacing the one he has killed, or be eaten.

The tormented jeweler weighs his choices. Leave his wife and daughter alone in the world? Hunt with the pack and profit from the spoils taken from their prey? Become one of the children of the night— and be damned?

For a year Brenryk hunts and kills with his new brothers. He learns more about the master, whom he realizes is a "wampyr," a creature who lives on a diet of blood alone. The master appears to be

H. WARNER MUNN, by Don Herron

"incredibly aged,...an immortal.... His face was like a crinkled, seamed piece of time-worn parchment, coal black with age," but his eyes glistened with an ever-renewing youth. In time the men the master has shaped into wolves grow more like him in their taste for blood and savagery. In time, they covet his immortality and seek to usurp it.

> "Fools!" he shrilled. "Cursed, peasant fools; you who thought you could kill me whom even the elements cannot harm! Idiots who tried to plot against the accumulated intelligence of a thousand years, listen to me.... I have made an example of one of you to warn the rest, and there he stands!... All of you have children, wives, or parents dependent upon you. I saw to that before I chose you.... I can at any time change any one of you to a beast by the power of my will, wherever I may be."

Brenryk, the example, awakes in human form one morning to find his wife mutilated, his daughter missing. He surrenders himself into the custody of the villagers of Ponkert.

To make amends, the cursed jeweler agrees to help entrap the werewolf pack. With eighty men—soldiers, some armed with guns ("but these new weapons are too slow to be of practical use"), rustics carrying clubs and pitchforks—Brenryk summons the pack one night to the ruins of a castle. The soldiers, knowing this wolf-brother will betray them when he is transmuted, stone the peddler as his shape changes. His howl of agony brings the unsuspecting pack rushing to his aid, and to death in close quarter combat. Only the master fights free, tearing away throats, leaping three times the length of a man to grasp the top of a wall, scrambling away into the darkness.

In the following weeks Brenryk, his broken bones mending, details his history of lycanthropy to a priest. And when he is well enough, he is taken from his cell and flayed alive for his crimes. His flayed hide is tanned, and on the four leaves or parchment made of his skin the tale of the werewolf of Ponkert is written.

Munn—sometimes called "young Brenryk" by HPL—immediately became an active member of what today is known as the Lovecraft Circle, the group of writers and amateur press publishers gravitating around the Rhode Island supernaturalist. In a letter to Maurice Moe dated July 30, 1927, Lovecraft noted that Donald Wandrei was visiting and W. Paul Cook and "his weird-literary protégé" H. Warner Munn had come down to Providence in Munn's car to join them. Lovecraft described Munn as "a splendid young chap—blond and burly, and just now sporting a gold medal awarded him for saving a man from drowning in the Hudson a couple of months ago." He also mentions how he, Wandrei, Munn, and Cook "all sat till two-thirty a.m. on a flat-topped tomb in St. John's hidden hillside churchyard which Poe used to love," looking over an unfinished copy of the magazine *The Recluse* which Cook had brought along. In an October 17, 1933 letter to Helen Sully, Lovecraft recalled how nervous Munn had become sitting among the benighted tombstones.

The lone issue of *The Recluse* which Cook published in 1927 often is held up as the earliest forerunner of today's many fantasy and science fiction fan magazines, and is especially noteworthy because it contains the first version of Lovecraft's now classic study, "Supernatural Horror in Literature." Writing to Vincent Starrett on December 6, 1927, Lovecraft spoke of other proposed literary surveys for subsequent issues of *The Recluse* which Cook had planned—issues that never came about—and said, "The next in the series will be a very informal paper on *popular* fantastic tales (of the *All-Story*, *Argosy* or *Weird Tales* grade) by H. Warner Munn, who has had the patience to search out endless and arid reams of that sort of thing." In a letter to Clark Ashton Smith of November 7, 1930, HPL describes Munn's collection of "popular weird material" as one of the "really big libraries owned by our crowd—beside which mine sinks into insignificance."

This interest in "popular" writing lasted to the end of Munn's life, and serves as a cornerstone to the contribution he made to fantastic literature. His immediate choice of the byline "H. Warner Munn" instead of simply Harold Munn underscores his admiration of such popular authors as H. Rider Haggard, by the 1920s the acknowledged master of the adventure novel, and the prolific H. Bedford-Jones, the leading adventure writer for the contemporary pulp magazines. In the last letter he wrote to me, some six months before his death, Munn acknowledged receipt of some paperbacks I had found for him, from the Antares interplanetary series written by Kenneth Bulmer as by "Alan Burt Akers." Of the twenty-two novels then available in that series, Munn lacked only #19, 20 and 21—he was reading his collection in order, as of that day, June 30, 1980, "working on no. 11." He said he found these books "reminiscent of Burroughs at his best," and "way ahead" of the Gor interplanetaries by John Norman.

I had visited Munn the month before, in his home in the 5000 block of Vassault, almost upon Point Defiance Park in Tacoma, Washington. On one of many excursions during that week we visited the book dealer Bob Brown in Seattle. In addition to his for-sale stock, Brown had a wall filled with his personal collection of H. Rider Haggard and another wall devoted to a specialty interest, End-of-the-World novels. Munn was drawn to this collection of post-apocalyptic fiction—books such as M. P. Shiel's *The Purple Cloud*, George R. Stewart's *Earth Abides*, Stephen King's *The Stand*. He recognized some of the books, novels dating from the Edwardian English period when fictionalizing how the world might end was something of a fad—several he had once had in his own collection, a couple of others he had heard

H. WARNER MUNN, by Don Herron

of but never seen actual copies of before. Obviously, Munn burned with a wish to read these novels he'd known of for fifty or sixty years.

During that visit he told me what became of his library, whose mass so impressed Lovecraft. He made the move from Athol to Tacoma in a couple of steps, retaining his place in Massachusetts until he finally decided to settle in the west later in the 1950s. Munn had the thought that something might happen to the books he left behind—the most obvious danger being a leak in the roof. He asked one of his four sons to go into his library and pull all the books two inches away from the wall in case a leak should occur and seep down into the building. The son never got around to it. A leak poured down a wall and the books butted into it soaked up the rainwater. Munn, much regret evident in his voice, said that he ended up literally shoveling ruined books from the room. A few favorites he managed to dry out and save. The bulk of what was left he sold to the fantasy fan Donald M. Grant.

Munn's natural inclination certainly seems to have been toward the fantastic adventure story. Even in "The Werewolf of Ponkert," with its fine detailing of horror, a pulse of adventure beats—the jeweler joins the pack in large degree for the sheer thrill of roaming the night: "I should have high adventure to season my prosaic existence." Munn's only "sympathy with the devil" to whom Brenryk has sold his soul, a sympathy demanded by Lovecraft when he suggested the idea for a new type of werewolf tale, occurs when the master storms the ruined castle to retrieve his apparently trapped follower—and when the fiend makes his dazzling leap to the top of the wall and freedom.

Lovecraft largely disdained the use of adventurous elements in horror fiction, feeling they marred the most important function of such tales, the creation of atmosphere. Writing to Clark Ashton Smith on October 17, 1930 on the subject of cosmic horror, HPL singled out Munn and August Derleth as writers who "simply don't know what it's all about." He further wrote to Emil Petaja on April 5, 1935: "Of the cheap magazine weirdists, the only orthodox religionist I know of is the peculiar H. Warner Munn."

These comments saw print in Lovecraft's *Selected Letters* from Arkham House, and by the time I visited Munn in May, 1980, he surely knew of them. At one point I asked him what kind of person Lovecraft had impressed him as being—not for further recounting of antiquarian jaunts he and Cook and HPL had made, or the stories about how in the late afternoon Lovecraft still would be lounging about dressed in his night-clothes—just for his opinion on the man. He said Lovecraft was a great guy.

Religious differences aside, Lovecraft surely recognized Munn from time to time as an equal among his peers. Munn paid Lovecraft back his debt of the story idea of "The Werewolf of Ponkert." Fascinated as he was with fantastic adventure novels, Munn undertook the task of completing Edgar Allan Poe's fragmentary *The Narrative of A.*

Gordon Pym. In time he realized that he was not going to be able to bring it off, but he suggested the idea to Lovecraft and turned over to him his notes, from which in 1931 Lovecraft developed his short novel *At the Mountains of Madness,* placed by some critics among the top ranks of his work. And writing to Robert H. Barlow on July 23, 1936, Lovecraft mentions a definitive habit of his, an "all-ice-cream dinner at Maxfield's (that famous gang headquarters where Cook, Morton, Munn, Wandrei, and many another titan has gorged)...."

Unlike most of the writers in the Lovecraft Circle, Munn ultimately did very little fiction derivative of HPL—instead of contributions to the Cthulhu Mythos, a couple of his best known stories for *Weird Tales* are the *contes cruels* "The Chain" from 1928 and "The Wheel" from 1933. The horror in these stories is situational, with no trace of cosmicism: in "The Chain" a man is imprisoned in a pit by a cuckolded husband, who lowers upon him a massive chain—a chain which he can *heat,* torturing his victim with crushing weight and burns; in "The Wheel" another victim is trapped on an upright wheel—which may be speeded up, slowed, reversed, or allowed to spin out of control—and the wheel revolves over a lake of boiling pitch. In the memoir "Writing for Weird Tales," Munn says the idea for "The Chain" came from playing a cat at the end of a string. "The Wheel" was "suggested by watching a fly fall into pitch and becoming hopelessly embedded. If the pitch was hot, I thought, beneath a man—a whole lake of it surrounding an upright wheel on which he must try to keep his balance.... There was such a wheel in a lake of water, where I was lifeguard at that time, and I knew how hard it was to stay on it."

In his foreword to the collection *Weird Tales: 32 Unearthed Terrors* (1988), Stefan R. Dziemianowitz notes that the early years of this magazine are not highly rated—most anthologists select material from 1930s issues, few choose from the 1920s. Still, he writes, "some exceptional authors, such as Henry S. Whitehead and H. Warner Munn, produced much of their best work in this period. Lop off the early years of *Weird Tales* and you lose two of the best storytellers to emerge from its pages." By the "golden age" of *Weird Tales* Munn largely had abandoned the idea of being a "horror" writer, and left a third *conte cruel,* "The Well," as uncompleted notes.

The essential themes which occupied Munn's writing for the next fifty-two years were evident in 1928 when a follow-up to his first story, "The Werewolf's Daughter," appeared in *Weird Tales.*

Brenryk's child had not been slain during the rampage in which his wife died: a hunter found her in the woods, and Dmitri Helgar, a Czech mercenary in the service of Hungary, raised her as his own. But Helgar has grown old, and his wardenship of Ivga Brenryk no longer stays the evil looks and curses the villagers of Ponkert direct toward the young woman, now that his sword arm is not so much to be feared. As the story opens, the handsome French troubadour Hugo

H. WARNER MUNN, by Don Herron

Gunnar comes to Ponkert with a traveling circus; Ivga catches his eye; Dmitri Helgar tells the werewolf's daughter the truth; and the master returns.

The *concept* for this novelette is not the relatively narrow evocation of horror—even the degree of grisliness becomes perceptably softer: in the original episode Brenryk is to be flayed alive, but now Munn suggests he met death on the gallows (going to his fate with "a smile on his lips and a jaunty tilt his hat"), and so presumably was flayed as an unfeeling corpse. The role of the master is given an expanded reading, also—he is no longer the ravenous, inimicable leader of a werewolf pack, a vampire, but something greater and less tangible, a hovering malignant spirit, some immortal *power*. The influence of Maturin's *Melmoth the Wanderer* (1820) on this additional interpretation of the master was noted by Donald M. Grant in 1958, when he published these first two stories of the Brenryks in one volume. In this story horror as such is not the issue. The Romantic love of Ivga and Hugo, the heroism and heroic sacrifice of Dmitri Helgar, holding a mountain pass against the enraged villagers so the young lovers may escape, these are concerns Munn plays out against the fantastic, curse-ridden stage-setting of medieval Ponkert. "The Werewolf's Daughter" announces the arrival of the complete H. Warner Munn, romantic fantasist.

Suddenly Munn's vision has expanded to encompass what we know today as epic fantasy, more than ten years before Tolkien would publish the opening of his great saga as *The Hobbit*, only two years after the publication of E. R. Eddison's *The Worm Ouroboros*. From his comments regarding "The Werewolf of Ponkert," Munn at first considered it a closed game; recalling his initial visit with Lovecraft, he says of the soon-to-be-published tale, "If it was published, what could I follow it with? One does not become a writer—an *author*—with one story. I did not realize that night, that the mere act of writing *creates* ideas. That one story will generate another, creating sequels." When he came to write "The Werewolf's Daughter," Munn approached it as the overture to a truly epic work. The villagers have chained Ivga with the book containing the record of her father's sins to a scaffold and piled wood and brush close by, so that they may burn "the witch" come daylight. Into her tortured thoughts the master steals—with an offer. Become his slave and he will free her, and punish the people of Ponkert who have reviled her throughout her life. Or keep her own freedom—he will free her nonetheless—and take his toll "...at your death, should you leave heirs, then they shall be my fair prey. One from each generation—perhaps more shall I take, until your line is stamped from the earth." All this to extract revenge for his betrayal by Wladislaw Brenryk.

So in 1928 began the series of "Tales of the Werewolf Clan," a story that runs through age after age and lands around the world, an epic saga Munn would work on until a couple of years before his death. Considering his theme of a haunted bloodline, it is ironic that the sale of "The Werewolf's Daughter" paid the birthing fee for Munn's first son. Three more Werewolf clan tales would appear in *Weird Tales*, beginning with the November 1930 issue.

In 1939 Munn opened his next epic in *Weird Tales* with the serial publication of his first novel, *King of the World's Edge*, a good adventure story of the type so well handled by Haggard, "Ganpat," Edgar Rice Burroughs, and others, but one which does little to suggest the imaginative epic fantasy which would follow. In this type of story, a group of adventurers arrive in a strange land where two opposing factions are at war. The adventurers invariably take sides with the underdog, and ultimately their leader wins the hand of a princess and sovereignty over a unified populace. Such stories usually are set in "lost lands" in Africa or Asia; the type comes under the classification of Lost Race Novels.

Munn displays originality, and gives his love for history and legend full workout, by having his band of adventurers be not modern-day scientists or explorers but a group of Anglo-Roman soldiers, defeated with King Arthur in the fall of Camelot, who follow the wizard Merlin across the Atlantic to North America. Ventidius Varro, the centurion in command of this ragtag legion, leads his men into a war fought among American Indians, helping to overthrow the Aztec-like Mias. Merlin is given the new name Quetzalcoatl, and so passes into the myth history of the New World as well as the Old. And Varro, now king of the world's edge, claims the land for Rome and takes the hand of the Indian princess Gold Flower of the Day.

The element of romantic love is no more emphasized here than in Burroughs or Haggard, perhaps less so. In subsequent novels in this series, love becomes the dominant concern and overriding theme for this epic. In a letter dated November 29, 1975 to John C. Moran, the editor of *The Romantist*, Munn explained why the "love interest is almost non-existent" in *King of the World's Edge*: he found that his wife *fixated* on his female characters. "She had a tendency," he stated, "if a woman was mentioned at all in anything I wrote, to identify completely with the character. Therefore, I was unable to have my charcaters do, or say, anything to which she could take offense. Had I not planned a sequel, in which a son was necessary to carry on the action—*Ship from Atlantis*—there would have been no woman in *King of the World's Edge*."

I cannot help but notice that in "The Werewolf of Ponkert" Brenryk's wife is described as having, like all people, "a weakness in one way or another, and she was no exception to the rule. She was jealous—insanely jealous!" I do not know if at the time Munn wrote that first tale he was married already, but from his comments to Moran it seems obvious that after he let his impulse for romantic love carry through "The Werewolf's Daughter," he discovered his wife's identification with his heroines and reined in any romantic situations that he may have wished to portray in his fiction.

In that letter Munn also says that he did not visualize Merlin the Magician as "the fuddy-duddy, inept—rather senile" character pictured by Mark Twain in *A Connecticut Yankee in King Arthur's Court*, nor according to Malory or Tennyson's *Idylls of the King*: "I went to *The Mabinogion* and the triads and anything that I could find pre-dating these sources, in the effort to present Merlin as something of a tragic adventurer—lonely, and courageous in his own right—anxious to do the right thing, but forced by circumstances to use magic against his will."

An interesting minor aspect of this novel is the appearance of the monstrous, manlike amphibian race called the Gronks, which attacks Merlin's forces. This race seems to be inspired by Lovecraft's batrachian hordes, seen in such tales as "The Shadow Over Innsmouth"—one of the few trace influences of his early idol in Munn's work.

Despite having a full-length novel behind him and the promise of a long series of stories concerning Brenryk's descendents, by the 1940s Munn decided to quit his financially insecure career as an author to find more reliable income for his family. His problem was that he *had* become an *author*, a man with certain statements he wanted to make, certain themes he wished to explore, and not just a *writer*, someone who quickly could turn out commercial product to pay for the week's groceries. Munn was too concerned with historic and scientific accuracy to burn the typewriter keys in the struggle to survive in the pulp jungle. In "Writing for *Weird Tales*" he says, "Accuracy comes through research. Don't trust to memory. Check, re-check, and if there is still doubt eliminate the dubious point, or the story will be ruined for someone.... I enjoy research—but it does slow up production." In these respects he was closely aligned with H. P. Lovecraft and his "gentleman's" method of writing fiction. Unlike Lovecraft, he had a wife and four children for whom to provide.

The despair of the artist forced to give up practising his art, yet never forgetting that he is an artist, comes out in line from Munn's HPL memoir: "...the mere act of living, experiencing, acquiring memories, despairing, striving—loving—*even of becoming buried in a withering heap of years*—all this gives each one of us a unique collection of thoughts...to draw upon creatively." The italics are mine: for almost two decades Munn put aside his writing.

In those years Munn labored in a number of workaday jobs. He told me stories of how sometimes difficult work was to come by. He once answered an ad that called for a high scaffolding painter. Munn had never done that sort of labor, but he needed a job and applied for it. The boss asked if he was afraid of working on a scaffold. Munn said no. Less than an hour into the job he was asked to tie off the scaffold. He tied the wrong kind of knot. A fellow worker caught the eye of the boss, glanced meaningfully at the knot. The boss exploded, "You could get us all killed! I thought you said you had high scaffolding experience."

"No, sir," Munn replied, "I said I wasn't afraid of heights."

Munn took me to look down on a small community he had lived in for awhile, a number of homes at the bottom of a cliff near Puget Sound. Precipitous wooden stairs dropped straight down through trees and brush to the houses far below. At one point when he was living here he could not find work, so he made work for himself, collecting scrap iron along the shore and hauling it up the cliff on his back. He hauled up hundreds and hundreds of pounds of iron. The exchange rate he quoted was appalling, something like a nickel for every ten or twenty pounds, maybe less. Munn said that if you borrowed a cup of sugar from a neighbor in that community, it was not acceptable just to pay for it later. *Everything* had to be carried in by those stairs. If you borrowed a cup of sugar, you *returned* a cup of sugar.

It would be unfair to his family and unfair to Munn to leave the impression that he worked ceaselessly for years, and that he did not *enjoy* those years. If the artist in him was tormented, the man knew full well the choice he had made. I doubt that he often begrudged his family this sacrifice—any more than Dmitri Helgar in his story regretted holding the pass, as at Thermopylae, so Ivga might escape. Munn loved his family and took pride in providing for them. To suggest otherwise would be to misrepresent his life and the way he lived it.

Beyond the love he had for his immediate family, Munn also was interested in *humanity*, in the ordinary lives of people, their sorrows and joys. I cannot read his description of the traveling circus in "The Werewolf's Daughter" without recalling the trip we made to the "Mai Fest" in Leavenworth, Washington, a small town in the Cascade Range that does its best to recreate an "Old World Bavarian Village." A couple of hours of imitation Old World Bavaria more than satisfied me, but Munn did not get bored with it. He really loved that sort of thing—the Calgary Stampede in Canada was one of his favorite such entertainments.

We also visited Old Fort Nisqually in Point Defiance Park, containing the oldest extant buildings in Washington state. I think now of the similar antiquarian excursions Munn drove Lovecraft on. Both these writers knew history and appreciated its pageant, but I suspect that a place such as Fort Nisqually would have inspired HPL with its architecture and role in the settlement of the northwest—an *intellectual* and aesthetic impression, whereas Munn in such a place identified viscerally with the settlers, saw their day-to-day existence ghostlike within the fort's walls.

A curiosity of Munn's career, considering his success as a fantasist in the pages of *Weird Tales* and his friendship with Lovecraft,

H. Warner Munn, by Don Herron

is that August Derleth never picked up any of his fiction for book publication. By the time Munn abandoned writing in the 1940s, Arkham House was a going publishing concern for Derleth; in 1947 alone he issued the first book collections of three *Weird Tales* alumni: Ray Bradbury's *Dark Carnival*, Carl Jacobi's *Revelations in Black*, and Fritz Leiber's *Night's Black Agents*—Jacobi and Leiber both had been correspondents of Lovecraft. I cannot help but think that had Munn had a book published in this period he might have tried a return to writing. Out of those members of the Lovecraft Circle who developed careers as writers, by his death in 1971 Derleth had issued many books by Lovecraft, Clark Ashton Smith, Henry S. Whitehead, Frank Belknap Long, and Donald Wandrei (with illustrations by his brother Howard Wandrei, another of the Lovecraft crowd during the New York years), not to mention numerous volumes he himself wrote or edited, as well as titles from Robert E. Howard, E. Hoffmann Price, and Robert Bloch. Munn is the only major writer among Lovecraft's frequent associates missing from the Arkham House stocklist.

Munn came into book publication by another route, one that now has a corner on the collector's dollar which vies strongly with the Arkham House mystique orchestrated by Derleth. In 1945 in Lovecraft's native Providence the fan Donald M. Grant, with Thomas P. Hadley, edited and published the booklet *Rhode Island on Lovecraft*. That lone title from Grant-Hadley of course is a collectors item today, and so too is *The Werewolf of Ponkert*, Munn's first book, which appeared in 1958 under Grant's original imprint of The Grandon Company, a modest precursor to Grant's current deluxe editions of Stephen King, which bring many hundreds of dollars on the market. Grant issued this small hardcover containing "The Werewolf of Ponkert" and "The Werewolf's Daughter" in an edition of only 350 copies, all signed "Best wishes/H. Warner Munn" in blue ballpoint pen on the front free endpaper. (I had my copy along on my visit, and before my eyes Munn took up a blue ballpoint and added "to Don Herron/May 7, 1980" below his original blank inscription—looking at the page today I cannot discern any notable difference between the lines written in 1958 and the words added twenty-two years later.)

Seeing a book finally in print thirty-three years after the publication of his first story no doubt revived some of Munn's interest in writing, but in his November 29, 1975 letter to John Moran he gives another reason which could not have been anticipated. In the early 1960s Munn was hospitalized for pneumonia. He told Moran, "I have always been fascinated with the tragedy of Joan of Arc, convinced of her sublime and unswerving faith, of the truth and validity of Christianity, encouraged by her courage and upheld by her endurance in the face of adversity and pain—to the point that I have been able to withstand what pain and adversity have come to me much better...." Naturally in the hospital thoughts of Joan, "his adopted patron saint," would come to him. And his long-standing interest in the Joan legend finds easy corroboration in "The Werewolf's Daughter," where the threat to burn Ivga at the stake is a nod toward Joan's fate, as well as a prefiguration of Joan of Arc's return to Munn's work throughout his life.

I suspect that the student nurse attending him seemed almost like an incarnation of Joan to Munn. She was interested in poetry, it turned out, and also was a contestant in the Miss Tacoma beauty pageant. Their discussions of poetry stimulated Munn's interest in writing, and he was after all in a hospital, with nothing else to do but write. Additionally, in a letter dated November 8, 1977, Munn told me that the specific spur to writing, after they had talked generally on poetry for awhile, came when the woman recited for benefit of his comments the poem she would give in the beauty pageant, Don Blanding's "Little Glass Ship." Munn knew Blanding's style quite well, and wrote for her another poem of the same name. He rhymed a couple of other poems to amuse her—and then Munn wrote four poems concerning Joan of Arc.

The young nurse was transferred for a month on exchange with a hospital in Vancouver, B.C. When she returned Munn had thirty-six more poems in his Joan cycle ready for her—all published as *The Banner of Joan* in 1975 by Don Grant.

For a couple of years Munn returned to writing in his spare time. He managed to sell *King of the World's Edge* to Ace Books in 1966. I recall a thumbnail description of this novel somewhere down the years which seemed to dismiss it in the phrase, "King Arthur meets Hiawatha." Still, it created enough interest at Ace that Don Wollheim bought a sequel, *The Ship from Atlantis*, issued in 1967 as one half of an Ace Double, bound with Emil Petaja's *The Stolen Sun.*

By this time Munn told Moran that his wife's "thinking had somewhat changed," and he could "cautiously" open his main theme of immortal love. He also in this second novel moved closer to finding his perfect vehicle of expression. The formula of the "lost race" novel used in the first Merlin book—with the voyage to the new land, disasters befalling the adventurers, friends won among the enemy, and betrayals within the band—was no longer useful. Here Munn tries out the "quest" novel, sending Gwalchmai, the son of Ventidius Varro, on a mission across the Ocean Sea to inform the Emperor of Rome of the new world that has been claimed for his colonies. A powerful irony is at work here: unknown to Varro, the Roman Empire has fallen under waves of barbarian invaders fifty years before his son sets out.

Gwalchmai wears Merlin's ring and carries along a chest full of magical devices to aid him in his travels, but his voyage immediately encounters disaster as the last survivors of the amphibian Gronks attack and destroy his company of warriors. Gwalchmai alone escapes in his ship, but injuries sustained during battle cause him to lose his memory. His vessel drifts into the weed-choked leagues of the Sargasso Sea.

H. WARNER MUNN, by Don Herron

Sick and suffering from thirst, Gwalchmai searches through Merlin's chest and comes across a vial of syrup. "It was pleasantly sweet and pungent and he drank it all." Unwittingly, he drains the only vial ever to contain the Elixir of life and becomes at that moment almost immortal.

For purposes of this short novel, Gwalchmai's near immortality and even his intended voyage to Rome largely are irrelevant. Munn is experimenting, introducing concepts for later use. The Sargasso Sea itself, famous in fantasy literature through such tales as the sea stories of William Hope Hodgson, is not a *necessary* setting, although Munn uses it extremely well as a writer approaching his mastership, giving an added flourish to a scenario already brimming with the fantastic simply to show his ability to utilize various materials and myths in one tale.

(Perhaps I should add here that Munn is the only person I ever recall talking with who *liked* the romance Hodgson introduces into his epic *The Night Land*, and liked the archly sentimental way it is handled—without exception, everyone else I've sounded out feels the romance element is terribly overdone. When this Hodgson novel was issued in paperback in the Adult Fantasy Series Ballantine editor Lin Carter took it upon himself to delete much of the romance material.)

The main plot of *The Ship from Atlantis* begins when Gwalchmai discovers a large golden ship in the shape of a swan. In this unusual vessel he meets Corenice, the only survivor of the foundering of Atlantis. She transferred her soul into a body of orichalcum, the labled living metal, when the evil alien force known as Oduarpa brought destruction to her land. Now she has but one mission: to go north to Nor-Um-Bega, the penal colony of lost Atlantis, and to destroy it before its evils are let loose upon the world. Gwalchmai, memory restored, joins her in this effort and comes to love her. Once the land of murderers is put to rest, she pledges to aid him in his own quest. In the rousing climax, Nor-Um-Bega is submerged beneath Arctic waves, but Corenice seems lost, her orichalcum body disintegrating from exposure to forces set loose during the destruction. She vows to meet her true love again, even if centuries should pass. And Gwalchmai becomes trapped within a massive glacier as the novel ends.

The Ship from Atlantis is much too short a novel for full display of the possibilities of character and action that Munn introduces. Taken alone, it is very unsatisfying, because the reader is left wanting much more, and knows that more should follow: "We shall meet and love again—though it be two hundred year!"

During this return to writing Munn was holding down a job in a door factory, but in the late 1960s he lost a kneecap, and with his mobility went the job. He took a year off and looked over various story notes. He wrote Moran that "I destroyed much of my previous writing and I do not understand yet why I bothered to keep notes I had made on *Merlin's Ring—The Lost Legion*, and another, as yet only in notes; a combination pair of shorter novels—*Treasure of Chenar* and *Land of the Dark Sun*—certain leads which I deliberately have built into this trilogy as a sort of preamble."

Instead of starting in on *Merlin's Ring*, the next novel of Gwalchmai and Corenice, he took up *The Lost Legion*, a historical romance which imagines the fate of Rome's thirteenth legion. Munn said he wrote every day, finishing the novel at about 350,000 words—yet this epic would not see print until 1980.

The premise for Munn's longest novel is that the Thirteenth Legion, under command of Manlius Varro (doubtless another case of family lines crossing the imagined history in Munn's fiction), falls into disfavor with the crazed Emperor Caligula. They are sent forth to follow the Silk Road into Asia and to recover the standard carried by the legendary "lost legion," an army from Rome which had vanished into the East a century before—an assignment that equals banishment, one that means suicide to the soldiers.

Munn's sympathy with the ordinary fighting man of Rome whose sword carved an empire is magnificent. Here obviously is a writer who savors the purely heroic as much as did Robert E. Howard—more, here is a writer who personally has known heroism. Meeting Munn in his seventies I had no trouble appreciating that this was the same man who had leaped into the Hudson River in 1927 to rescue another man from drowning. H. Warner Munn was one of the kindest people I ever expect to meet, a gentleman in the full sense of the word, but when push comes to shove, I think he would not have been a man to push.

Driving in Tacoma we happened to go through an underpass where two traffic lanes merge suddenly into one narrow funnel between concrete walls. Munn mentioned an incident when he was driving into this underpass and another car threw on speed and recklessly cut him off, almost forcing his machine into the concrete. He said he followed the car until the driver stopped in a gas station. Munn parked and walked over to the man. Munn told him that perhaps he did not realize his driving had endangered not only Munn but also his own wife and child he had in the car—or perhaps he did realize it and did not care. Munn made the man this offer: put his wife and child safely out at the gas station, the two them would drive their cars back to the other side of the funnel—*and then they would see who got through first.* The man declined this offer, mumbling an apology.

As much as he admired heroism, however, I believe Munn was too keenly aware of human fallibilities to ever succumb to vainglory. Of the many excursions we made during my visit, I recall most fondly a drive across the new Tacoma Narrows Bridge to Gig Harbor. Munn wanted to take me to a shop that sold nautical supplies and antiques, a place he liked because the owner talked only nautical talk, never breaking his routine, like a refined pirate. Somehow at this shop Munn ended up telling a tale of frontier life in New England. His own ancestors were not prosperous enough to have dwellings within the fort—instead, they sheltered in the lean-to shacks thrown up against outer walls. One winter a storm buried their shacks under drifts of snow, and over these drifts ran an army of red Indians, leaping the stockade and killing everyone inside the fort. The proto-Munns huddled inside the snow drifts and were careful to make no sounds that might attract attention. "Ahoy there, mate!" exclaimed the shop owner. "You mean to tell me they *hid* there the while all those people were *slaughtered*! I don't think I hold kindly to that...." Munn grinned, smart enough to know that, all things being equal, if his ancestors had crawled bravely from their shelter to their deaths, he would not have been there to tell that tale. I believe he understood far better than Robert E. Howard and many another adventure writer all the possible ramifications and drawbacks to heroism.

In *The Lost Legion* are Varro and his men any less heroic because they are dispatched, under orders of a madman, to complete an insane mission? An interesting question, considering the years during which Munn composed this novel, in the late 1960s and early 1970s. I sometimes wonder if the war in Vietnam reinforced in any way his vision of an army sent to its doom deep in Asia. Whether it did or not, I feel certain that Munn would have supported the memorials that have been erected in recent years to honor *the soldiers* of that war—whether the war itself was insane or not.

One of the most telling episodes was edited out before Doubleday published the novel, and appears in the H. Warner Munn memorial issue of *The Romantist* from 1982. After one of the book's many battles, the Roman soldier Galba, a farmer, lies dying in the field, beside him a Parthian he has wounded mortally. As their lives fade they begin to talk, and learn they are both farmers, and their feelings on nature and life are quite the same. Spiritual brother has slain spiritual brother. A profound vignette, it shows Munn's full understanding of the lives of people and their hopes, and the follies they become prey to. The Parthian's last words are "Good soil." Galba replies, as their blood soaks into the ground, "Yes, Brother, good soil. It will be better now—."

Another vignette cut from the published book offers a scene of prophecy in a witch's tent, which aligns *The Lost Legion* more closely with Munn's supernatural fantasies. And even in the Doubleday edition genuine fantasy intrudes as the heroine Lilia enters a grove sacred to the great god Pan. Munn's rendering of the Pan-ic which follows is among the best fantastic moments in any of his work—a scene which effects the last movement of what otherwise might be read strictly as a historical novel. And in the acknowledgments to the book Munn once again makes clear his lifelong appreciation of popular fantastic writing, and of his practise of shrewdly taking up and elaborating on clues from other writers, by thanking "Andre Norton, whom I have never met but who unwittingly suggested the theme in the Foreword to one of her fine books."

From *The Lost Legion* Munn moved into work on *Merlin's Ring*. According to his letter to John Moran, he had done most of his research for this novel soon after completing *The Ship from Atlantis*, but found that he had no "empathy with Corenice.... I could not *see* her.... So I dropped the story."

Munn goes on to suggest that until he met a specific young woman in Tacoma, he had no "model" for Corenice. The fact is that he already had used this character in a short novel and he had much of *Merlin's Ring* completed before he met the woman in question. Munn sometimes suggested that Lilia in *The Lost Legion* was also inspired by this woman—sometimes that she was inspired by another young woman he met later; in the acknowledgments he says that "a drum majorette who came strutting, head held high, by me in a parade...immediately became Lilia in my mind." Without various drafts of these novels to consult, it is impossible here to say how greatly Munn may have modified descriptions of his heroines to reflect any particular woman, but my own feeling is that Munn throughout his career had one vision of an idealized woman on the spiritual plane, his Joan archetype, and another vision of an idealized woman on the physical plane—Ivga, Lilia, Corenice—all, I suspect, reflections in some way of his love for his wife, who was with him for all those years.

Certainly the death of his wife in 1972 hit Munn hard. The grief and the lonely months that followed surely are reflected in the emotional force Munn brings to *Merlin's Ring*, which stands without question as his masterwork, an expansive volume of more than three hundred pages in which Munn takes Gwalchmai and Corenice through an amazing profusion of lands and ages, myths and histories, and throws them into encounters with peasants, noblemen, kings, and even gods.

Merlin's Ring appeared in paperback in 1974 as the final volume in the Ballantine Adult Fantasy Series, the last book in that line to be introduced by series editor Lin Carter, who had found the romance in Hodgson's *The Night Land* so unpalatable. He offers no objections to Munn's greatest work of romance, instead saying, "Seldom have I encountered a more ambitious narrative in my exploration of fantasy, and seldom has a gripping human drama of such strength and vigor invested a story of such sweep and scope and vaulting imaginative power.... Prose epics of this magnitude are most often the work of a writer in the first enthusiasm of his creative power...now it can be seen that the career of H. Warner Munn is that of a writer slowly and meticulously developing and testing his powers, in anticipation of a masterpiece."

H. WARNER MUNN, by Don Herron

Carter notes that this novel follows others which portray immortal adventurers through the ages: *Phra the Phoenician, Valdar the Oft-Born, My First Two Thousand Years*. With this scope to work in, Munn moves comfortably into a perfect form for his novelistic needs, an episodic work which recalls the picaresque novel exemplified by Spain's *Lazarillo de Tormes* from 1554—in which the main character, in this case not the usual rogue or *picaro*, proceeds from one loosely connected scenario to the next. By this time Gwalchmai's mission to inform the Roman Emperor of the New World is largely forgotten, and I cannot imagine that the reader of this book minds the neglect very much. In sharp contrast to *The Ship from Atlantis*, this novel stands very much on its own—one need never read the prequels to appreciate *Merlin's Ring*.

Gwalchmai eventually discovers that Rome has lost its empire, of course. Following the advice of the ghost of Merlin, he decides to carry his tidings to a suitable Christian monarch (even Merlin is a convert, at least in part, to the new religion). His wanderings are impelled by another force, as well—Oduarpa, the dark lord, who seeks revenge on Corenice for her part in the destruction of Nor-Um-Bega.

A creature such as Oduarpa, master of all ills, has become a standard fixture in epic fantasy since J. R. R. Tolkien introduced Sauron in *The Lord of the Rings*. Munn's creation in no way rivals Sauron—as one of the few required elements for an "epic fantasy," Oduarpa impresses me as possibly the weakest part of this novel, although his presence helps motivate Gwalchmai across land and sea and the passing centuries.

Munn begins with a boat of Nordic fisher folk tossed on the north seas, and throughout this novel he returns to the common man, describing the pleasures and hardships that he realizes change little with time, whether in medieval England, feudal Japan, fifteenth-century France, or twentieth-century Tacoma where this novel was written. Corenice's immortal spirit can assume command of living forms—"So she lived on, sometimes temporarily housed in the bodies of fish or seals, or in the airy apartments of the mind known to the falcon, kittiwakes, and gulls."—and now she inhabits a Norse girl, who leads her followers to rescue Gwalchmai from his icy prison, an exciting last-minute escape as the glacier crumbles about them.

Munn alternates between such episodes of high adventure and interludes of peace, when Gwalchmai and Corenice find quiet moments together. The dry wit of his native New England frequently appears—in a comic China, for example, where an experiment with gunpowder gives birth to fiery little dragons, or in Elveron where the faeries lament mankind's inroads, singing "Naiad and Undine pine and sigh/For pollution slew the Lorelei." Munn's insect-sized elves are not those of Tolkien, but hark back to Shakespeare's *A Midsummer Night's*

Dream (1595-1596), and the elf-prince Huon appears once to Gwalchmai in the meadows of France as a butterfly.

He juxtaposes these lighter moments with darker scenes: comic China precedes stark tragedy in feudal Japan; to help the elves, Gwalchmai incurs the wrath of the thunder god Thor, "an honest, blunt, straightforward hater." Munn draws at will on myth and on man's treatment of myth, moving between comic effects worthy of T. H. White's *The Sword in the Stone* (1938) to an encounter with a sorcerer in the hills of Spain that is as action-packed as any Sword-and-Sorcery tale by Robert E. Howard. Munn, coming to this work with nearly fifty years as a fantasy writer behind him, and with more than fifty years as a reader and appreciator of the field, moves through these pages with mastery in every step.

His economy of style reflects this mastery—he simply bypasses the ornate prose forms preferred by so many fantasy writers, and captures in simple language images that draw one's imagination away from the everyday into delightful reveries. For example, consider this description: "On a black strand they saw where a careless whale had found its end, for broad ribcages upthrust out of the crumbling lava beach, like the bones of a wrecked dragon-ship." This prose is not at all difficult to read or understand, gives a precise image, yet an image that is quite complex, dealing as it does with the kindred natures of ship and ocean beast and the way their fates are interchangeable. A lesser writer might have pictured a wrecked dragon-ship and compared the skeleton of the hull to whale bones, but Munn is able to capture that very feeling *and more* by reversing the order. His description of a berserker is simple, too, but extremely evocative: "He bit the edge of his buckler until his teeth splintered and his mouth bled. He howled like a wolf and rushed, foaming, in great leaps and bounds, against his enemies under a bloody and setting sun." In a line describing a spae-wife Munn comes up with one of the most interesting turns of meaning on a word I have ever encountered: "Folk wondered if she were a turn-coat and ran the woods at night as either wolf or cat." *A turncoat and ran the woods at night*—in my opinion, the author of "The Werewolf of Ponkert" achieves a moment of *Zen* mastery in the evocation of lycanthropy with that image.

In Gwalchmai's wanderings, he sees and experiences the valor and cowardice, the humor and gloom, the love and hatreds of man. Munn invests his characters, whether of the nobility or the peasantry, with epic qualities, suggesting that to survive in any age brings out the heroic qualities in men and women. The mythic figures—Thor, Huon, Oduarpa—of course are reflections of *man's imagination*, gods and demigods created, revered, and forgotten. The form Munn's thoughts about the human condition take in *Merlin's Ring* implies that romance is a necessary part of man's makeup and mind. If Atlantis, Camelot, and

H. WARNER MUNN, by Don Herron

Elveron did not actually exist, they nevertheless live in man's mind and culture, and Munn's writings bear witness to this fact.

Significantly, Gwalchmai's conflict with the evil Oduarpa draws to a climax in the chapters set in the France of Joan of Arc. The presentation of Joan's struggle to free her land from England's domination gives us a picture of honor and nobility that was a model for Munn in the manner in which he faced his own life, and which becomes for Gwalchmai in the novel an ideal which he strives to emulate.

Munn realizes, of course, that the model of St. Joan and her heroic death by fire is a romantic goal for which to reach—but one difficult or impossible for most people to attain. He contrasts her heroic campaign with an episode which portrays the most depraved actions to which man can sink. Gilles de Rais, Joan's lieutenant, sees in her execution the death of his God and throws himself into the service of evil. His slaughter of hundreds of children made him infamous as the historical Bluebeard. Munn could not have selected a more appropriate servant of darkness, a genuine monster whose deeds make the imagined horrors of an Oduarpa, of a Sauron, seem as nothing.

Thus Munn brings his epic from its roots in the legends of Camelot and Atlantis, moves it through the early years of history when mythical figures such as Thor still lived in man's mind, and places it firmly in historical reality with his account of the transcendent Joan of Arc and the fallen de Rais—figures whose respective nobility and depravity are of as genuinely mythic proportions to modern man as are the legends of a King Arthur or a Loki. Munn shows that those qualities respected or reviled in myth are possible for man even today: men and women can be heroes, or they can be monsters.

Gwalchmai, after the defeat of de Rais and the routing of Oduarpa, finally passes his information about the New World to an Italian sailor called Columbus and himself passes into eternity with the spirit of Corenice. Munn, a true romantic, suggests heroism will triumph; still, he does not underestimate the power for evil in man's imagination. He suggests only that man may struggle and occasionally win, and that love such as that of Gwalchmai and Corenice makes the struggle endurable.

In *Merlin's Ring* Munn reaches the apex of his art, creating a synthesis of myth and history as a showcase for the heroic qualities by which the human spirit endures. With this novel he clearly transcends the limitations of the cult of *Weird Tales* to stand among the major practitioners of modern fantasy, the high fantasy of Tolkien and the Inklings, the only member of the Lovecraft Circle who lived long enough to bring this about and who also had the reach and determination to make such a work from imagination and blank paper. Since Munn was "the only orthodox religionist" Lovecraft knew of among his peers, it seems obvious enough now that Munn's place within fantastic

145

literature more naturally falls in beside the Christian mythopoeia of the Inklings than the cosmic terrors of his friend H. P. Lovecraft.

Merlin's Ring rapidly went through three printings for Ballantine, but at the time Munn wrote John Moran in November 1975 *The Ship from Atlantis* with Ace was still available in first printing and had not yet earned royalties beyond the advance. The sales of Munn's blockbuster epic were not to be argued with, however; in 1976 Ballantine Books picked up both *King of the World's Edge* and *The Ship from Atlantis* and reissued them in one volume as a "prequel" to *Merlin's Ring*, under the title *Merlin's Godson*.

Munn was on a roll. Once again he looked to the plight of all those generations descended from Wladislaw Brenryk and finished a full thirteen Tales of the Werewolf Clan to follow "The Werewolf of Ponkert" and "The Werewolf's Daughter." Several of these appeared in *Lost Fantasies*, edited by Robert Weinberg; others appeared as separate chapbooks before ultimately being gathered into two hardcover volumes published by Donald M. Grant.

Munn follows the lycanthrope-tainted bloodline over the centuries, a narrative device which allows him, as in *Merlin's Ring*, an astounding historical sweep in which unfolds a panorama of human life to raise this series far above the level of the ordinary werewolf yarn. Munn anticipates and in my opinion succinctly equals such later horror series with historical canvases, which typically feature an immortal vampire as the central character—such as Les Daniels's saga of Don Sebastian de Villanueva, Chelsea Quinn Yarbro's novels and stories about Ragoczy, Count de Saint-Germain, or Anne Rice with her sequels to *Interview with the Vampire*. Amid the horrors engendered by the fiendish machinations of the master, Munn portrays the *true* horrors of evolution and war that humanity has endured to establish and maintain civilization. He shows bloody periods such as the Inquisition or the frontier settlement of America to be as horrific as any agent of the supernatural.

In a foreword to the collected tales Munn explains the origins of "the master." As is the case with the dark lord Oduarpa in his Merlin cycle, the master is extraterrestrial, from the star Algol, a "sentient knot of energy" summoned by a Babylonian witch's spells to earth to inhabit a living body:

> Into the body of her servant, Althusar, came an eager, inquisitive intelligence..., anxious to experience the wonder called life, meaning to displace Althusar's ego for a few hours only, it thought, and then to return, sated with knowledge.
> It had no other desire.
> The witch thought otherwise. Swift the binding spells were cast....

H. Warner Munn, by Don Herron

It knew its fate—it knew anger....
The neighbors of the witch heard her screams....

This cosmic overture is well-done, but ultimately unconvincing—why would such an entity, even if earthbound, bother with the children and children's children of *one man* who over all those centuries incurred its disfavor? Why would Oduarpa bother with Corenice and Gwalchmai? I must agree with Lovecraft's assessment of Munn as having no idea of what cosmic horror is all about; in fact, given his Christian orthodoxy in terms of God, it is curious to see that Munn in his fiction does embrace the usual concept of Satan. I suspect that Munn as a romanticist, while clearly aware of the evil that men do and have done throughout history, could not accept a two-sided coin of God/Satan—and opted to have evil incursions as "alien" to mankind.

Munn's return to writing in 1974 included making up chapbooks of verse and sending them out as seasonal greetings. He inaugurated this series with *Christmas Comes to the Little House* (1974), and followed it with *To All Amis* (1975), *Season's Greeting's with Spooky Stuff* (1976), *There Was a Man* (1977), and *Of Life and Love and Loneliness* (1979). Other poetry chapbooks—*The Pioneers, Twenty-Five Poems*—also appeared in this period, with Munn's collected verse gathered into hardcover in 1979 in *The Book of Munn*.

Munn was a self-admitted traditionalist, and saw no point in writing poems that did not rhyme or, ballad-like, tell a tale. And as he said in his letter to John Moran, he considered himself not only a romanticist but also "a sentimentalist"—thus it follows that among the strong poems he composed are as many more that are unbearably sweet and sappy, and I'm sure Munn knew it when he was writing them. In one of his songs *about* country music, Hank Williams Jr. says fans of country *know* when the music rocks, *and they know when it's slow.* Munn could likewise openly embrace the sentimental, but was never in danger of becoming a slave to "sweetness and light" platitudinizing. (All I need do to reassure myself of this is to remember stopping with Munn at a small zoo in Tacoma: as we stood before a mountain lion's cage Munn recalled taking his youngest son as a plump baby to look a cougar—he said the infant was delighted with the beast and the cat equally fascinated with the possibilities of young Munn, its tongue rolling across its teeth.)

In 1975 Munn attended the first World Fantasy Convention held in his old haunt of Providence, Rhode Island. He would attend each annual World Fantasy Convention until his death, as well as many smaller regional conventions. Munn was a well-liked figure at these gatherings, and the source of a certain amount of awe from the male conventioneers because he usually went in company with a strikingly beautiful young woman. At least two of Munn's friends worked professionally as exotic dancers and he delighted in their companionship—as he wrote to me on March 26, 1980, he would soon be attending a science fiction convention with one of his friends, "to whom usually all eyes turn—to her with admiration—to me, with envy. Alas, that I am not younger!"

In a memoir in *The Chicago Fantasy Newsletter*, Jessica Amanda Salmonson mentions that Munn "once introduced me to a friend of his who was a woman his own age, a poet; she was attractive and interesting. When I asked him why he didn't try to get something going with her, he said, 'She's too old for me.' And he meant it." I think in that instance Munn was saying that he already had lived his life with his wife, and in his seventies had no interest in starting over again. He told me that his interest in the young women, given the realities of a five-decade difference in ages, was platonic—and if attending conventions with his dazzling protégées was in some sense living out a fantasy, who's to say H. Warner Munn was not entitled?

I went with Munn to see one of his friends perform—I found it hard to believe how quickly it became boring, watching topless dancers who had no particular talent for the art. Munn's pal, however, was not among those without talent, and as he warned me, when she did her table dance the only thing you could do to keep from embarrassing yourself was to sit on your hands.

Inspired by his new associates, Munn turned out most of his published poetry in these years, and also wrote a number of stories and essays in addition to the werewolf series. He took up his notes from the 1930s and finished his third *conte cruel*, "The Well," which appeared in DAW's *Year's Best Horror Stories* under the editorship of Gerald Page. "The Affair of the Cuckolded Warlock" was issued as a chapbook.

During this period Munn made several other story sales to W. Paul Ganley's *Weirdbook*, returning in a series of three novelettes to the Lovecraftian theme of batrachian hybrid life forms which seemed to interest him; and used "the Deep Ones" in his fiction fully for the first and final time, although still not managing to catch the hint of cosmicism Lovecraft invested in his stories. He also took up a long-standing idea based on a thirteenth-century reference to "a mysterious iron box, held in the hands of a wooden statue of David, patron Saint of Wales," for a five-part novella, "The Melldrum Box."

When I visited him in May, 1980, Munn said that no matter how long he lived from that point on there would be "no more horror stories from me"—he felt the world had had enough of horror. Instead, he spoke of other things he wished to write. Among those concepts he tossed out as we sat talking in his attic studio would be his own variation on the End-of-the-World novel; as gloomy as that category sounds, could such a book written by H. Warner Munn be anything but filled with romance and wonder and hope?

H. WARNER MUNN, by Don Herron

Yet ironically, in the realm of the full-length novel, Munn became trapped by the success of *Merlin's Ring*. Obviously he wrote *King of the World's Edge, The Ship from Atlantis,* and *Merlin's Ring* over a period of decades as a loosely connected trilogy. Since Tolkien's *The Lord of the Rings* was first broken down into a "trilogy" simply because of the inadvisable economics of publishing a one-volume edition in the 1950s, "trilogies" (or, today, *sets* of "trilogies") have become the standard marketing tactic for epic fantasy. But the first two books in Munn's Merlin cycle were too short to individually pad out to the usual 300-plus page count for "epic fantasy." Thus, both were packaged together as *Merlin's Godson.* Then there was *Merlin's Ring,* but no third volume for display with the others on the racks.

As Salmonson noted in *The Chicago Fantasy Newsletter* memoir, Ballantine discouraged Munn from taking up one of his other ideas for a novel: "You see, trilogies were hot stuff. They wanted a third book about Merlin, so they'd have a trilogy, so they could put three books in a neat-and-keen box for Christmas. No matter that he didn't want to write it, never had such a book in mind...." So Munn skirted the issue of completing his contract for the "third" novel in his trilogy, *The Sword of Merlin,* by working instead on poems and short stories.

Of course it is unknowable whether or not Munn might have finished other novels if he had not had *The Sword of Merlin* hanging over him. He *did* do many shorter works, but he also spent a good amount of time enjoying himself at conventions, and seemed quite happy to kick about all over the northwest with me for a week. And he still had children and grandchildren—when I arrived in Tacoma, a note on his screen door directed me a few blocks over to the home of one of his sons, where we had dinner and a great time. As was the case in the 1940s and '50s, if Munn the artist experienced some torment after 1974 because he was balked on certain projects, I am sure the man made the best of those years. The obituary which ran in *Locus* for January 1981 backs up this observation in the comment, "He was 77, but seemed much younger." Much younger, indeed.

Toward the end of 1980 Munn became very ill and was diagnosed with cancer. He had told John Moran in that letter of November 29, 1975, that he had asked his adopted patron saint, Joan of Arc, only to be present "in the hour of my death." That hour came on January 10, 1981.

Munn had prepared another seasonal chapbook, his child's fantasy *The Baby Dryad,* with illustrations by Victoria Poyser, to send out that Christmas, but his final illness prevented his mailing copies. This last offering from H. Warner Munn, of Athol and Tacoma, was made posthumously by his family.

Munn left behind two novels, *The Lost Legion* and *Merlin's Ring,* which truly are epic in their scope and achievement, and the same may be said for his Tales of the Werewolf Clan. Looking over his work today, I find one of the best recommendations for reading Munn is that in meeting the novels and stories on the page you very definitely will meet the man who wrote them. Like H. P. Lovecraft, he was *an author*. And as he said of Lovecraft, I'll say of H. Warner Munn—he was a great guy, well worth your acquaintance.

NOTES

CHAPTER ONE

Throughout this paper, in order to keep footnotes to a minimum, I have cited Dunsany's tales (most of which are quite short) merely by the collection in which they appear (*The Gods of Pegana* by the page numbers of the Luce edition); uncollected stories, of course, have been be cited to their original appearances, and the plays by act and scene (the one-act plays, being very short, receive no special citation); novels are cited by chapter.

[1]Letter to Fritz Leiber, November 15, 1936, in *Selected Letters 1934-1937*, by H. P. Lovecraft, edited by August Derleth and James Turner. Sauk City, WI: Arkham House, 1976, p. 354.

[2]I should note here that I have no intention of discussing Dunsany's poetry at all. Meritorious as some of it is, it is on the whole clearly inferior to his prose work, and when fantastic it rarely expresses ideas better than his tales, novels, and plays. It is astonishing that Dunsany could allow himself to commit such aesthetic disasters as *A Journey* (1944) or *The Year* (1946), two "epic" poems in Byronic stanzas—something Dunsany found apparently as easy to write as Lovecraft did heroic couplets—of a perfectly contentless nature.

[3]A tendency unfortunately echoed in Mark Amory's *Biography of Lord Dunsany* (1972).

[4]"Lord Dunsany and His Work" (1922), in *Marginalia*, by H. P. Lovecraft. Sauk City, WI: Arkham House, 1944, p. 151, 155.

[5]*The Gods of Pegana*, by Lord Dunsany. Boston: Luce, n.d., p. 5.

[6]*Ibid.*, p. 21.

[7]*Ibid.*, p. 81.

[8]*Life of Johnson*. London: Oxford University Press, 1970, p. 426.

[9]*The Gods of Pegana*, p. 11.

[10]*Ibid.*, p. 5.

[11]*Ibid.*, p. 46-47.

[12]*Ibid.*, p. 76.

[13]*Ibid.*, p. 17.

[14]*Patches of Sunlight*, by Lord Dunsany. London: William Heinemann, 1938, p. 30.

[15]*The Gods of Pegana*, p. 16.

[16]*Aeneid*, translated by James Rhoades. London: Oxford University Press, 1921, p. 44-45.

[17]"Romance and the Modern Stage," in *National Review* No. 341 (July 1911): 831.

[18]"Jetsam," in *Saturday Review* (London) (25 June 1910): 819.

[19]*Selected Letters 1934-1937*, p. 354.

[20]I avoid discussion here of the peculiar non-fantasy novel, *Up in the Hills* (1935), since the point of this novel appears to be merely to make fun of

the Irish; a tendency found also in many of Dunsany's humorous sketches for *Punch* in the 1940s and 1950s.

[21]H. P. Lovecraft to James F. Morton (February 3, 1932), in *Selected Letters 1932-1934*, edited by August Derleth and James Turner. Sauk City, WI: Arkham House, 1976, p. 13.

[22]"Four Poets" (1957), in *The Ghosts of the Heaviside Layer and Other Fantasms*, by Lord Dunsany, edited by Darrell Schweitzer. Philadelphia: Owlswick Press, 1980, p. 157.

[23]*Ibid.*, p. 96.

[24]"Romance and the Modern Stage," p. 830.

[25]"Told under Oath" (1952), in *The Ghosts of the Heaviside Layer*, p. 33-45.

[26]"Introduction" to *A Dreamer's Tales*. New York: Modern Library, 1917, p. xvii.

[27]*The Sirens Wake*, by Lord Dunsany. London: Jarrolds, 1945, p. 24.

[28]*The Donnellan Lectures*, by Lord Dunsany. London: William Heinemann, 1945, p. 46.

[29]*Patches of Sunlight*, p. 158.

[30]*Ibid.*, p. 74.

[31]*The Sirens Wake*, p. 22.

[32]"The Use of Man," in *Harper's Bazaar* No. 2626 (August 1931): 85, 108.

[33]*Spectator* (October 3, 1952): 420-421.

[34]*Poetry Review* 44 (July-Sept. 1953): 375-377.

[35]"Notes on Writing Weird Fiction" (c. 1932), in *Marginalia*, p. 138.

[36]*The Sirens Wake*, p. 6.

[37]*The Ghosts of the Heaviside Layer*, p. 97-102.

[38]"Lord Dunsany and His Work," p. 159-160.

CHAPTER FOUR

[1]*The John Collier Reader*, p. 157.

[2]Anthony Burgess, "Introduction" to *The John Collier Reader*, p. xii.

[3]"Hell Hath No Fury."

[4]"The Devil, George, and Rosie."

[5]"Halfway to Hell."

[6]"Fallen Star."

[7]*Fancies and Goodnights*. Garden City, New York: Doubleday & Co., p. 34.

[8]*Ibid.*, p. 442.

[9]*The John Collier Reader*, p. 223.

[10]*Ibid.*, p. 228.

[11]*Ibid.*, p. 266.

[12]*Fancies and Goodnights*, p. 5.

[13]*Ibid.*, p. 10.

[14]*Milton's Paradise Lost*, p. viii.

[15]*Ibid.*, p. x.

[16]*Ibid.*, p. 3.

[17]*Ibid.*, p. 7.

[18]*Ibid.*, p. viii.

CHAPTER FIVE

[1]A. Merritt's brief autobiography, written by him in the third person, appeared originally as one of a series of its authors in "The Men Who Make the *Argosy*" in that magazine, and was revised for *Famous Fantastic Mysteries* (May-June 1940).

NOTES

2A fragment found among Merritt's papers after his death, entitled "The White Road," was presumed to be a possible attempt at a sequel to "Through the Dragon Glass" by Donald A. Wollheim, who edited a book of Merritt's short fiction, *The Fox Woman and Other Stories* (Avon, 1949). There are slight elements in common. Merritt had written in the *FFM* biography that he had "three novels under way," one of which was a "story of Chinese sorcery." While this might be applicable to the title story, stylistic comparisons favor "The White Road."

3In his excellent discussion and anthology of favorite Munseyarns in *Under the Moons of Mars* (Holt, Rinehart & Winston, 1970), Sam Moskowitz points out that Merritt would have been making $25,000 on *The American Weekly* by 1919, a considerable wage, so that "the fifty dollars sent him...for the short story could not have been his prime motivation. Likewise, subsequent payments of $60 for "The People of the Pit," $75 for "Three Lines of Old French," and such (reported by Moskowitz in *A. Merritt: Reflections in the Moon Pool* [Oswald Train, 1985] indicate that the desire to write fiction was Merritt's sole motivation. However, it should be noted that his novels would very soon be bringing the author several thousand dollars each. Furthermore, nearly all appeared in hardcover form subsequently, some in condensed form (see the Bibliography), and two were made into films.

4Merritt was partial to certain words, and they recur in his work frequently: "corruscating," "opalescent," "elfin." Indeed, "elfin" is to Merritt as "eldritch" was to Lovecraft. They are code words which haunt a new reader and acquaint familiar readers with the author's intent.

5That Merritt, so renowned for slights of sheer fantasy, might utilize the devices of more mundane science fiction, and even be considered a science fiction writer, was so obvious to pioneer editor Hugo Gernsback that he had no qualms about reprinting *The Metal Monster* and *The Moon Pool* in his publications. In a lengthy letter printed in *Argosy* shortly before the appearance of *Dwellers in the Mirage*, the author expressed his pique with readers who criticized his "scientific accuracy." He stated: "There is not a single scientific statement in *The Snake Mother* that cannot be substantiated." And he continues, in regard to *Dwellers in the Mirage* and the ethnic accuracy of its dwarf people, that a "little people" had been reported in Florida. In addition, concerning Khalk'ru, Merritt had seen the appearances of the Kraken "carved high on the Andean peaks by hands thousands of years dead." Finally, he justifies his valley of the "mirage" with a report of a *New York Times* story on the discovery of a tropical valley in an area otherwise experiencing a normal temperature of 40° below zero.

6*Burn, Witch, Burn* was filmed in 1936 as *The Devil Doll*, being ably directed by Todd Browning, but substantially altered by him in plot. Madame Mandilip suffered an extreme sex change when her part was played by Lionel Barrymore, all of it much to Merritt's distaste. Curiously, Merritt's own title was appropriated in 1962 for a film version of Fritz Leiber's *Conjure Wife*, an excellent novel with an already excellent title.

7"The Pool of the Stone God" was first brought to light as a Merrittale in Sam Moskowitz's anthology, *Horrors Unknown* (Walker, 1971), and reprinted with a fuller discussion in *A. Merritt: Reflections in the Moon Pool* (Oswald Train, 1985). The latter is a valuable study of Merritt, with biography, commentary, poetry, and several more previously unpublished fragments by the author.

8Merritt's *FFM* autobiography mentioned a novel he was writing about Yucatan. "When Old Gods Wake" has a Mayan reference, and might well the piece being referred to. It is, however, far from the polished style of his writing.

9A word should be said about Merritt's artists. Virgil Finlay came from Rochester to draw for his newspaper, and did indeed find work with the company, but his dilatory habits, and the time he required to complete his detailed stipple art at times exasperated the older man. However, Finlay first illustrated Merritt's own work in the late 1930s reprint in *Argosy* of *Seven Footprints to Satan*, and became for innumerable fans permanently associated with the author in the pages of *FFM*, commencing with its second issue. Much of the finest work the artist ever did was for these stories, where his own magic illuminated the author's. On the West Coast, a young artist who called himself Hannes Bok was so enamored of Merritt that he copied excerpts of "The Metal Emperor" (Merritt's revision) longhand from Gernsback's pre-*Amazing Stories* magazine, *Science and Invention*. He dreamed of professionally illustrating Merritt, his favorite writer, but did not receive the opportunity. When his associate Paul Dennis O'Connor got the opportunity to publish the uncompleted stories, *The Fox Woman* and *The Black Wheel* (for his New Collectors Group), he had Bok complete the tales (Bok had already had fiction published, sometimes in the manner of Merritt), and also illustrate them. For Bok it was the opportunity of a lifetime, and in his art he at least justified the faith Merritt himself had once expressed. The lithographs he produced for the two books were superb.

10The second story Merritt wrote for a fan magazine was "The Drone," inspired by his pleasure with bees. For *TWS* he retitled it "The Drone Man."

11See *Selected Letters, Volume IV*, by H. P. Lovecraft. Sauk City, WI: Arkham House, 1976, p. 341-342.

12*Ibid.*, p. 390.

CHAPTER SEVEN

1*The Centaur*, by Algernon Blackwood. London: Macmillan, 1911, p. 72.

2*Ibid.*, p. 144.

3*Jimbo: A Fantasy*, by Algernon Blackwood. London: Macmillan, 1909, p. 13.

4*A Prisoner in Fairyland: (The Book That 'Uncle Paul' Wrote)*, by Algernon Blackwood. London: Macmillan, 1913, p. 61.

5*The Extra Day*, by Algernon Blackwood. London: Macmillan, 1915, p. 5.

6*Ibid.*, p. 61.

7*The Education of Uncle Paul*, by Algernon Blackwood. London: Macmillan, 1909, p. 52-53.

8*Ibid.*, p. 131.

CHAPTER TEN

1Moskowitz, Sam, *Seekers of Tomorrow*. New York: Ballantine Books, 1967.

2Briney, R. E., commentary on Henry Kuttner in *Twentieth-Century Science-Fiction Authors*, edited by Curtis C. Smith. Chicago: St. James Press, 1986, p. 415-416.

3Cited in Briney.

4*Ibid.*

BIBLIOGRAPHY

CHAPTER ONE: LORD DUNSANY

The Blessing of Pan. London: G. P. Putnam's Sons, 1927.
The Book of Wonder. London: William Heinemann, 1912.
The Charwoman's Shadow. London: G. P. Putnam's Sons, 1926.
The Curse of the Wise Woman. London: William Heinemann, 1933.
Don Rodriguez: The Chronicles of Shadow Valley (aka *The Chronicles of Rodriguez*). London: G. P. Putnam's Sons, 1922.
A Dreamer's Tales. London: George Allen & Sons, 1910.
Five Plays. London: Grant Richards, 1914.
The Fourth Book of Jorkens. London: Jarrolds, 1947.
The Ghosts of the Heaviside Layer, edited by Darrell Schweitzer. Philadelphia: Owlswick Press, 1980.
The Gods of Pegana. London: Elkin Mathews, 1905.
If. London: G. P. Putnam's Sons, 1921.
Jorkens Borrows Another Whiskey. London: Michael Joseph, 1954.
Jorkens Has a Large Whiskey. London: G. P. Putnam's Sons, 1940.
Jorkens Remembers Africa. London: Longmans, Green, & Co, 1934.
The King of Elfland's Daughter. London: G. P. Putnam's Sons, 1924.
The Last Revolution. London: Jarrolds, 1953.
Little Tales of Smethers. London: Jarrolds, 1952.
Lord Adrian. London: Golden Cockerel Press, 1933.
The Man Who Ate the Phoenix. London: Jarrolds, 1949.
My Talks with Dean Spanley. London: William Heinemann, 1936.
The Old Folk of the Centuries. London: Elkin Mathews and Marrot, 1930.
Patches of Sunlight. London: William Heinemann, 1938.
Plays for Earth and Air. London: William Heinemann, 1937.
Plays of Gods and Men. Dublin: The Talbot Press, 1917.
Seven Modern Comedies. London: G. P. Putnam's Sons, 1928.
The Sirens Wake. London: Jarrolds, 1945.
The Story of Mona Sheehy. London: G. P. Putnam's Sons, 1939.
The Strange Journeys of Colonel Polders. London: Jarrolds, 1950.
The Sword of Welleran. London: George Allen & Sons, 1908.
Tales of Three Hemispheres. Boston: John Luce, 1919.
Tales of Wonder (aka *The Last Book of Wonder*). London: Elkin Mathews, 1916.
Time and the Gods. London: William Heinemann, 1906.
The Travel Tales of Mr. Joseph Jorkens. London: G. P. Putnam's Sons, 1931.
When the Sirens Slept. London: Jarrolds, 1944.

CHAPTER TWO: JAMES BRANCH CABELL

Beyond Life. New York: Robert M. McBride Co., 1919.

The Certain Hour: (Dizain des Poëtes). New York: Robert M. McBride Co., 1916.

Chivalry. New York: Robert M. McBride Co., 1909.

The Cords of Vanity. New York: Robert M. McBride Co., 1909.

The Cream of the Jest: A Comedy of Evasions. New York: Robert M. McBride Co., 1917.

The Devil's Own Dear Son: A Comedy of the Fatted Calf. New York: Farrar, Strauss, & Co., 1949.

Domnei: A Comedy of Woman-Worship. New York: Robert M. McBride Co., 1920.

The Eagle's Shadow. New York: Robert M. McBride Co., 1914.

Figures of Earth: A Comedy of Appearances. New York: Robert M. McBride Co., 1921.

From the Hidden Way. New York: Robert M. McBride Co., 1916.

Gallantry. New York: Robert M. McBride Co., 1907.

Hamlet Had an Uncle: A Comedy of Honor. New York: Farrar & Rinehart, New York, 1940.

The High Place: A Comedy of Disenchantment. New York: Robert M. McBride Co., 1923.

The Jewel Merchants. New York: Robert M. McBride Co., 1921.

The Judging of Jurgen. Chicago: Bookfellows, 1920.

Jurgen: A Comedy of Justice. New York: Robert M. McBride Co., 1919.

The Line of Love: Dizain des Mariages. New York: Harper & Brothers, 1905. Also: New York: Robert M. McBride Co., 1921 (adds "The Wedding Guest").

The Lineage of Lichfield: An Essay in Eugenics. New York: Robert M. McBride Co., 1922.

The Music from Behind the Moon: An Epitome. New York: John Day, New York, 1926.

The Nightmare Has Triplets: An Author's Note on Smire. Garden City, NY: Doubleday, Doran, & Co., 1937.

Preface to the Past. New York: Robert M. McBride Co., 1936.

The Rivet in Grandfather's Neck. New York: Robert M. McBride Co., 1915.

The Silver Stallion: A Comedy of Redemption. New York: Robert M. McBride Co., 1926.

Smire: An Acceptance in the Third Person. Garden City, NY: Doubleday, Doran & Co., 1937.

Smirt: An Urbane Nightmare. New York: Robert M. McBride Co., 1934.

Smith: A Sylvan Interlude. New York: Robert M. McBride Co., 1935.

Something About Eve: A Comedy of Fig-Leaves. New York: Robert M. McBride Co., 1927.

The Soul of Melicent. New York: Frederick A. Stokes, 1913. Retitled *Domnei* (see above).

Straws and Prayer Books. New York: Robert M. McBride Co., 1924.

Taboo: A Legend Retold from the Dirghis of Saevius Nicanor. New York: Robert M. McBride Co., 1921.

There Were Two Pirates: A Comedy of Division. New York: Farrar, Straus & Co, 1946.

These Restless Heads: A Trilogy of Romantics. New York: Robert M. McBride Co., 1932.

Townsend of Lichfield: Dizain des Adieux. New York: Robert M. McBride Co., 1930.

The Way of Ecben: A Comedietta Involving a Gentleman. New York: Robert M. McBride Co., 1929.

The White Robe: A Saint's Summary. New York: Robert M. McBride Co., 1928.

The Witch-Woman: A Trilogy about Her. New York: Farrar, Straus & Co, 1948. Includes *The Music from Behind the Moon*, *The Way of Ecben*, and *The White Robe*.

CHAPTER THREE: MERVYN WALL

The Complete Fursey. Dublin: Wolfhound Press, 1985.

A Flutter of Wings. Dublin: Talbot Press, 1974.

"The Garden of Echoes," in *The Journal of Irish Literature* XL:1/2 (January-May 1982).

The Garden of Echoes. Dublin: Fingal Books, 1988.

The Return of Fursey. London: Pilot Press, 1948.

The Unfortunate Fursey. London: Pilot Press, 1946. New York: Crown Publishers, 1947. Dublin: Helicon, 1965.

CHAPTER FOUR: JOHN COLLIER

The Best of John Collier. New York: Pocket Books, 1975. Short stories.

Defy the Foul Fiend. London: Macmillan, 1934.

The Devil and All. London: Nonesuch Press, 1934. Short stories.

Fancies and Goodnights. Garden City, New York: Doubleday & Co., 1951. Short stories, including: "Bottle Party," "De Mortuis," "Evening Primrose," "Witch's Money," "Are You Too Late or Was I Too Early," "Fallen Star," "The Touch of Nutmeg Makes It," "Three Bears Cottage," "Pictures in the Fire," "Wet Saturday," "Squirrels Have Bright Eyes," "Halfway to Hell," "The Lady on the Grey," "Incident on a Lake," "Over Insurance," "Old Acquaintance," "The Frog Prince," Season of Mists," "Great Possibilities," "Without Benefit of Galsworthy," "The Devil George and Rosie," "Ah, the University," "Back for Christmas," "Another American Tragedy," "Collaboration," "Midnight Blue," "Gavin O'Leary," "If Youth Knew If Age Could," "Thus I Refute Beelzy," "Special Delivery," "Rope Enough," "Little Memento," "Green Thoughts," "Romance Lingers, Adventure Lives," "Bird of Prey," "Variation on a Theme," "Night Youth Paris and the Moon," "The Steel Cat," "Sleeping Beauty," "Interpretation of a Dream," "Mary," "Hell Hath No Fury," "In the Cards," "The Invisible Dove Dancer of Strathpeen Island," "The Right Side," "Spring Fever," "Youth from Vienna," "Possession of Angela Bradshaw," "Cancel All I Said," and "'The Chaser."

Gemini. London: Ulysses Press, 1931. Poetry.

Green Thoughts. London: William Jackson, 1932. Short story.

His Monkey Wife; or, Married to a Chimp. London: Peter Davies, 1930; New York: D. Appleton-Century, 1931.

The John Collier Reader. New York: Alfred A. Knopf, 1972. Includes: *His Monkey Wife*, Chapters 8 and 9 from *Defy the Foul Fiend*, and the short stories "Bottle Party," "Evening Primrose," "Witch's Money," "Are You Too Late or Was I Too Early," "Fallen Star," "Three Bears Cottage," "Pictures in the Fire," "Wet Saturday," "Squirrels Have Bright Eyes," "Halfway to Hell," "The Lady on the Gray," "Incident on a Lake," "Over Insurance," "The Frog Prince," "Season of Mists," "Without Benefit of Galsworthy," "The Devil George and Rosie," "Ah, the University," "Back for Christmas," "Another American Tragedy," "Collaboration," "Gavin O'Leary," "If Youth Knew, If Age Could," "Thus I Refute Beelzy,"

"Special Delivery," "Rope Enough," "Green Thoughts," "Romance Lingers, Adventure Lives," "Bird of Prey," "Variation on a Theme," "Night! Youth! Paris! And the Moon!," "The Steel Cat," "Sleeping Beauty," "Interpretation of a Dream," "Mary," "Hell Hath no Fury," "In the Cards," "Spring Fever," "Youth From Vienna," "Possession of Angela Bradshaw," "The Chaser," "Mademoiselle Kiki," "Son of Kiki," "A Matter of Taste," "A Dog's a Dog," "Man Overboard," and "The Tender Age."

Milton's Paradise Lost. New York: Alfred A. Knopf, 1973. Screenplay.

No Traveler Returns. London: White Owl Press, 1931. Short story.

Of Demons and Darkness. London: Corgi Books, 1965. Short stories.

Pictures in the Fire. London: Rupert Hart-Davis, 1958. Short stories.

Presenting Moonshine. London: Macmillan, 1941; New York: Viking Press, 1941. Short stories.

Tom's a-Cold: A Tale. London: Macmillan, 1933. as: *Full Circle: A Tale.* New York: D. Appleton-Century, 1933.

The Touch of Nutmeg, and Other Unlikely Stories. New York: Press of The Readers Club, 1943. Short stories.

Variation on a Theme. London: Grayson and Grayson, 1935. Short story.

Witch's Money. New York: Viking Press, 1940.

CHAPTER FIVE: A. MERRITT

The Black Wheel, with Hannes Bok. New York: New Collector's Group, 1947.

Burn Witch Burn! New York: Liveright Publishers, 1933.

Creep, Shadow! Garden City, New York: Doubleday, Doran & Co., 1934. As: *Creep, Shadow, Creep!* London: Methuen, 1935.

The Drone Man. Sedalia, CO: M. Doreal, 1948.

Dwellers in the Mirage. New York: Liveright Publishers, 1932.

The Face in the Abyss. New York: Horace Liveright, 1931.

The Fox Woman & Other Stories. New York: Avon Books, 1949. Includes: "The Fox Woman," "The People of the Pit," "Through the Dragon Glass," "The Drone," "The Last Poet and the Robots," "Three Lines of Old French," "The White Road," "When Old Gods Wake," and "The Women of the Wood."

The Fox Woman; The Blue Pagoda, with Hannes Bok. Denver, CO: New Collector's Group, 1946.

The Metal Monster. New York: Avon Books, 1946.

The Moon Pool. New York: G. P. Putnam's Sons, 1919.

Rhythm of the Spheres. Sedalio, CO: M. Doreal, 1948.

7 Footprints to Satan. New York: Boni & Liveright, 1928.

The Ship of Ishtar. New York: G. P. Putnam's Sons, 1926.

Three Lines of Old French. Millheim, PA: The Bizarre Series, 1937.

Thru the Dragon Glass. Jamaica, NY: ARRA Printers, 1933. Originally published 1917.

SHORTER WORKS AND SERIALIZATIONS

"Through the Dragon Glass," in *All-Story Weekly* (November 24, 1917).

"The People of the Pit," in *All-Story Weekly* (January 5, 1918).

"The Moon Pool," in *All-Story Weekly* (June 22, 1918).

"The Conquest of the Moon Pool," published in six installments in *All-Story Weekly* (February 15, 1919) to (March 22, 1919).

"Three Lines of Old French," in *Argosy* (August 9, 1919).

"The Metal Monster," published in eight installments beginning in *Argosy All-Story Weekly* (August 7, 1920).

"The Face in the Abyss," in *Argosy All-Story* (September 8, 1923).

"The Pool of the Stone God," as W. FENIMORE, in *The American Weekly* (September 23, 1923).

"The Ship of Ishtar," published in six installments in *Argosy All-Story* from (November 8, 1924) to (December 13, 1924).

"The Women of the Wood," in *Weird Tales* (August 1926).

"Seven Footprints to Satan," published in five installments in *Argosy All-Story* from (July 2, 1927) to (August 1, 1927).

"The Snake Mother," published in seven installments in *Argosy* from (October 25, 1930).

"Dwellers in the Mirage," published in six installments in *Argosy* from (January 23, 1932) to (February 25, 1932).

"Burn, Witch, Burn!", published in six installments in *Argosy* from (October 22, 1932) to (November 20, 1932).

"The Last Poet and the Robots," Chapter 11 of *Cosmos*, a round-robin novel, published in *Fantasy Magazine* (previously *Science Fiction Digest*) (April 1934).

"The Drone," published in *Fantasy Magazine* (September 1934).

"Creep, Shadow!," published in seven installments in *Argosy* from (September 8, 1934) to (October 20, 1934).

"The Challenge from Beyond," a brief segment in a round-robin novel, published in *Fantasy Magazine* (September 1935).

"The Drone Man," (retitled from "The Drone"), published in *Thrilling Wonder Stories* (August 1936).

"Rhythm of the Spheres" (retitled with minor changes from "The Last Poet and the Robots"), published in *Thrilling Wonder Stories* (October 1936).

"When Old Gods Wake," published in *Avon Fantasy Reader No. 7*, edited by Donald A. Wollheim. New York: Avon Books, 1948.

Other fragments and ephemera include: "Pilgrimage; or, Obi Giese," a short story; "Bootleg and Witches," a fragment; and "The Devil in the Heart," an outline. These are printed in *A. Merritt: Reflections in the Moon Pool*, by Sam Moskowitz. Philadelphia: Oswald Train: Publisher, 1985.

CHAPTER SIX: E. R. EDDISON

A Fish Dinner in Memison. New York: E. P. Dutton, 1941.

The Mezentian Gate. Plaistow: Curwen Press, 1958.

Mistress of Mistresses: A Vision of Zimiamvia. London: Faber & Faber, 1935.

Styrbiorn the Strong. London: Jonathan Cape, 1926.

The Worm Ouroboros: A Romance. London: Jonathan Cape, 1922.

CHAPTER SEVEN: ALGERNON BLACKWOOD

The Bright Messenger. London: Cassell, 1921.

The Centaur. London: Macmillan, 1911.

Dudley & Gilderoy: A Nonsense. London: Ernest Benn, 1929.

The Education of Uncle Paul. London: Macmillan, 1909.

The Extra Day. London: Macmillan, 1915.

The Fruit Stoners: Being the Adventures of Maria Among the Fruit Stoners. London: Grayson & Grayson, 1934.

Full Circle. London: Elkin Mathews & Marrot, 1929.

The Garden of Survival. London: Macmillan, 1918.

The Human Chord. London: Macmillan, 1910.
Jimbo: A Fantasy. London: Macmillan, 1909.
Julius LeVallon: An Episode. London: Cassell, 1916.
Karma: A Reincarnation Play. London: Macmillan, 1918.
The Prisoner in Fairyland: (The Book That 'Uncle Paul' Wrote). London: Macmillan, 1913.
The Promise of Air. London: Macmillan, 1918.
Sambo and Snitch. Oxford: Basil Blackwell, 1927.
The Wave: An Egyptian Aftermath. London: Macmillan, 1916.

CHAPTER EIGHT: DAVID LINDSAY

Adventures of M. de Mailly. London: Andrew Melrose, 1926; as *A Blade for Sale: The Adventures of Monsieur de Mailly*, New York: Robert M. McBride, 1927.
Devil's Tor. London: G. P. Putnam's Sons, 1932; New York: Arno Press, 1978.
The Haunted Woman. London: Methuen, 1922; London: Victor Gollancz, 1964; Hollywood, CA: Newcastle Publishing Co., 1975.
Sphinx. London: John Long, 1923; New York, Carroll & Graf, 1978.
The Violet Apple. London: Sidgwick & Jackson, 1978.
The Violet Apple; &, The Witch. Chicago: Chicago Review Press, 1976, edited by J. B. Pick, introduction by Colin Wilson.
A Voyage to Arcturus. London: Methuen, 1920; London: Victor Gollancz, London, 1946, 1963, 1968; New York: Macmillan, 1963, with an introduction by Loren Eiseley; New York: Ballantine Books, November 1968, April 1973, September 1973.

BIOGRAPHY AND CRITICISM

David Lindsay, by Gary K. Wolfe. Mercer Island, WA: Starmont House, 1982.
David Lindsay's Vision, by David Power. Nottingham, England: Paupers' Press, 1991.
The Life and Works of David Lindsay, by Bernard Sellin. Cambridge: Cambridge University Press, 1981.
The Strange Genius of David Lindsay, by J. B. Pick, Colin Wilson, and E. H. Visiak. London: John Baker, 1970. Wilson's essay from this book was reprinted with slight amendations as *The Haunted Man: The Strange Genius of David Lindsay*. San Bernardino, CA: The Borgo Press, 1979. A series of essays and critiques on Lindsay and his visionary novels. Visiak's reminiscences are first-hand, as he knew Lindsay personally. This volume was the first book written on Lindsay. All quotes from his notebooks are excerpted from this book. As a reference and document, its value is inestimable.

CHAPTER NINE: L. FRANK BAUM

Dorothy and the Wizard in Oz. Chicago: Reilly & Britton, 1908.
The Emerald City of Oz. Chicago: Reilly & Britton, 1910.
The Enchanted Island of Yew. Indianapolis, IN: Bobbs-Merrill, 1903.
Glinda of Oz. Chicago: Reilly & Britton, 1920.
The Land of Oz. Chicago: Reilly & Britton, 1904.

The Last Egyptian: A Romance of the Nile. Philadelphia: Edward Stern, 1908.
The Lost Princess of Oz. Chicago: Reilly & Britton, 1917.
The Magic of Oz. Chicago: Reilly & Britton, 1919.
The Master Key: An Electrical Fairy Tale Founded Upon the Mysteries of Electricity and the Optimism of Its Devotees. Indianapolis, IN: Bowen-Merrill, 1901.
Ozma of Oz. Chicago: Reilly & Britton, 1907.
The Patchwork Girl of Oz. Chicago: Reilly & Britton, 1913.
Queen Zixi of Ix; or, The Story of the Magic Cloak. New York: Century Co., 1905.
Rinkitink in Oz. Chicago: Reilly & Britton, 1916.
The Road to Oz. Chicago: Reilly & Britton, 1909.
The Scarecrow of Oz. Chicago: Reilly & Britton, 1915.
The Sea Fairies. Chicago: Reilly & Britton, 1911.
Sky Island. Chicago: Reilly & Britton, 1912.
The Surprising Adventures of the Magical Monarch of Mo. Indianapolis, IN: Bowen-Merrill, 1901.
The Tin Woodman of Oz. Chicago: Reilly & Britton, 1918.
The Wonderful Wizard of Oz. Chicago: G. M. Hill, 1900.

CHAPTER TEN: HENRY KUTTNER

Some of the fantasy stories listed below made their magazine appearances under pseudonyms (*e.g.*, "Call Him Demon" as by KEITH HAMMOND and numerous uses of the LEWIS PADGETT byline in *Unknown*), but they are usually reprinted under Kuttner's own name, with the exception, again, of many of the Padgett items, some of which may be found in the 1950 Simon & Schuster collection, *A Gnome There Was* (bylined Padgett).

"Before I Wake," in *Famous Fantastic Mysteries* (March 1945).
Beyond Earth's Gates, by Henry Kuttner and C. L. Moore. New York: Ace Books, 1954. Originally published in *Startling Stories* (September 1949), as "The Portal in the Picture."
"Beyond the Phoenix," in *Weird Tales* (October 1938). Elak.
"The Black Kiss," with Robert Bloch, in *Weird Tales* (June 1937).
"By These Presents," in *Fantastic* (March 1953).
"Call Him Demon," in *Thrilling Wonder Stories* (Fall 1946).
"Compliments of the Author," in *Unknown* (October 1942).
The Dark World. New York: Ace Books, 1965. Originally published in *Startling Stories* (Summer 1946).
"The Devil We Know," in *Unknown* (August 1941).
"A Gnome There Was," in *Unknown Worlds* (October 1941).
"The Graveyard Rats," in *Weird Tales* (March 1936).
"Housing Problem," in *Charm* (October 1944).
"I, the Vampire," in *Weird Tales* (February 1937).
"It Walks by Night," in *Weird Tales* (December 1936).
The Mask of Circe. New York: Ace Books, 1971. Originally published in *Startling Stories* (May 1948).
"Masquerade," in *Weird Tales* (May 1942).
"The Misguided Halo," in *Unknown* (August 1939).
"The Salem Horror," in *Weird Tales* (May 1937).
"Spawn of Dagon," in *Weird Tales* (July 1938). Elak.
"Threshold," in *Unknown* (December 1940).
"Thunder in the Dawn," in *Weird Tales* (May-June 1938). Elak.

The Time Axis. New York: Ace Books, 1965. Originally published in *Startling Stories* (January 1949).

"Time to Kill," in *Strange Stories* (June 1940).

The Well of the Worlds. New York: Galaxy Novels, 1953; New York: Ace Books, 1965. Originally published in *Startling Stories* (March 1952).

"Wet Magic," in *Unknown Worlds* (February 1943).

CHAPTER ELEVEN: H. WARNER MUNN

The Banner of Joan. Providence, Rhode Island: Donald M. Grant, 1975. Verse cycle.

The Book of Munn. Sacramento, CA: Outre House, 1979. Collected poems.

King of the World's Edge. New York: Ace Books, 1966.

The Lost Legion. Garden City, NY: Doubleday & Co,, 1980.

Merlin's Godson. New York: Ballantine Books, 1976. An omnibus gathering *King of the World's Edge* and *The Ship from Atlantis.*

Merlin's Ring. New York: Ballantine Books, 1974. With an introduction by Lin Carter.

The Ship from Atlantis. New York: Ace Books, 1967.

Tales of the Werewolf Clan, Volume I. Providence, RI: Donald M. Grant, 1979.

Tales of the Werewolf Clan, Volume II. Providence, RI: Donald M. Grant, 1980.

The Werewolf of Ponkert. Providence, RI: The Grandon Company, 1958. With an introduction by Donald M. Grant. Reprinted: Providence, RI: Centaur Books, 1976. Paperback reprint, with a new introduction by Grant.

ABOUT THE CONTRIBUTORS

DON D'AMMASSA has been reviewing books for *Science Fiction Chronicle* for many years. He is almost legendary as one of the few people in science-fiction/fantasy circles who has read virtually everything. He has been a prolific essayist for many years, and has recently turned to writing fiction, and his short stories have appeared in numerous anthologies and magazines. *D'Ammassa's Guide to Modern Horror Fiction: An Annotated Bibliography of Works in English*, is forthcoming from Borgo Press.

GALAD ELFLANDSSON is a Canadian, and author of the fantasy horror novel *The Black Wolf* (published by Donald M. Grant), plus many distinguished short stories.

JEFFREY GODDIN is the author of several horror novels. His short fiction has appeared in *Twilight Zone* magazine and elsewhere. He is a rare book dealer, formerly assistant in the Louisville University Library's rare books department, and the author of numerous scholarly essays.

DON HERRON has edited the letters of Philip K. Dick. He is an expert on Clark Ashton Smith and California writers in general, and is the author of books as varied as *Literary San Francisco and Its Environs* and *Echoes from the Vaults of Yoth-Vombis* (a biography of George Haas). He edited a superb critical anthology about Robert E. Howard, *The Dark Barbarian*, for Greenwood Press and the last of the Underwood-Miller Stephen King criticism collections, *Reign of Fear*. His work appears in *Discovering Modern Horror 1* (on Russell Kirk) and *Discovering Stephen King*.

BEN P. INDICK maintains his record of appearing in every Darrell Schweitzer essay anthology. Considering the quality of his work, your editor hopes to keep that record going into the indefinite future. Ben is the author of *Ray Bradbury: Dramatist* (1989) and *Geo. Alec Effinger* for Borgo Press (1993), as well as being a playwright, the publisher of the fanzine *Ibid*, a distinguished essayist, and a retired pharmacist in real life.

S. T. JOSHI is the editor of *Lovecraft Studies* and *Studies in Weird Fiction*, and is the leading Lovecraft scholar of the present time, being responsible for the restored and corrected texts of Lovecraft's work. His books include *The Weird Tale, The Modern Weird Tale, H. P. Lovecraft: The Decline of the West, H. P. Lovecraft: Four Decades of Criticism, Lord Dunsany, Master of the Anglo-Irish Imagination,* and *A Subtler Magick: The Writings and Philosophy of H. P. Lovecraft* (Borgo Press, 1996).

DARRELL SCHWEITZER is the author of *The Mask of the Sorcerer, The Shattered Goddess, The White Isle, We Are All Legends,* and *Tom O'Bedlam's Night Out,* plus over a hundred fantasy short stories. His 1993 collection, *Transients,* was a finalist for the World Fantasy Award. He has edited several volumes of essays for Starmont House, including *Discovering H. P. Lovecraft, Discovering Classic Horror,* and *Discovering Modern Horror* (2 vols.). He has also written critical studies on Lord Dunsany, H. P. Lovecraft, and Robert E. Howard. A widely-published essayist, reviewer, and interviewer, he co-edited the revived *Weird Tales,* and now edits its successor magazine, *Worlds of Fantasy & Horror.*

ALAN WARREN is a San Francisco-area writer, who has published fiction in *Mike Shayne's Mystery Magazine, Isaac Asimov's Science Fiction Magazine,* and elsewhere. He has written film criticism, essays for previous volumes of Schweitzer's *Discovering Modern Horror 1* and *2,* and *Roald Dahl: From the Gremlins to the Chocolate Factory* (Borgo Press, 1994).

NEAL WILGUS, limerickist extraordinaire, also interviews authors, contributes to Libertarian publications, and is represented in *Discovering Modern Horror 1* with an essay on Fred Saberhagen. He is the compiler and interviewer of *Seven by Seven: Interviews with American Science Fiction Writers of the West and Southwest* (Borgo Press, 1996).

INDEX

INDEX

CHARACTER INDEX